PIMLICO

386

THE RISE OF THE NOVEL

Ian Watt is Jackson Eli Reynolds Professor of Humanities at Stanford University. He served as Chairman of the English Department (1968–71), and of the Program in Modern Thought and Literature (1977–80), and was Director of the Stanford Humanities Center from 1980 to 1985. His books include *Conrad in the Nineteenth Century* (1979), *Conrad: Nostromo* (1988) and *Myths of Individualism: Faust, Don Quixote, Don Juan and Robinson Crusoe* (1998).

THE RISE OF
THE NOVEL

Studies in Defoe,
Richardson and Fielding

———

IAN WATT

PIMLICO

Published by Pimlico 2000

12

Copyright © Ian Watt 1957

First published in Great Britain by
Chatto & Windus 1957
Pimlico edition 2000

Pimlico
Random House, 20 Vauxhall Bridge Road,
London SW1V 2SA

www.randomhouse.co.uk

Addresses for companies within
The Random House Group Limited can be found at:
www.randomhouse.co.uk/offices.htm

The Random House Group Limited Reg. No. 954009

A CIP catalogue record for this book
is available from the British Library

ISBN 9780712664271

The Random House Group Limited supports the Forest Stewardship
Council ® (FSC®), the leading international forest certification organisation.
All our titles that are printed on Greenpeace approved FSC® certified
paper carry the FSC® logo. Our paper procurement policy can be found at
www.randomhouse.co.uk/environment

Printed and bound in Great Britain by
CPI Antony Rowe, Chippenham, Wiltshire

CONTENTS

ABBREVIATIONS USED

ELH	*Journal of English Literary History*
HLQ	*Huntington Library Quarterly*
JEGP	*Journal of English and Germanic Philology*
J. Comp. Psychology	*Journal of Comparative Psychology*
MLN	*Modern Language Notes*
MLR	*Modern Language Review*
MP	*Modern Philology*
N & Q	*Notes and Queries*
PMLA	*Publications of the Modern Language Association of America*
PQ	*Philological Quarterly*
Proc. Amer. Antiquarian Soc.	*Proceedings of the American Antiquarian Society*
RES	*Review of English Studies*
SP	*Studies in Philology*

PREFACE

IN 1938 I began a study of the relation between the growth of the reading public and the emergence of the novel in eighteenth-century England; and in 1947 it eventually took shape as a Fellowship Dissertation for St. John's College, Cambridge. Two wider problems, however, remained unresolved. Defoe, Richardson and Fielding were no doubt affected by the changes in the reading public of their time; but their works are surely more profoundly conditioned by the new climate of social and moral experience which they and their eighteenth-century readers shared. Nor could one say much about how this was connected with the emergence of the new literary form without deciding what the Novel's distinctive literary features were and are.

These are the problems with which I am here concerned, and they are so large that their treatment is necessarily selective. I have not, for example, made more than incidental reference to the earlier traditions of fiction, nor to the more immediate precursors and contemporaries of my central figures; equally regrettably, my treatment of Fielding is briefer than that of Defoe and Richardson—since most of the new elements of the novel had by then appeared, there seemed no need to go beyond an analysis of how he combined them with the classical literary tradition. Finally, although my main effort has been to elucidate in a fairly systematic fashion the enduring connections between the distinctive literary qualities of the novel and those of the society in which it began and flourished, I have not limited myself to such considerations: partly because I also wanted to give a general critical assessment of Defoe, Richardson and Fielding; and partly because my studies had confronted me with the monitory example of how that rigorously systematic thinker Walter Shandy would 'twist and torture everything in nature to support his hypothesis'.

I am obliged to William Kimber and Co. for permission to quote an extract from Peter Quennell's *Mayhew's London*; also to the editors and publishers of the *Review of English Studies* and of *Essays in Criticism* for allowing me to use, especially in chapters I, III and VIII, material which originally appeared in their pages. I gladly acknowledge the skill and devotion which Cecilia Scurfield and Elizabeth Walser exhibited both as typists and cryptographers; and I am deeply grateful for the financial and other assistance which I have received as Scholar, research student and Fellow of St. John's College, Cambridge, and as holder of Fellowships from the Commonwealth Fund of New York and from the President of the University of California.

Most of my scholarly obligations are, I hope, adequately detailed in footnotes: but I must here acknowledge the great stimulus I received at the outset of my research from Q. D. Leavis's *Fiction and the Reading Public*. My other debts are extensive. Mrs. A. D. M. de Navarro, Eric Twist and Hugh Sykes Davies early interested themselves in my work; I am very grateful to them, and to the many scholars in diverse fields of interest who later read and criticised the various drafts which led to this book—Miss M. G. Lloyd Thomas, Miss Hortense Powdermaker, Theodore Adorno, Louis B. Wright, Henry Nash Smith, Leonard Broom, Bertrand H. Bronson, Alan D. McKillop, Ivor Richards, Talcott Parsons, Peter Laslett, Hrothgar Habakkuk and John H. Raleigh. I owe much to them, and also to those who in a more official but equally friendly capacity directed my studies at various times and places: to Louis Cazamian and the late F. T. Blanchard, with both of whom I worked only too briefly; and especially to John Butt, Edward Hooker and George Sherburn, whose judicious encouragement combined with unanswerable criticism have saved me from a variety of ill courses.

I. P. W.

University of California,
Berkeley.
February 1956

CHAPTER I

Realism and the Novel Form

THERE are still no wholly satisfactory answers to many of the general questions which anyone interested in the early eighteenth-century novelists and their works is likely to ask: Is the novel a new literary form? And if we assume, as is commonly done, that it is, and that it was begun by Defoe, Richardson and Fielding, how does it differ from the prose fiction of the past, from that of Greece, for example, or that of the Middle Ages, or of seventeenth-century France? And is there any reason why these differences appeared when and where they did?

Such large questions are never easy to approach, much less to answer, and they are particularly difficult in this case because Defoe, Richardson and Fielding do not in the usual sense constitute a literary school. Indeed their works show so little sign of mutual influence and are so different in nature that at first sight it appears that our curiosity about the rise of the novel is unlikely to find any satisfaction other than the meagre one afforded by the terms 'genius' and 'accident', the twin faces on the Janus of the dead ends of literary history. We cannot, of course, do without them: on the other hand there is not much we can do with them. The present inquiry therefore takes another direction: assuming that the appearance of our first three novelists within a single generation was probably not sheer accident, and that their geniuses could not have created the new form unless the conditions of the time had also been favourable, it attempts to discover what these favourable conditions in the literary and social situation were, and in what ways Defoe, Richardson and Fielding were its beneficiaries.

For this investigation our first need is a working definition of the characteristics of the novel—a definition sufficiently narrow to exclude previous types of narrative and yet broad enough to apply to whatever is usually put in the novel category. The novelists themselves do not help us very much here. It is true that both Richardson and Fielding saw themselves as founders of a new kind of writing, and that both viewed their work as involving a break with the old-fashioned romances; but neither they nor their contemporaries provide us with the kind of characterisation of the new genre that we need; indeed they did not even canonise the changed nature of their fiction by a change in nomenclature—our usage of the term 'novel' was not fully established until the end of the eighteenth century.

With the help of their larger perspective the historians of the novel have been able to do much more to determine the idiosyncratic features of the new form. Briefly, they have seen 'realism' as the defining characteristic which differentiates the work of the early eighteenth-century novelists from previous fiction. With their picture—that of writers otherwise different but alike in this quality of 'realism'—one's initial reservation must surely be that the term itself needs further explanation, if only because to use it without qualification as a defining characteristic of the novel might otherwise carry the invidious suggestion that all previous writers and literary forms pursued the unreal..

The main critical associations of the term 'realism' are with the French school of Realists. 'Réalisme' was apparently first used as an aesthetic description in 1835 to denote the 'vérité humaine' of Rembrandt as opposed to the 'idéalité poétique' of neo-classical painting; it was later consecrated as a specifically literary term by the foundation in 1856 of *Réalisme*, a journal edited by Duranty.[1]

Unfortunately much of the usefulness of the word was soon lost in the bitter controversies over the 'low' subjects and allegedly immoral tendencies of Flaubert and his successors. As a result, 'realism' came to be used primarily as the antonym of 'idealism', and this sense, which is actually a reflection of the position taken by the enemies of the French Realists, has in fact coloured much critical and historical writing about the novel. The prehistory of the form has commonly been envisaged as a matter of tracing the continuity between all earlier fiction which portrayed low life: the story of the Ephesian matron is 'realistic' because it shows that sexual appetite is stronger than wifely sorrow; and the fabliau or the picaresque tale are 'realistic' because economic or carnal motives are given pride of place in their presentation of human behaviour. By the same implicit

[1] See Bernard Weinberg, *French Realism: the Critical Reaction 1830–1870* (London, 1937), p. 114.

premise, the English eighteenth-century novelists, together with Furetière, Scarron and Lesage in France, are regarded as the eventual climax of this tradition: the 'realism' of the novels of Defoe, Richardson and Fielding is closely associated with the fact that Moll Flanders is a thief, Pamela a hypocrite, and Tom Jones a fornicator.

This use of 'realism', however, has the grave defect of obscuring what is probably the most original feature of the novel form. If the novel were realistic merely because it saw life from the seamy side, it would only be an inverted romance; but in fact it surely attempts to portray all the varieties of human experience, and not merely those suited to one particular literary perspective: the novel's realism does not reside in the kind of life it presents, but in the way it presents it.

This, of course, is very close to the position of the French Realists themselves, who asserted that if their novels tended to differ from the more flattering pictures of humanity presented by many established ethical, social, and literary codes, it was merely because they were the product of a more dispassionate and scientific scrutiny of life than had ever been attempted before. It is far from clear that this ideal of scientific objectivity is desirable, and it certainly cannot be realised in practice: nevertheless it is very significant that, in the first sustained effort of the new genre to become critically aware of its aims and methods, the French Realists should have drawn attention to an issue which the novel raises more sharply than any other literary form—the problem of the correspondence between the literary work and the reality which it imitates. This is essentially an epistemological problem, and it therefore seems likely that the nature of the novel's realism, whether in the early eighteenth century or later, can best be clarified by the help of those professionally concerned with the analysis of concepts, the philosophers.

I

By a paradox that will surprise only the neophyte, the term 'realism' in philosophy is most strictly applied to a view of reality diametrically opposed to that of common usage—to the view held by the scholastic Realists of the Middle Ages that it is universals, classes or abstractions, and not the particular, concrete objects of sense-perception, which are the true 'realities'.

This, at first sight, appears unhelpful, since in the novel, more than in any other genre, general truths only exist *post res*; but the very unfamiliarity of the point of view of scholastic Realism at least serves to draw attention to a characteristic of the novel which is analogous to the changed philosophical meaning of 'realism' today: the novel arose in the modern period, a period whose general intellectual orientation was most decisively separated from its classical and mediaeval heritage by its rejection—or at least its attempted rejection—of universals.[1]

Modern realism, of course, begins from the position that truth can be discovered by the individual through his senses: it has its origins in Descartes and Locke, and received its first full formulation by Thomas Reid in the middle of the eighteenth century.[2] But the view that the external world is real, and that our senses give us a true report of it, obviously does not in itself throw much light on literary realism; since almost everyone, in all ages, has in one way or another been forced to some such conclusion about the external world by his own experience, literature has always been to some extent exposed to the same epistemological naïveté. Further, the distinctive tenets of realist epistemology, and the controversies associated with them, are for the most part much too specialised in nature to have much bearing on literature. What is important to the novel in philosophical realism is much less specific; it is rather the general temper of realist thought, the methods of investigation it has used, and the kinds of problems it has raised.

The general temper of philosophical realism has been critical, anti-traditional and innovating; its method has been the study of the particulars of experience by the individual investigator, who, ideally at least, is free from the body of past assumptions and traditional beliefs; and it has given a peculiar importance to semantics, to the problem of the nature of the correspondence between words and reality. All of these features of philosophical realism have analogies to distinctive features of the novel form, analogies which draw attention to the characteristic kind of correspondence between life and literature which has obtained in prose fiction since the novels of Defoe and Richardson.

[1] See R. I. Aaron, *The Theory of Universals* (Oxford, 1952), pp. 18-41.
[2] See S. Z. Hasan, *Realism* (Cambridge, 1928), chs. 1 and 2.

(a)

The greatness of Descartes was primarily one of method, of the thoroughness of his determination to accept nothing on trust; and his *Discourse on Method* (1637) and his *Meditations* did much to bring about the modern assumption whereby the pursuit of truth is conceived of as a wholly individual matter, logically independent of the tradition of past thought, and indeed as more likely to be arrived at by a departure from it.

The novel is the form of literature which most fully reflects this individualist and innovating reorientation. Previous literary forms had reflected the general tendency of their cultures to make conformity to traditional practice the major test of truth: the plots of classical and renaissance epic, for example, were based on past history or fable, and the merits of the author's treatment were judged largely according to a view of literary decorum derived from the accepted models in the genre. This literary traditionalism was first and most fully challenged by the novel, whose primary criterion was truth to individual experience—individual experience which is always unique and therefore new. The novel is thus the logical literary vehicle of a culture which, in the last few centuries, has set an unprecedented value on originality, on the novel; and it is therefore well named.

This emphasis on the new accounts for some of the critical difficulties which the novel is widely agreed to present. When we judge a work in another genre, a recognition of its literary models is often important and sometimes essential; our evaluation depends to a large extent on our analysis of the author's skill in handling the appropriate formal conventions. On the other hand, it is surely very damaging for a novel to be in any sense an imitation of another literary work: and the reason for this seems to be that since the novelist's primary task is to convey the impression of fidelity to human experience, attention to any pre-established formal conventions can only endanger his success. What is often felt as the formlessness of the novel, as compared, say, with tragedy or the ode, probably follows from this: the poverty of the novel's formal conventions would seem to be the price it must pay for its realism.

But the absence of formal conventions in the novel is unimportant compared to its rejection of traditional plots. Plot, of course, is not a simple matter, and the degree of its originality or otherwise is never easy to determine; nevertheless a broad and necessarily summary comparison between the novel and previous literary forms reveals an important difference: Defoe and Richardson are the first great writers in our literature who did not take their plots from mythology, history, legend or previous literature. In this they differ from Chaucer, Spenser, Shakespeare and Milton, for instance, who, like the writers of Greece and Rome, habitually used traditional plots; and who did so, in the last analysis, because they accepted the general premise of their times that, since Nature is essentially complete and unchanging, its records, whether scriptural, legendary or historical, constitute a definitive repertoire of human experience.

This point of view continued to be expressed until the nineteenth century; the opponents of Balzac, for example, used it to deride his preoccupation with contemporary and, in their view, ephemeral reality. But at the same time, from the Renaissance onwards, there was a growing tendency for individual experience to replace collective tradition as the ultimate arbiter of reality; and this transition would seem to constitute an important part of the general cultural background of the rise of the novel.

It is significant that the trend in favour of originality found its first powerful expression in England, and in the eighteenth century; the very word 'original' took on its modern meaning at this time, by a semantic reversal which is a parallel to the change in the meaning of 'realism'. We have seen that, from the mediaeval belief in the reality of universals, 'realism' had come to denote a belief in the individual apprehension of reality through the senses: similarly the term 'original' which in the Middle Ages had meant 'having existed from the first' came to mean 'underived, independent, first-hand'; and by the time that Edward Young in his epoch-making *Conjectures on Original Composition* (1759) hailed Richardson as 'a genius as well moral as original',[1] the word could be used as a term of praise meaning 'novel or fresh in character or style'.

The novel's use of non-traditional plots is an early and probably independent manifestation of this emphasis. When Defoe,

[1] *Works* (1773), V, 125; see also Max Scheler, *Versuche zu einer Soziologie des Wissens* (München and Leipzig, 1924), pp. 104 ff.; Elizabeth L. Mann, 'The Problem of Originality in English Literary Criticism, 1750–1800', *PQ*, XVIII (1939), 97-118.

for example, began to write fiction he took little notice of the dominant critical theory of the day, which still inclined towards the use of traditional plots; instead, he merely allowed his narrative order to flow spontaneously from his own sense of what his protagonists might plausibly do next. In so doing Defoe initiated an important new tendency in fiction: his total subordination of the plot to the pattern of the autobiographical memoir is as defiant an assertion of the primacy of individual experience in the novel as Descartes's *cogito ergo sum* was in philosophy.

After Defoe, Richardson and Fielding in their very different ways continued what was to become the novel's usual practice, the use of non-traditional plots, either wholly invented or based in part on a contemporary incident. It cannot be claimed that either of them completely achieved that interpenetration of plot, character and emergent moral theme which is found in the highest examples of the·art of the novel. But it must be remembered that the task was not an easy one, particularly at a time when the established literary outlet for the creative imagination lay in eliciting an individual pattern and a contemporary significance from a plot that was not itself novel.

(b)

Much else besides the plot had to be changed in the tradition of fiction before the novel could embody the individual apprehension of reality as freely as the method of Descartes and Locke allowed their thought to spring from the immediate facts of consciousness. To begin with, the actors in the plot and the scene of their actions had to be placed in a new literary perspective: the plot had to be acted out by particular people in particular circumstances, rather than, as had been common in the past, by general human types against a background primarily determined by the appropriate literary convention.

This literary change was analogous to the rejection of universals and the emphasis on particulars which characterises philosophic realism. Aristotle might have agreed with Locke's primary assumption, that it was the senses which 'at first let in particular ideas, and furnish the empty cabinet' of the mind.[1] But he would have gone on to insist that the scrutiny of particular cases was of little value in itself; the proper intellectual task

[1] *Essay Concerning Human Understanding* (1690), Bk. I, ch. 2, sect. xv.

of man was to rally against the meaningless flux of sensation, and achieve a knowledge of the universals which alone consti-tuted the ultimate and immutable reality.[1] It is this generalising emphasis which gives most Western thought until the seven-teenth century a strong enough family resemblance to outweigh all its other multifarious differences: similarly when in 1713 Berkeley's Philonous affirmed that 'it is an universally received maxim, that *everything which exists is particular*',[2] he was stating the opposite modern tendency which in turn gives modern thought since Descartes a certain unity of outlook and method.

Here, again, both the new trends in philosophy and the related formal characteristics of the novel were contrary to the domin-ant literary outlook. For the critical tradition in the early eight-eenth century was still governed by the strong classical prefer-ence for the general and universal: the proper object of literature remained *quod semper quod ubique ab omnibus creditum est.* This preference was particularly pronounced in the neo-Platonist tendency, which had always been strong in the romance, and which was becoming of increasing importance in literary criti-cism and aesthetics generally. Shaftesbury, for instance, in his *Essay on the Freedom of Wit and Humour* (1709), expressed the dis-taste of this school of thought for particularity in literature and art very emphatically: 'The variety of Nature is such, as to dis-tinguish every thing she forms, by a *peculiar* original character; which, if strictly observed, will make the subject appear unlike to anything extant in the world besides. But this effect the good poet and painter seek industriously to prevent. They hate *minuteness*, and are afraid of *singularity*.'[1] He continued: 'The mere Face-Painter, indeed, has little in common with the Poet; but, like the mere Historian, copies what he sees, and minutely traces every feature, and odd mark'; and concluded confidently that ''Tis otherwise with men of invention and design'.

Despite Shaftesbury's engaging finality, however, a contrary aesthetic tendency in favour of particularity soon began to assert itself, largely as a result of the application to literary problems of the psychological approach of Hobbes and Locke. Lord Kames was perhaps the most forthright early spokesman of this tendency. In his *Elements of Criticism* (1762) he declared

---

[1] See *Posterior Analytics*, Bk. I, ch. 24; Bk. II, ch. 19.
[2] First *Dialogue between Hylas and Philonous*, 1713 (Berkeley, *Works*, ed. Luce and Jessop (London, 1949), II, 192). [3] Pt. IV, sect. 3.

that 'abstract or general terms have no good effect in any composition for amusement; because it is only of particular objects that images can be formed';[1] and Kames went on to claim that, contrary to general opinion, Shakespeare's appeal lay in the fact that 'every article in his descriptions is particular, as in nature'.

In this matter, as in that of originality, Defoe and Richardson established the characteristic literary direction of the novel form long before it could count on any support from critical theory. Not all will agree with Kames that 'every article' in Shakespeare's descriptions is particular; but particularity of description has always been considered typical of the narrative manner of *Robinson Crusoe* and *Pamela*. Richardson's first biographer, indeed, Mrs. Barbauld, described his genius in terms of an analogy which has continually figured in the controversy between neo-classical generality and realistic particularity. Sir Joshua Reynolds, for example, expressed his neo-classical orthodoxy by preferring the 'great and general ideas' of Italian painting to the 'literal truth and . . . minute exactness in the detail of nature modified by accident' of the Dutch school;[2] whereas the French Realists, it will be remembered, had followed the 'vérité humaine' of Rembrandt, rather than the 'idéalité poétique' of the classical school. Mrs. Barbauld accurately indicated Richardson's position in this conflict when she wrote that he had 'the accuracy of finish of a Dutch painter . . . content to produce effects by the patient labour of minuteness'.[3] Both he and Defoe, in fact, were heedless of Shaftesbury's scorn, and like Rembrandt were content to be 'mere face-painters and historians'.

The concept of realistic particularity in literature is itself somewhat too general to be capable of concrete demonstration: for such demonstration to be possible the relationship of realistic particularity to some specific aspects of narrative technique must first be established. Two such aspects suggest themselves as of especial importance in the novel—characterisation, and presentation of background: the novel is surely distinguished from

---

[1] 1763 ed., III, 198-199.

[2] *Idler*, No. 79 (1759). See also Scott Elledge, 'The Background and Development in English Criticism of the Theories of Generality and Particularity', *PMLA*, LX (1945), 161-174.

[3] *Correspondence of Samuel Richardson*, 1804, I, cxxxvii. For similar comments by contemporary French readers, see Joseph Texte, *Jean-Jacques Rousseau and the Cosmopolitan Spirit in Literature* (London, 1899), pp. 174-175.

other genres and from previous forms of fiction by the amount of attention it habitually accords both to the individualisation of its characters and to the detailed presentation of their environment.

(c)

Philosophically the particularising approach to character resolves itself into the problem of defining the individual person. Once Descartes had given the thought processes within the individual's consciousness supreme importance, the philosophical problems connected with personal identity naturally attracted a great deal of attention. In England, for example, Locke, Bishop Butler, Berkeley, Hume and Reid all debated the issue, and the controversy even reached the pages of the *Spectator*.[1]

The parallel here between the tradition of realist thought and the formal innovations of the early novelists is obvious: both philosophers and novelists paid greater attention to the particular individual than had been common before. But the great attention paid in the novel to the particularisation of character is itself such a large question that we will consider only one of its more manageable aspects: the way that the novelist typically indicates his intention of presenting a character as a particular individual by naming him in exactly the same way as particular individuals are named in ordinary life.

Logically the problem of individual identity is closely related to the epistemological status of proper names; for, in the words of Hobbes, 'Proper names bring to mind one thing only; universals recall any one of many'.[2] Proper names have exactly the same function in social life: they are the verbal expression of the particular identity of each individual person. In literature, however, this function of proper names was first fully established in the novel.

Characters in previous forms of literature, of course, were usually given proper names; but the kind of names actually used showed that the author was not trying to establish his characters as completely individualised entities. The precepts of classical and renaissance criticism agreed with the practice of their literature in preferring either historical names or type names. In either case, the names set the characters in the context of a large body of expectations primarily formed from past

[1] No. 578 (1714).   [2] *Leviathan* (1651), Pt. I, ch. 4.

literature, rather than from the context of contemporary life. Even in comedy, where characters were not usually historical but invented, the names were supposed to be 'characteristic', as Aristotle tells us,[1] and they tended to remain so until long after the rise of the novel.

Earlier types of prose fiction had also tended to use proper names that were characteristic, or non-particular and unrealistic in some other way; names that either, like those of Rabelais, Sidney or Bunyan, denoted particular qualities, or like those of Lyly, Aphra Behn or Mrs. Manley, carried foreign, archaic or literary connotations which excluded any suggestion of real and contemporary life. The primarily literary and conventional orientation of these proper names was further attested by the fact that there was usually only one of them—Mr. Badman or Euphues; unlike people in ordinary life, the characters of fiction did not have both given name and surname.

The early novelists, however, made an extremely significant break with tradition, and named their characters in such a way as to suggest that they were to be regarded as particular individuals in the contemporary social environment. Defoe's use of proper names is casual and sometimes contradictory; but he very rarely gives names that are conventional or fanciful—one possible exception, Roxana, is a pseudonym which is fully explained; and most of the main characters such as Robinson Crusoe or Moll Flanders have complete and realistic names or aliases. Richardson continued this practice, but was much more careful and gave all of his major characters, and even most of his minor ones, both a given name and a surname. He also faced a minor but not unimportant problem in novel writing, that of giving names that are subtly appropriate and suggestive, yet sound like ordinary realistic ones. Thus the romance-connotations of Pamela are controlled by the commonplace family name of Andrews; both Clarissa Harlowe and Robert Lovelace are in many ways appropriately named; and indeed nearly all Richardson's proper names, from Mrs. *Sin*clair to Sir Charles *Grand*ison, sound authentic and are yet suited to the personalities of the bearers.

Fielding, as an anonymous contemporary critic pointed out, christened his characters 'not with fantastic high-sounding Names, but such as, tho' they sometimes had some reference to

[1] *Poetics*, ch. 9.

the Character, had a more modern termination'.[1] Such names as Heartfree, Allworthy and Square are certainly modernised versions of the type name, although they are just credible; even Western or Tom Jones suggest very strongly that Fielding had his eye as much on the general type as on the particular individual. This, however, does not controvert the present argument, for it will surely be generally agreed that Fielding's practice in the naming, and indeed in the whole portrayal of his characters, is a departure from the usual treatment of these matters in the novel. Not, as we have seen in Richardson's case, that there is no place in the novel for proper names that are in some way appropriate to the character concerned: but that this appropriateness must not be such as to impair the primary function of the name, which is to symbolise the fact that the character is to be regarded as though he were a particular person and not a type.

Fielding, indeed, seems to have realised this by the time he came to write his last novel, *Amelia*: there his neo-classical preference for type-names finds expression only in such minor characters as Justice Thrasher and Bondum the bailiff; and all the main characters—the Booths, Miss Matthews, Dr. Harrison, Colonel James, Sergeant Atkinson, Captain Trent and Mrs. Bennet, for example—have ordinary and contemporary names. There is, indeed, some evidence that Fielding, like some modern novelists, took these names somewhat at random from a printed list of contemporary persons—all the surnames given above are in the list of subscribers to the 1724 folio edition of Gilbert Burnet's *History of His Own Time*, an edition which Fielding is known to have owned.[2]

Whether this is so or not, it is certain that Fielding made considerable and increasing concessions to the custom initiated by Defoe and Richardson of using ordinary contemporary proper names for their characters. Although this custom was not always followed by some of the later eighteenth-century novelists, such as Smollett and Sterne, it was later established as part of the tradition of the form; and, as Henry James pointed out with respect to Trollope's fecund cleric Mr. Quiverful,[3] the

[1] *Essay on the New Species of Writing Founded by Mr. Fielding*, 1751, p. 18. This whole question is treated more fully in my 'The Naming of Characters in Defoe, Richardson and Fielding', *RES*, XXV (1949), 322-338.

[2] See Wilbur L. Cross, *History of Henry Fielding* (New Haven, 1918), I, 342-343.

[3] *Partial Portraits* (London, 1888), p. 118.

novelist can only break with the tradition at the cost of destroy-ing the reader's belief in the literal reality of the character concerned.

(d)

Locke had defined personal identity as an identity of con-sciousness through duration in time; the individual was in touch with his own continuing identity through memory of his past thoughts and actions.[1] This location of the source of personal identity in the repertoire of its memories was continued by Hume: 'Had we no memory, we never should have any notion of causation, nor consequently of that chain of causes and effects, which constitute our self or person'.[2] Such a point of view is characteristic of the novel; many novelists, from Sterne to Proust, have made their subject the exploration of the person-ality as it is defined in the interpenetration of its past and present self-awareness.

Time is an essential category in another related but more external approach to the problem of defining the individuality of any object. The 'principle of individuation' accepted by Locke was that of existence at a particular locus in space and time: since, as he wrote, 'ideas become general by separating from them the circumstances of time and place',[3] so they become particular only when both these circumstances are specified. In the same way the characters of the novel can only be individualised if they are set in a background of particular-ised time and place.

Both the philosophy and the literature of Greece and Rome were deeply influenced by Plato's view that the Forms or Ideas were the ultimate realities behind the concrete objects of the temporal world. These forms were conceived as timeless and unchanging,[4] and thus reflected the basic premise of their civil-isation in general that nothing happened or could happen whose fundamental meaning was not independent of the flux of time. This premise is diametrically opposed to the outlook which has established itself since the Renaissance, and which views time,

---

[1] *Human Understanding*, Bk. II, ch. 27, sects. ix, x.
[2] *Treatise of Human Nature*, Bk. I, pt. 4, sect. vi.
[3] *Human Understanding*, Bk. III, ch. 3, sect. vi.
[4] Plato does not specifically state that the Ideas are timeless, but the notion, which dates from Aristotle (*Metaphysics*, Bk. XII, ch. 6), underlies the whole system of thought with which they are associated.

not only as a crucial dimension of the physical world, but as the shaping force of man's individual and collective history.

The novel is in nothing so characteristic of our culture as in the way that it reflects this characteristic orientation of modern thought. E. M. Forster sees the portrayal of 'life by time' as the distinctive role which the novel has added to literature's more ancient preoccupation with portraying 'life by values';[1] Spengler's perspective for the rise of the novel is the need of 'ultrahistorical' modern man for a literary form capable of dealing with 'the whole of life';[2] while more recently Northrop Frye has seen the 'alliance of time and Western man' as the defining characteristic of the novel compared with other genres.[3]

We have already considered one aspect of the importance which the novel allots the time dimension: its break with the earlier literary tradition of using timeless stories to mirror the unchanging moral verities. The novel's plot is also distinguished from most previous fiction by its use of past experience as the cause of present action: a causal connection operating through time replaces the reliance of earlier narratives on disguises and coincidences, and this tends to give the novel a much more cohesive structure. Even more important, perhaps, is the effect upon characterisation of the novel's insistence on the time process. The most obvious and extreme example of this is the stream of consciousness novel which purports to present a direct quotation of what occurs in the individual mind under the impact of the temporal flux; but the novel in general has interested itself much more than any other literary form in the development of its characters in the course of time. Finally, the novel's detailed depiction of the concerns of everyday life also depends upon its power over the time dimension: T. H. Green pointed out that much of man's life had tended to be almost unavailable to literary representation merely as a result of its slowness;[4] the novel's closeness to the texture of daily experience directly depends upon its employment of a much more minutely discriminated time-scale than had previously been employed in narrative.

The role of time in ancient, mediaeval and renaissance

[1] *Aspects of the Novel* (London, 1949), pp. 29-31.
[2] *Decline of the West*, trans. Atkinson (London, 1928), I, 130-131.
[3] 'The Four Forms of Fiction', *Hudson Review*, II (1950), 596.
[4] 'Estimate of the Value and Influence of Works of Fiction in Modern Times' (1862), *Works*, ed. Nettleship (London, 1888), III, 36.

literature is certainly very different from that in the novel. The restriction of the action of tragedy to twenty-four hours, for example, the celebrated unity of time, is really a denial of the importance of the temporal dimension in human life; for, in accord with the classical world's view of reality as subsisting in timeless universals, it implies that the truth about existence can be as fully unfolded in the space of a day as in the space of a lifetime. The equally celebrated personifications of time as the winged chariot or the grim reaper reveal an essentially similar outlook. They focus attention, not on the temporal flux, but on the supremely timeless fact of death; their role is to overwhelm our awareness of daily life so that we shall be prepared to face eternity. Both these personifications, in fact, resemble the doctrine of the unity of time in that they are fundamentally a-historical, and are therefore equally typical of the very minor importance accorded to the temporal dimension in most literature previous to the novel.

Shakespeare's sense of the historical past, for example, is very different from the modern one. Troy and Rome, the Plantagenets and the Tudors, none of them are far enough back to be very different from the present or from each other. In this Shakespeare reflects the view of his age: he had been dead for thirty years before the word 'anachronism' first appeared in English,[1] and he was still very close to the mediaeval conception of history by which, whatever the period, the wheel of time churns out the same eternally applicable *exempla*.

This a-historical outlook is associated with a striking lack of interest in the minute-by-minute and day-to-day temporal setting, a lack of interest which has caused the time scheme of so many plays both by Shakespeare and by most of his predecessors from Aeschylus onwards, to baffle later editors and critics. The attitude to time in early fiction is very similar; the sequence of events is set in a very abstract continuum of time and space, and allows very little importance to time as a factor in human relationships. Coleridge noted the 'marvellous independence and true imaginative absence of all particular space or time in the "Faerie Queene" ';[2] and the temporal dimension of Bunyan's allegories or the heroic romances is equally vague and unparticularised.

---

[1] See Herman J. Ebeling, 'The Word Anachronism', *MLN*, LII (1937), 120-121.   [2] *Selected Works*, ed. Potter (London, 1933), p. 333.

Soon, however, the modern sense of time began to permeate many areas of thought. The late seventeenth century witnessed the rise of a more objective study of history and therefore of a deeper sense of the difference between the past and the present.[1] At the same time Newton and Locke presented a new analysis of the temporal process;[2] it became a slower and more mechanical sense of duration which was minutely enough discriminated to measure the falling of objects or the succession of thoughts in the mind.

These new emphases are reflected in the novels of Defoe. His fiction is the first which presents us with a picture both of the individual life in its larger perspective as a historical process, and in its closer view which shows the process being acted out against the background of the most ephemeral thoughts and actions. It is true that the time scales of his novels are sometimes both contradictory in themselves, and inconsistent with their pretended historical setting, but the mere fact that such objections arise is surely a tribute to the way the characters are felt by the reader to be rooted in the temporal dimension. We obviously could not think of making such objections seriously to Sidney's *Arcadia* or *The Pilgrim's Progress*; there is not enough evidence of the reality of time for any sense of discrepancies to be possible. Defoe does give us such evidence. At his best, he convinces us completely that his narrative is occurring at a particular place and at a particular time, and our memory of his novels consists largely of these vividly realised moments in the lives of his characters, moments which are loosely strung together to form a convincing biographical perspective. We have a sense of personal identity subsisting through duration and yet being changed by the flow of experience.

This impression is much more strongly and completely realised in Richardson. He was very careful to locate all his events of his narrative in an unprecedentedly detailed timescheme: the superscription of each letter gives us the day of the week, and often the time of the day; and this in turn acts as an objective framework for the even greater temporal detail of the letters themselves—we are told, for example, that Clarissa died

---

[1] See G. N. Clark, *The Later Stuarts, 1660–1714* (Oxford, 1934), pp. 362–366; René Wellek, *The Rise of English Literary History* (Chapel Hill, 1941), ch. 2.

[2] See especially Ernst Cassirer, 'Raum und Zeit', *Das Erkenntnisproblem . . .* (Berlin, 1922–23), II, 339–374.

at 6.40 P.M. on Thursday, 7th September. Richardson's use of the letter form also induced in the reader a continual sense of actual participation in the action which was until then unparalleled in its completeness and intensity. He knew, as he wrote in the 'Preface' to *Clarissa*, that it was 'Critical situations . . . with what may be called *instantaneous* descriptions and reflections' that engaged the attention best; and in many scenes the pace of the narrative was slowed down by minute description to something very near that of actual experience. In these scenes Richardson achieved for the novel what D. W. Griffith's technique of the 'close-up' did for the film: added a new dimension to the representation of reality.

Fielding approached the problem of time in his novels from a more external and traditional point of view. In *Shamela* he poured scorn on Richardson's use of the present tense: 'Mrs. Jervis and I are just in bed, and the door unlocked; if my master should come—Ods-bobs! I hear him just coming in at the door. You see I write in the present tense, as Parson William says. Well, he is in bed between us . . .'[1] In *Tom Jones* he indicated his intention of being much more selective than Richardson in his handling of the time dimension: 'We intend . . . rather to pursue the method of those writers who profess to disclose the revolutions of countries, than to imitate the painful and voluminous historian, who, to preserve the regularity of his series, thinks himself obliged to fill up as much paper with the detail of months and years in which nothing remarkable happened, as he employs upon those notable eras when the greatest scenes have been transacted on the human stage'.[2] At the same time, however, *Tom Jones* introduced one interesting innovation in the fictional treatment of time. Fielding seems to have used an almanac, that symbol of the diffusion of an objective sense of time by the printing press: with slight exceptions, nearly all the events of his novel are chronologically consistent, not only in relation to each other, and to the time that each stage of the journey of the various characters from the West Country to London would actually have taken, but also in relation to such external considerations as the proper phases of the moon and the time-table of the Jacobite rebellion in 1745, the supposed year of the action.[3]

[1] Letter 6.   [2] Bk. II, ch. 1.
[3] As was shown by F. S. Dickson (Cross, *Henry Fielding*, II, 189-193).

(e)

In the present context, as in many others, space is the necessary correlative of time. Logically the individual, particular case is defined by reference to two co-ordinates, space and time. Psychologically, as Coleridge pointed out, our idea of time is 'always blended with the idea of space'.[1] The two dimensions, indeed, are for many practical purposes inseparable, as is suggested by the fact that the words 'present' and 'minute' can refer to either dimension; while introspection shows that we cannot easily visualise any particular moment of existence without setting it in its spatial context also.

Place was traditionally almost as general and vague as time in tragedy, comedy and romance. Shakespeare, as Johnson tells us, 'had no regard to distinction of time or place';[2] and Sidney's *Arcadia* was as unlocalized as the Bohemian limbos of the Elizabethan stage. In the picaresque novel, it is true, and in Bunyan, there are many passages of vivid and particularised physical description; but they are incidental and fragmentary. Defoe would seem to be the first of our writers who visualised the whole of his narrative as though it occurred in an actual physical environment. His attention to the description of milieu is still intermittent; but occasional vivid details supplement the continual implication of his narrative and make us attach Robinson Crusoe and Moll Flanders much more completely to their environments than is the case with previous fictional characters. Characteristically, this solidity of setting is particularly noticeable in Defoe's treatment of movable objects in the physical world: in *Moll Flanders* there is much linen and gold to be counted, while Robinson Crusoe's island is full of memorable pieces of clothing and hardware.

Richardson, once again occupying the central place in the development of the technique of narrative realism, carried the process much further. There is little description of natural scenery, but considerable attention is paid to interiors throughout his novels. Pamela's residences in Lincolnshire and Bedfordshire are real enough prisons; we are given a highly detailed description of Grandison Hall; and some of the descriptions in

---

[1] *Biographia Literaria*, ed. Shawcross (London, 1907), I, 87.
[2] 'Preface' (1765), *Johnson on Shakespeare*, ed. Raleigh (London, 1908), pp. 21-22.

Clarissa anticipate Balzac's skill in making the setting of the novel a pervasive operating force—the Harlowe mansion becomes a terrifyingly real physical and moral environment.

Here, too, Fielding is some way from Richardson's particularity. He gives us no full interiors, and his frequent landscape descriptions are very conventionalised. Nevertheless *Tom Jones* features the first Gothic mansion in the history of the novel:[1] and Fielding is as careful about the topography of his action as he is about its chronology; many of the places on Tom Jones's route to London are given by name, and the exact location of the others is implied by various other kinds of evidence.

In general, then, although there is nothing in the eighteenth-century novel which equals the opening chapters of *Le Rouge et le noir* or *Le Père Goriot*, chapters which at once indicate the importance which Stendhal and Balzac attach to the environment in their total picture of life, there is no doubt that the pursuit of verisimilitude led Defoe, Richardson and Fielding to initiate that power of 'putting man wholly into his physical setting' which constitutes for Allen Tate the distinctive capacity of the novel form;[2] and the considerable extent to which they succeeded is not the least of the factors which differentiate them from previous writers of fiction and which explain their importance in the tradition of the new form.

(f)

The various technical characteristics of the novel described above all seem to contribute to the furthering of an aim which the novelist shares with the philosopher—the production of what purports to be an authentic account of the actual experiences of individuals. This aim involved many other departures from the traditions of fiction besides those already mentioned. What is perhaps the most important of them, the adaptation of prose style to give an air of complete authenticity, is also closely related to one of the distinctive methodological emphases of philosophical realism.

Just as it was the Nominalist scepticism about language

[1] See Warren Hunting Smith, *Architecture in English Fiction* (New Haven, 1934), p. 65.
[2] 'Techniques of Fiction', in *Critiques and Essays on Modern Fiction, 1920–1951*, ed. Aldridge (New York, 1952), p. 41.

which began to undermine the attitude to universals held by the scholastic Realists, so modern realism soon found itself faced with the semantic problem. Words did not all stand for real objects, or did not stand for them in the same way, and philosophy was therefore faced with the problem of discovering their rationale. Locke's chapters at the end of the third Book of the *Essay Concerning Human Understanding* are probably the most important evidence of this trend in the seventeenth century. Much of what is said there about the proper use of words would exclude the great bulk of literature, since, as Locke sadly discovers, 'eloquence, like the fair sex', involves a pleasurable deceit.[1] On the other hand, it is interesting to note that although some of the 'abuses of language' which Locke specifies, such as figurative language, had been a regular feature of the romances, they are much rarer in the prose of Defoe and Richardson than in that of any previous writer of fiction.

The previous stylistic tradition for fiction was not primarily concerned with the correspondence of words to things, but rather with the extrinsic beauties which could be bestowed upon description and action by the use of rhetoric. Heliodorus's *Aethiopica* had established the tradition of linguistic ornateness in the Greek romances and the tradition had been continued in the Euphuism of John Lyly and Sidney, and in the elaborate conceits, or 'phébus', of La Calprenède and Madeleine de Scudéry. So even if the new writers of fiction had rejected the old tradition of mixing poetry with their prose, a tradition which had been followed even in narratives as completely devoted to the portrayal of low life as Petronius's *Satyricon*, there would still have remained a strong literary expectation that they would use language as a source of interest in its own right, rather than as a purely referential medium.

In any case, of course, the classical critical tradition in general had no use for the unadorned realistic description which such a use of language would imply. When the 9th *Tatler* (1709) introduced Swift's 'Description of the Morning' as a work where the author had 'run into a way perfectly new, and described things as they happen', it was being ironical. The implicit assumption of educated writers and critics was that an author's skill was shown, not in the closeness with which he made his

[1] Bk. III, ch. 10, sects. xxxiii-xxxiv.

words correspond to their objects, but in the literary sensitivity with which his style reflected the linguistic decorum appropriate to its subject. It is natural, therefore, that it is to writers outside the circle of wit that we should have to turn for our earliest examples of fictional narrative written in a prose which restricts itself almost entirely to a descriptive and denotative use of language. Natural, too, that both Defoe and Richardson should have been attacked by many of the better educated writers of the day for their clumsy and often inaccurate way of writing.

Their basically realistic intentions, of course, required something very different from the accepted modes of literary prose. It is true that the movement towards clear and easy prose in the late seventeenth century had done much to produce a mode of expression much better adapted to the realistic novel than had been available before; while the Lockean view of language was beginning to be reflected in literary theory—John Dennis, for example, proscribed imagery in certain circumstances on the ground that it was unrealistic: 'No sort of imagery can ever be the language of grief. If a man complains in simile, I either laugh or sleep.'[1] Nevertheless the prose norm of the Augustan period remained much too literary to be the natural voice of Moll Flanders or Pamela Andrews: and although the prose of Addison, for example, or Swift, is simple and direct enough, its ordered economy tends to suggest an acute summary rather than a full report of what it describes.

It is therefore likely that we must regard the break which Defoe and Richardson made with the accepted canons of prose style, not an incidental blemish, but rather as the price they had to pay for achieving the immediacy and closeness of the text to what is being described. With Defoe this closeness is mainly physical, with Richardson mainly emotional, but in both we feel that the writer's exclusive aim is to make the words bring his object home to us in all its concrete particularity, whatever the cost in repetition or parenthesis or verbosity. Fielding, of course, did not break with the traditions of Augustan prose style or outlook. But it can be argued that this detracts from the authenticity of his narratives. Reading *Tom Jones* we do not imagine that we are eavesdropping on a new exploration of

[1] Preface, *The Passion of Byblis, Critical Works*, ed. Hooker (Baltimore, 1939–43), I, 2.

reality; the prose immediately informs us that exploratory operations have long since been accomplished, that we are to be spared that labour, and presented instead with a sifted and clarified report of the findings.

There is a curious antinomy here. On the one hand, Defoe and Richardson make an uncompromising application of the realist point of view in language and prose structure, and thereby forfeit other literary values. On the other hand, Fielding's stylistic virtues tend to interfere with his technique as a novelist, because a patent selectiveness of vision destroys our belief in the reality of report, or at least diverts our attention from the content of the report to the skill of the reporter. There would seem to be some inherent contradiction between the ancient and abiding literary values and the distinctive narrative technique of the novel.

That this may be so is suggested by a parallel with French fiction. In France, the classical critical outlook, with its emphasis on elegance and concision, was not fully challenged until the coming of Romanticism. It is perhaps partly for this reason that French fiction from *La Princesse de Clèves* to *Les Liaisons dangereuses* stands outside the main tradition of the novel. For all its psychological penetration and literary skill, we feel it is too stylish to be authentic. In this Madame de La Fayette and Choderlos de Laclos are the polar opposites of Defoe and Richardson, whose very diffuseness tends to act as a guarantee of the authenticity of their report, whose prose aims exclusively at what Locke defined as the proper purpose of language, 'to convey the knowledge of things',[1] and whose novels as a whole pretend to be no more than a transcription of real life—in Flaubert's words, 'le réel écrit'.

It would appear, then, that the function of language is much more largely referential in the novel than in other literary forms; that the genre itself works by exhaustive presentation rather than by elegant concentration. This fact would no doubt explain both why the novel is the most translatable of the genres; why many undoubtedly great novelists, from Richardson and Balzac to Hardy and Dostoevsky, often write gracelessly, and sometimes with downright vulgarity; and why the novel has less need of historical and literary commentary than other genres—its formal convention forces it to supply its own footnotes.

[1] *Human Understanding*, Bk. III, ch. 10, sect. xxiii.

II

So much for the main analogies between realism in philosophy and literature. They are not proposed as exact; philosophy is one thing and literature is another. Nor do the analogies depend in any way on the presumption that the realist tradition in philosophy was a cause of the realism of the novel. That there was some influence is very likely, especially through Locke, whose thought everywhere pervades the eighteenth-century climate of opinion. But if a causal relationship of any importance exists it is probably much less direct: both the philosophical and the literary innovations must be seen as parallel manifestations of larger change—that vast transformation of Western civilisation since the Renaissance which has replaced the unified world picture of the Middle Ages with another very different one—one which presents us, essentially, with a developing but unplanned aggregate of particular individuals having particular experiences at particular times and at particular places.

Here, however, we are concerned with a much more limited conception, with the extent to which the analogy with philosophical realism helps to isolate and define the distinctive narrative mode of the novel. This, it has been suggested, is the sum of literary techniques whereby the novel's imitation of human life follows the procedures adopted by philosophical realism in its attempt to ascertain and report the truth. These procedures are by no means confined to philosophy; they tend, in fact, to be followed whenever the relation to reality of any report of an event is being investigated. The novel's mode of imitating reality may therefore be equally well summarised in terms of the procedures of another group of specialists in epistemology, the jury in a court of law. Their expectations, and those of the novel reader coincide in many ways: both want to know 'all the particulars' of a given case—the time and place of the occurrence; both must be satisfied as to the identities of the parties concerned, and will refuse to accept evidence about anyone called Sir Toby Belch or Mr. Badman—still less about a Chloe who has no surname and is 'common as the air'; and they also expect the witnesses to tell the story 'in his own words'. The jury, in fact, takes the 'circumstantial view of life', which T. H. Green[1] found to be the characteristic outlook of the novel.

[1] 'Estimate', *Works*, III, 37.

The narrative method whereby the novel embodies this circumstantial view of life may be called its formal realism; formal,
because the term realism does not here refer to any special
literary doctrine or purpose, but only to a set of narrative procedures which are so commonly found together in the novel,
and so rarely in other literary genres, that they may be regarded
as typical of the form itself. Formal realism, in fact, is the narrative embodiment of a premise that Defoe and Richardson
accepted very literally, but which is implicit in the novel form
in general: the premise, or primary convention, that the novel
is a full and authentic report of human experience, and is
therefore under an obligation to satisfy its reader with such
details of the story as the individuality of the actors concerned,
the particulars of the times and places of their actions, details
which are presented through a more largely referential use of
language than is common in other literary forms.

Formal realism is, of course, like the rules of evidence, only a
convention; and there is no reason why the report on human
life which is presented by it should be in fact any truer than those
presented through the very different conventions of other literary genres. The novel's air of total authenticity, indeed, does
tend to authorise confusion on this point: and the tendency of
some Realists and Naturalists to forget that the accurate transcription of actuality does not necessarily produce a work of any
real truth or enduring literary value is no doubt partly responsible for the rather widespread distaste for Realism and all its
works which is current today. This distaste, however, may also
promote critical confusion by leading us into the opposite error;
we must not allow an awareness of certain shortcomings in the
aims of the Realist school to obscure the very considerable
extent to which the novel in general, as much in Joyce as in
Zola, employs the literary means here called formal realism.
Nor must we forget that, although formal realism is only a convention, it has, like all literary conventions, its own peculiar
advantages. There are important differences in the degree to
which different literary forms imitate reality; and the formal
realism of the novel allows a more immediate imitation of
individual experience set in its temporal and spatial environment than do other literary forms. Consequently the novel's
conventions make much smaller demands on the audience than
do most literary conventions; and this surely explains why the

majority of readers in the last two hundred years have found in the novel the literary form which most closely satisfies their wishes for a close correspondence between life and art. Nor are the advantages of the close and detailed correspondence to real life offered by formal realism limited to assisting the novel's popularity; they are also related to its most distinctive literary qualities, as we shall see.

In the strictest sense, of course, formal realism was not discovered by Defoe and Richardson; they only applied it much more completely than had been done before. Homer, for example, as Carlyle pointed out,[1] shared with them that outstanding 'clearness of sight' which is manifested in the 'detailed, ample and lovingly exact' descriptions that abound in their works; and there are many passages in later fiction, from *The Golden Ass* to *Aucassin and Nicolette*, from Chaucer to Bunyan, where the characters, their actions and their environment are presented with a particularity as authentic as that in any eighteenth-century novel. But there is an important difference: in Homer and in earlier prose fiction these passages are relatively rare, and tend to stand out from the surrounding narrative; the total literary structure was not consistently oriented in the direction of formal realism, and the plot especially, which was usually traditional and often highly improbable, was in direct conflict with its premises. Even when previous writers had overtly professed a wholly realistic aim, as did many seventeenth-century writers, they did not pursue it wholeheartedly. La Calprenède, Richard Head, Grimmelshausen, Bunyan, Aphra Behn, Furetière,[2] to mention only a few, had all asserted that their fictions were literally true; but their prefatory asseverations are no more convincing than the very similar ones to be found in most works of mediaeval hagiography. The aim of verisimilitude had not been deeply enough assimilated in either case to bring about the full rejection of all the non-realistic conventions that governed the genre.

For reasons to be considered in the next chapter, Defoe and Richardson were unprecedentedly independent of the literary conventions which might have interfered with their primary intentions, and they accepted the requirements of literal truth

[1] 'Burns', *Critical and Miscellaneous Essays* (New York, 1899), I, 276-277.
[2] See A. J. Tieje, 'A Peculiar Phase of the Theory of Realism in Pre-Richardsonian Prose-Fiction', *PMLA*, XXVII (1913), 213-252.

much more comprehensively. Of no fiction before Defoe's could Lamb have written, in terms very similar to those which Hazlitt used of Richardson,[1] 'It is like reading evidence in a court of Justice'.[2] Whether that is in itself a good thing is open to question; Defoe and Richardson would hardly deserve their reputation unless they had other and better claims on our attention. Nevertheless there can be little doubt that the development of a narrative method capable of creating such an impression is the most conspicuous manifestation of that mutation of prose fiction which we call the novel; the historical importance of Defoe and Richardson therefore primarily depends on the suddenness and completeness with which they brought into being what may be regarded as the lowest common denominator of the novel genre as a whole, its formal realism.

[1] 'He sets about describing every object and transaction, as if the whole had been given in on evidence by an eye-witness' (*Lectures on the English Comic Writers* (New York, 1845), p. 138).

[2] Letter to Walter Wilson, Dec. 16, 1822, printed in the latter's *Memoirs of the Life and Times of Daniel de Foe* (London, 1830, III, 428).

CHAPTER II

The Reading Public and the Rise of the Novel

THE novel's formal realism, we have seen, involved a many-sided break with the current literary tradition. Among the many reasons which made it possible for that break to occur earlier and more thoroughly in England than elsewhere, considerable importance must certainly be attached to changes in the eighteenth-century reading public. In his *English Literature and Society in the Eighteenth Century*, for example, Leslie Stephen long ago suggested that 'the gradual extension of the reading class affected the development of the literature addressed to them',[1] and he pointed to the rise of the novel, together with that of journalism, as prime examples of the effect of changes in the audience for literature. The nature of the evidence is such, however, that a reasonably full analysis would be inordinately long and yet fall far short of completeness in some important matters where information is scanty and difficult to interpret: what is offered here, therefore, is only a brief and tentative treatment of a few of the possible connections between changes in the nature and organisation of the reading public, and the emergence of the novel.

I

Many eighteenth-century observers thought that their age was one of remarkable and increasing popular interest in reading. On the other hand, it is probable that although the reading public was large by comparison with previous periods, it was still very far from the mass reading public of today. The most convincing evidence of this is statistical, although it must, of course, be remembered that all the numerical estimates available are, to varying but always considerable degrees, both untrustworthy in themselves and problematic in their application.

[1] London, 1904, p. 26. See also Helen Sard Hughes, 'The Middle Class Reader and the English Novel', *JEGP*, XXV (1926), 362-378.

The only contemporary estimate of the size of the reading public was made very late in the century: Burke estimated it at 80,000 in the nineties.[1] This is small indeed, out of a population of at least six millions, and would probably imply an even smaller figure for the earlier part of the century with which we are most concerned. Such is certainly the implication of the most reliable evidence available on the circulation of newspapers and periodicals: one figure, that of 43,800 copies sold weekly in 1704,[2] implies less than one newspaper buyer per hundred persons per week; and another later figure, of 23,673 copies sold daily in 1753,[3] suggests that although the newspaper-buying public tripled in the first half of the century, it remained a very small percentage of the total population. Even if we accept the highest contemporary estimate of the number of readers per copy, that of twenty made by Addison in the *Spectator*,[4] we are left with a maximum newspaper-reading public of less than half a million—at most one in eleven of the total population; and since the estimate of twenty readers per copy seems a wild (and not disinterested) exaggeration, the real proportion was probably no more than half of this, or less than one in twenty.

The sale of the most popular books in the period suggests a book-buying public that is still numbered only in tens of thousands. Most of the very few secular works with sales of over ten thousand were topical pamphlets, such as Swift's *Conduct of the Allies* (1711), with a sale of 11,000 copies,[5] and Price's *Observations on the Nature of Civil Liberty* (1776), with a sale of 60,000 in a few months.[6] The highest figure recorded for a single work, that of 105,000, for Bishop Sherlock's 1750 *Letter from the Lord Bishop of London to the Clergy and People of London on the Occasion of the Late Earthquakes . . .*,[7] was for a somewhat sensational religious pamphlet, many of which were distributed free for evangelical purposes. Sales of full-length, and therefore more expensive, works were much smaller, especially when they were of a secular nature.

[1] *Cit.* A. S. Collins, *The Profession of Letters* (London, 1928), p. 29.
[2] J. Sutherland, 'The Circulation of Newspapers and Literary Periodicals, 1700–1730', *Library*, 4th ser., XV (1934), 111-113.
[3] A. S. Collins, *Authorship in the Days of Johnson* (London, 1927), p. 255.
[4] No. 10 (1711).   [5] Swift, *Journal to Stella*, Jan. 28, 1712.
[6] Collins, *Profession of Letters*, p. 21.
[7] E. Carpenter, *Thomas Sherlock* (London, 1936), pp. 286-287.

Figures showing the growth of the reading public are an even more unreliable guide than those indicating its size; but two of the least dubious suggest that a very considerable increase occurred during the period. In 1724 Samuel Negus, a printer, complained that the number of printing presses in London had increased to 75;[1] but by 1757 another printer, Strahan, estimated that there were between 150 and 200 'constantly employed'.[2] A modern estimate of the average annual publication of new books, excluding pamphlets, suggests that an almost fourfold increase occurred during the century; annual output from 1666 to 1756 averaging less than 100, and that from 1792 to 1802, 372.[3]

It is likely, therefore, that when, in 1781, Johnson spoke of a 'nation of readers',[4] he had in mind a situation which had to a large extent arisen after 1750, and that, even so, his phrase must not be taken literally: the increase in the reading public may have been sufficiently marked to justify hyperbole, but it was still on a very limited scale.

A brief survey of the factors which affected the composition of the reading public will show why it remained so small by modern standards.

The first and most obvious of these factors was the very limited distribution of literacy; not literacy in its eighteenth-century sense—knowledge of the classical languages and literatures, especially Latin—but literacy in the modern sense of a bare capacity to read and write the mother-tongue. Even this was far from universal in eighteenth-century England. James Lackington, for example, towards the end of the century reported that 'in giving away religious tracts I found that some of the farmers and their children, and also three-fourths of the poor could not read';[5] and there is much evidence to suggest that in the country many small farmers, their families, and the majority of labourers, were quite illiterate, while even in the towns certain sections of the poor—especially soldiers, sailors and the rabble of the streets—could not read.

---

[1] Collins, *Authorship*, p. 236.
[2] R. A. Austen-Leigh, 'William Strahan and His Ledgers', *Library*, 4th ser., III (1923), 272.
[3] Marjorie Plant, *The English Book Trade* (London, 1939), p. 445.
[4] *Lives of the Poets*, ed. Hill (Oxford, 1905), III, 19.
[5] *Confessions* (London, 1804), p. 175.

In the towns, however, it is likely that semi-literacy was much commoner than total illiteracy. In London especially: the general spread of shop names instead of signs, which struck a Swiss visitor, Carl Philipp Moritz, as unusual, in 1782,[1] surely implies that it was being increasingly assumed that written communications would be understood by a large enough proportion even of the denizens of Gin Lane to be worth addressing to them.

Opportunities for learning to read seem to have been fairly widely available, although the evidence strongly suggests that popular schooling was at best casual and intermittent. An educational system as such hardly existed; but a miscellaneous network of old endowed grammar schools and English schools, charity schools and non-endowed schools of various kinds, notably dame schools, covered the country, with the exception of some outlying rural areas and some of the new industrial towns of the north. In 1788, the first year for which adequate figures are available, about a quarter of the parishes of England had no school at all, and nearly a half had no endowed schools.[2] The coverage earlier in the century was probably a little, but not much, greater.

Attendance at these schools was usually too short and irregular to give the poor anything but the rudiments of reading. Children of the lower classes often left school at the age of six or seven, and if they continued, it was only for a few months in the year when there was no work in the fields or the factories. The fees of 2d. to 6d. a week charged at the commonest type of elementary school, the dame schools, would be a considerable drain on many incomes, and completely beyond the normal range of the million or more persons who were regularly on poor relief throughout the century.[3] For some of these, especially in London and the larger towns, Charity Schools provided free educational facilities: but their main emphasis was on religious education and social discipline; the teaching of reading, writing and arithmetic—the 'three R's'—was a secondary aim and it was rarely pursued with much expectation of success:[4] for this and other reasons it is very unlikely that the Charity School movement made any considerable contribution to the effective

---

[1] *Travels*, ed. Matheson (London, 1924), p. 30.
[2] M. G. Jones, *The Charity School Movement* . . . (Cambridge, 1938), p. 332.
[3] Dorothy Marshall, *The English Poor in the Eighteenth Century* (London, 1926), p. 27-29, 76-77.   [4] Jones, *Charity School Movement*, pp. 80, 304.

literacy of the poor, much less to the growth of the reading public.

There was in any case no general agreement that this would be desirable. Throughout the eighteenth century utilitarian and mercantilist objections to giving the poor a literate education increased. The current attitude was expressed by Bernard Mandeville with his usual forthrightness in his *Essay on Charity and Charity Schools* (1723): 'Reading, writing and arithmetic, are . . . very pernicious to the Poor . . . Men who are to remain and end their days in a laborious, tiresome and painful station of life, the sooner they are put upon it at first, the more patiently they'll submit to it for ever after.'[1]

This point of view was widely held, not only by employers and economic theorists, but by many of the poor themselves, both in the town and the country. Stephen Duck, the thresher poet, for example, was taken away from school at the age of fourteen by his mother 'lest he become too fine a gentleman for the family that produced him';[2] and many other children of the country poor attended school only when they were not needed for work in the fields. In the towns there was one factor at least which was even more hostile to popular education: the increasing employment of children from the age of five onwards to offset the shortage of industrial labour. Factory work was not as subject to seasonal factors, and the long hours left little or no time for schooling; and as a result it is likely that in some textile and other manufacturing areas the level of popular literacy tended to fall throughout the eighteenth century.[3]

There were, then, as is shown by the lives of the uneducated poets and self-made men, such as Duck, James Lackington, William Hutton and John Clare, many serious obstacles in the way of those members of the labouring classes who wanted to be able to read and write; while the most pervasive factor of all in restricting literacy was probably the lack of positive inducement to learn. Being able to read was a necessary accomplishment only for those destined to the middle-class occupations—commerce, administration and the professions; and since reading

---

[1] 'Essay on Charity and Charity Schools', *The Fable of the Bees*, ed. Kaye (Oxford, 1924), I, 288.
[2] *Poems on Several Occasions: Written by Stephen Duck . . .*, 1730, p. iv.
[3] Jones, *Charity School Movement*, p. 332; J. L. and Barbara Hammond, *The Town Labourer, 1760–1832* (London, 1919), pp. 54-55, 144-147.

is inherently a difficult psychological process and one which requires continual practice, it is likely that only a small proportion of the labouring classes who were technically literate developed into active members of the reading public, and further, that the majority of these were concentrated in those employments where reading and writing was a vocational necessity.

Many other factors tended to restrict the reading public. Perhaps the most significant of them from the writer's point of view was the economic one.

Two of the most reliable estimates of the average incomes of the main social groups, those of Gregory King in 1696[1] and of Defoe in 1709,[2] show that more than half of the population was short of the bare necessities of life. King specifies that some 2,825,000 people out of a total population of 5,550,500, constituted an 'unprofitable majority' who were 'decreasing the wealth of the kingdom'. This majority of the population was mainly composed of cottagers, paupers, labouring people and outservants; and King estimated that their average incomes ranged from £6 to £20 per annum per family. All these groups, it is clear, lived so close to subsistence level that they can have had little to spare for such luxuries as books and newspapers.

Both King and Defoe speak of an intermediate class, between the poor and the well-to-do. King lists 1,990,000 people with family incomes of between £38 and £60 per annum. They comprised: 1,410,000 'freeholders of the lesser sort, and farmers' with annual incomes of £55 and £42:10s.; 225,000 'shopkeepers and tradesmen', at £45 per annum; and 240,000 'artisans and handicrafts', with average incomes of £38 a year. None of these incomes would allow a large surplus for book-buying, especially when one considers that the income given is for a whole family; but some money would be available among the richer farmers, shopkeepers and tradesmen; and it is probable that changes within this intermediate class account for the main increases in the eighteenth-century reading public.

This increase was probably most marked in the towns, for the number of small yeoman farmers is thought to have diminished

---

[1] In *Natural and Political Observations and Conclusions upon the State and Condition of England*, 1696.   [2] *Review*, VI (1709), No. 36.

during the period, and their incomes probably either stayed stationary or decreased,[1] whereas there was a marked rise in the numbers and wealth of shopkeepers, independent tradesmen and administrative and clerical employees throughout the eighteenth century.[2] Their increasing affluence probably brought them within the orbit of the middle-class culture, previously the reserve of a smaller number of well-to-do merchants, shopkeepers and important tradesmen. It is probably from them that the most substantial additions to the book-buying public were drawn, rather than from the impoverished majority of the population.

The high cost of books in the eighteenth century emphasises the severity of economic factors in restricting the reading public. Prices were roughly comparable with those today, whereas average incomes were something like one-tenth of their present monetary value, with 10s. a week an average labourer's wage, and £1 a week a decent income for skilled journeymen or small shopkeepers.[3] Charles Gildon sneered that 'there's not an old woman that can go to the price of it, but buys *Robinson Crusoe*':[4] there can surely have been few poor women who were buyers of the original edition at five shillings a copy.

Just as there was a much greater contrast than today between the incomes of different classes, so there was a much greater range between the prices of different types of books. Magnificent folios for the libraries of the gentry and the rich merchants would cost a guinea a volume or more, whereas a duodecimo, with perhaps the same amount of reading, ranged from one to three shillings. Pope's *Iliad*, at six guineas the set, was far beyond the reach of many members of the book-buying public; but very soon a pirated Dutch duodecimo and other cheaper versions were provided 'for the gratification of those who were impatient to read what they could not yet afford to buy'.[5]

These less affluent readers would not have been able to afford the French heroic romances, usually published in expensive folios. But—significantly—novels were in the medium price

[1] H. J. Habakkuk, 'English Land Ownership, 1680–1740', *Economic History Review*, X (1940), 2-17.
[2] M. D. George, *London Life in the 18th Century* (London, 1926), p. 2.
[3] On this difficult subject, see E. W. Gilboy, *Wages in 18th Century England* (Cambridge, Mass., 1934), pp. 144 ff
[4] *Robinson Crusoe Examin'd and Criticis'd*, ed. Dottin (London and Paris, 1923), pp. 71-72.   [5] Johnson, 'Pope', *Lives of the Poets*, ed. Hill. III, 111.

range. They gradually came to be published in two or more small duodecimo volumes, usually at 3s. bound, and 2s. 3d. in sheets. Thus *Clarissa* appeared in seven and later eight volumes, *Tom Jones* in six. The prices of novels, then, though moderate compared to larger works, were still far beyond the means of any except the comfortably off: *Tom Jones*, for example, cost more than a labourer's average weekly wage. It is certain, therefore, that the novel's audience was not drawn from such a wide cross-section of society as, for example, that of the Elizabethan drama. All but the destitute had been able to afford a penny occasionally to stand in the pit of the Globe; it was no more than the price of a quart of ale. The price of a novel, on the other hand, would feed a family for a week or two. This is important. The novel in the eighteenth century was closer to the economic capacity of the middle-class additions to the reading public than were many of the established and respectable forms of literature and scholarship, but it was not, strictly speaking, a popular literary form.

For those on the lower economic fringes of the book-buying public there were, of course, many cheaper forms of printed entertainment; ballads at a halfpenny or a penny; chapbooks containing abbreviated chivalric romances, new stories of criminals, or accounts of extraordinary events, at prices ranging from a penny to sixpence; pamphlets at threepence to a shilling; and, above all, newspapers at the price of one penny until a tax was imposed in 1712, rising to three-halfpence or twopence until 1757, and eventually to threepence after 1776. Many of these newspapers contained short stories, or novels in serialised form—*Robinson Crusoe*, for example, was thus reprinted in the *Original London Post*, a thrice-weekly journal, as well as in cheap duodecimos and chapbooks. For our particular purposes, however, this poorer public is not very important; the novelists with whom we are concerned did not have this form of publication in mind, and the printers and publishers who specialised in it normally used works that had already been published in more expensive form, often without payment.

The extent to which economic factors retarded the expansion of the reading public, and especially that for the novel, is suggested by the rapid success of the non-proprietary or circulating libraries, as they were called after 1742 when the term was invented.[1] A few such libraries are recorded earlier, especially after 1725, but the rapid spread of the movement came after 1740, when the first circulating library was established in London, to be followed by at least seven others within a decade. Subscriptions were moderate: the usual charge was between half a guinea and a guinea a year, and there were often facilities for borrowing books at the rate of a penny a volume or threepence for the usual three-volume novel.

Most circulating libraries stocked all types of literature, but novels were widely regarded as their main attraction: and there can be little doubt that they led to the most notable increase in the reading public for fiction which occurred during the century. They certainly provoked the greatest volume of contemporary comment about the spread of reading to the lower orders. These 'slop-shops in literature'[2] were said to have debauched the minds of schoolboys, ploughboys, 'servant women of the better sort',[3] and even of 'every butcher and baker, cobbler and tinker, throughout the three kingdoms'.[4] It is likely, therefore, that until 1740 a substantial marginal section of the reading public was held back from a full participation in the literary scene by the high price of books; and further, that this marginal section was largely composed of potential novel readers, many of them women.

The distribution of leisure in the period supports and amplifies the picture already given of the composition of the reading public; and it also supplies the best evidence available to explain the increasing part in it played by women readers. For, while many of the nobility and gentry continued their cultural regress from the Elizabethan courtier to Arnold's 'Barbarians', there was a parallel tendency for literature to become a primarily feminine pursuit.

As so often, Addison is an early spokesman of a new trend. He wrote in the *Guardian* (1713): 'There are some reasons why learning is more adapted to the female world than to the male. As in the first place, because they have more spare time on their hands, and lead a more sedentary life. . . . There is another

---

[1] See especially Hilda M. Hamlyn, 'Eighteenth Century Circulating Libraries in England', *Library*, 5th ser., I (1946), 197.
[2] Mrs. Griffith, *Lady Barton*, 1771, Preface.
[3] Cit. John Tinnon Taylor, *Early Opposition to the English Novel* (New York, 1943), p. 25.
[4] Fanny Burney, *Diary*, March 26, 1778.

reason why those especially who are women of quality, should apply themselves to letters, namely, because their husbands are generally strangers to them.'[1] For the most part quite unashamed strangers, if we can judge by Goldsmith's busy man of affairs, Mr. Lofty, in *The Good Natur'd Man* (1768), who proclaims that 'poetry is a pretty thing enough for our wives and daughters; but not for us'.[2]

Women of the upper and middle classes could partake in few of the activities of their menfolk, whether of business or pleasure. It was not usual for them to engage in politics, business or the administration of their estates, while the main masculine leisure pursuits such as hunting and drinking were also barred. Such women, therefore, had a great deal of leisure, and this leisure was often occupied by omnivorous reading.

Lady Mary Wortley Montagu, for example, was an avid novel reader, asking her daughter to send a list of novels copied down from newspaper advertisements, and adding: 'I doubt not that at least the greater part of these are trash, lumber, etc. However, they will serve to pass away the idle time. . . .'[3] Later, and at a definitely lower social level, Mrs. Thrale recounted that by her husband's orders she 'was not to *think of the kitchen*' and explained that it was as a result of this enforced leisure that she was 'driven . . . on literature as [her] sole resource'.[4]

Many of the less well-to-do women also had much more leisure than previously. B. L. de Muralt had already found in 1694 that 'even among the common people the husbands seldom make their wives work';[5] and another foreign visitor to England, César de Saussure, observed in 1727 that tradesmen's wives were 'rather lazy, and few do any needlework'.[6] These reports reflect the great increase in feminine leisure which had been made possible by an important economic change. The old household duties of spinning and weaving, making bread, beer, candles and soap, and many others, were no longer necessary, since most necessities were now manufactured and could be bought at shops and markets. This connection between increased feminine leisure and the development of economic specialisation

[1] No. 155.   [2] Act II.
[3] *Letters and Works*, ed. Thomas (London, 1861), I, 203; II, 225-226, 305.
[4] *A Sketch of Her Life* . . ., ed. Seeley (London, 1908), p. 22.
[5] *Letters Describing the Character and Customs of the English and French Nations*, 1726, p. 11.
[6] *A Foreign View of England*, trans. Van Muyden (London, 1902), p. 206.

was noted in 1748 by the Swedish traveller, Pehr Kalm, who was surprised to find that in England 'one hardly ever sees a woman here trouble herself in the least about outdoor duties'; even indoors, he discovered, 'weaving and spinning is also in most houses a rare thing, because their many manufactures save them from the necessity of such'.[1]

Kalm probably conveys a somewhat exaggerated impression of the change, and he is in any case speaking only of the home counties. In rural areas further from London the economy changed much more slowly, and most women certainly continued to devote themselves almost entirely to the multifarious duties of a household that was still largely self-supporting. Nevertheless a great increase in feminine leisure certainly occurred in the early eighteenth century, although it was probably mainly restricted to London, its environs and the larger provincial towns.

How much of this increased leisure was devoted to reading is difficult to determine. In the towns, and especially in London, innumerable competing entertainments offered themselves: during the season there were plays, operas, masquerades, ridottos, assemblies, drums, while the new watering-places and resort towns catered for the summer months of the idle fair. However, even the most ardent devotees of the pleasures of the town must have had some time left for reading; and the many women who did not wish to partake of them, or could not afford to, must have had much more. For those with puritan backgrounds, especially, reading would be a much more unobjectionable resource. Isaac Watts, a very influential early eighteenth-century Dissenter, dwelt luridly on 'all the painful and dismal consequences of lost and wasted time',[2] but he encouraged his charges, very largely feminine, to pass their leisure hours in reading and literary discussions.[3]

There is in the early eighteenth century a good deal of outraged comment about how the labouring classes were bringing ruin upon themselves and the country by aspiring to the leisure pursuits of their betters. The implications of these jeremiads, however, must be largely discounted. Not only because genteel

[1] *Kalm's Account of His Visit to England* . . ., trans. Lucas (London, 1892), p. 326.
[2] 'The End of Time', *Life and Choice Works of Isaac Watts*, ed. Harsha (New York, 1857), p. 322.
[3] *Improvement of the Mind* (New York, 1885), pp. 51, 82.

dress and fashionable entertainments were much more expensive in relation to the standard of living than they are today, but because a very slight increase in the leisure of a few fortunate or improvident members of the populace would have been enough to arouse alarm and hostility of a kind we find difficult to understand today. The traditional view was that class distinctions were the basis of social order, and that consequently leisure pursuits were only proper for the leisure classes; and this outlook was strongly reinforced by the economic theory of the day which opposed anything which might keep the labouring classes away from their tasks. There was therefore considerable agreement among the spokesmen both of mercantilism and of traditional religious and social thought that even reading constituted a dangerous distraction from the proper pursuits of those who worked with their hands. Robert Bolton, Dean of Carlisle, for instance, in his *Essays on the Employment of Time* (1750), mentions the possibility of reading as a pastime for the peasant and mechanic, only to reject it summarily: 'No, the advice to him is, Observe what passes'.[1]

The opportunities of the poor for any extensive impropriety in this direction were in any case very small. Hours of work for labourers in the country included all the hours of daylight, and even in London they were from six in the morning to eight or nine at night. The usual holidays were only four—Christmas, Easter, Whitsun and Michaelmas, with the addition, in London, of the eight hanging days at Tyburn. It is true that labourers in favoured occupations, especially in London, could and did absent themselves from work fairly freely. But in the main conditions of work were not such as to give appreciable leisure except on Sundays; and then six days of *labor ipse voluptas* usually led to the seventh's being devoted to activities more extrovert than reading. Francis Place thought that drink was almost the only working-class recreation during the eighteenth century;[2] and it must be remembered that cheap gin made drunkenness available for less than the cost of a newspaper.

For those few who might have liked to read there were other difficulties besides lack of leisure and the cost of books. There was little privacy, as, in London especially, housing was appallingly overcrowded; and there was often not enough light to read by, even by day. The window tax imposed at the end of the

---

[1] P. 29.   [2] George, *London Life*, p. 289.

seventeenth century had reduced windows to a minimum, and those that remained were usually deepset, and covered with horn, paper or green glass. At night lighting was a serious problem, since candles, even farthing dips, were considered a luxury. Richardson was proud of the fact that as an apprentice he bought them for himself,[1] but others could not, or were not allowed to. James Lackington, for example, was forbidden to have light in his room by his employer, a baker, and claims to have read by the light of the moon![2]

There were, however, two large and important groups of relatively poor people who probably did have time and opportunity to read—apprentices and household servants, especially the latter. They would normally have leisure and light to read by; there would often be books in the house; if there were not, since they did not have to pay for their food and lodging, their wages and vails could be devoted to buying them if they chose; and they were, as ever, peculiarly liable to be contaminated by the example of their betters.

It is certainly remarkable how many contemporary declamations against the increased leisure, luxury and literary pretensions of the lower orders specifically refer to apprentices and domestic servants, especially footmen and waiting-maids. In assessing the literary importance of this latter group it must be remembered that they constituted a very large and conspicuous class, which in the eighteenth century probably constituted the largest single occupational group in the country, as was the case, indeed, until within living memory. Pamela, then, may be regarded as the culture-heroine of a very powerful sisterhood of literate and leisured waiting-maids. We note that her main stipulation for the new post she envisaged taking up after leaving Mr. B. was that it should allow her 'a little Time for Reading'.[3] This emphasis prefigured her triumph when, following a way of life rare in the class of the poor in general but less so in her particular vocation, she stormed the barriers of society and of literature alike by her skilful employment of what may be called conspicuous literacy, itself an eloquent tribute to the extent of her leisure.

Evidence on the availability and use of leisure thus confirms

[1] A. D. McKillop, *Samuel Richardson: Printer and Novelist* (Chapel Hill, 1936), p. 5.
[2] *Memoirs*, 1830, p. 65.   [3] *Pamela*, Everyman Edition, I, 65.

the previous picture given of the composition of the reading public in the early eighteenth century. Despite a considerable expansion it still did not normally extend much further down the social scale than to tradesmen and shopkeepers, with the important exception of the more favoured apprentices and indoor servants. Still, there had been additions, and they had been mainly recruited from among the increasingly prosperous and numerous social groups concerned with commerce and manufacture. This is important, for it is probable that this particular change alone, even if it was of comparatively minor proportions, may have altered the centre of gravity of the reading public sufficiently to place the middle class as a whole in a dominating position for the first time.

In looking for the effects of this change upon literature, no very direct or dramatic manifestations of middle-class tastes and capacities are to be expected, for the dominance of the middle class in the reading public had in any case been long preparing. One general effect of some interest for the rise of the novel, however, seems to follow from the change in the centre of gravity of the reading public. The fact that literature in the eighteenth century was addressed to an ever-widening audience must have weakened the relative importance of those readers with enough education and leisure to take a professional or semi-professional interest in classical and modern letters; and in return it must have increased the relative importance of those who desired an easier form of literary entertainment, even if it had little prestige among the literati.

People have always, presumably, read for pleasure and relaxation, among other things; but there seems to have arisen in the eighteenth century a tendency to pursue these ends more exclusively than before. Such, at least, was Steele's view, put forward in the *Guardian* (1713); he attacked the prevalence of:

> . . . this unsettled way of reading . . . which naturally seduces us into as undetermined a manner of thinking. . . . That assemblage of words which is called a style becomes utterly annihilated. . . . The common defence of these people is, that they have no design in reading but for pleasure, which I think should rather arise from reflection and remembrance of what one had read, than from the transient satisfaction of what one does, and we should be pleased proportionately as we are profited.[1]

[1] No. 60.

'The transient satisfaction of what one does' seems a peculiarly appropriate description of the quality of the reading which was called for by most examples of those two new eighteenth-century literary forms, the newspaper and the novel—both obviously encourage a rapid, inattentive, almost unconscious kind of reading habit. The effortlessness of the satisfaction afforded by fiction, indeed, had been urged in a passage from Huet's *Of the Origin of Romances* which prefaced Samuel Croxall's *Select Collection of Novels and Histories* (1720):

> . . . those discoveries which engage and possess [the mind] most effectually are such as are obtained with the least labour, wherein the imagination has the greatest share, and where the subject is such as is obvious to our senses . . . And of this sort are *romances*; which are to be comprehended without any great labour of the mind, or the exercise of our rational faculty, and where a strong fancy will be sufficient, with little or no burthen to the memory.[1]

The new literary balance of power, then, probably tended to favour ease of entertainment at the expense of obedience to traditional critical standards, and it is certain that this change of emphasis was an essential permissive factor for the achievements of Defoe and Richardson. That these achievements were also related to other and more positive features of the tastes and attitudes of the main accessions to the reading public during the period also seems likely: the outlook of the trading class, for instance, was much influenced by the economic individualism and the somewhat secularised puritanism which finds expression in the novels of Defoe; and the increasingly important feminine component of the public found many of its interests expressed by Richardson. Consideration of these relationships, however, must be deferred until we have concluded the present survey of the reading public with an account of some of the other changes in its taste and organisation.

II

By far the greatest single category of books published in the eighteenth century, as in previous centuries, was that composed of religious works. An average of over two hundred such works

[1] 1729 ed., I, xiv.

was published annually throughout the century. *The Pilgrim's Progress*—although little noted by polite authors, and then usually with derision—went through one hundred and sixty editions by 1792;[1] while at least ten devotional manuals had sales of over thirty editions during the eighteenth century, and many other religious and didactic works were equally popular.[2]

These enormous sales, however, do not refute the view that eighteenth-century readers had increasingly secular tastes. To begin with, the number of religious publications does not seem to have increased in proportion either to the growth of the population or to the sales of other types of reading matter.[3] Further, the public for religious reading seems to have been rather independent of that for secular literature. 'Nobody reads sermons but Methodists and Dissenters', says Smollett's Henry Davis, the London bookseller in *Humphrey Clinker* (1771),[4] and his view is partly supported by the paucity of references to popular works of piety in the polite letters of the period.

On the other hand, many readers, especially those from the less educated strata of society, began with religious reading and passed on to wider literary interests. Defoe and Richardson are representative figures in this trend. Their forebears, and those of many of their readers, would in the seventeenth century have indulged in little but devotional reading; but they themselves combined religious and secular interests. Defoe, of course, wrote both novels and works of piety such as his *Family Instructor*; while Richardson was conspicuously successful in carrying his moral and religious aims into the fashionable and predominantly secular field of fiction. This compromise, between the wits and the less educated, between the belles-lettres and religious instruction, is perhaps the most important trend in eighteenth-century literature, and finds earlier expression in the most famous literary innovations of the century, the establishment of the *Tatler* in 1709 and of the *Spectator* in 1711.

These periodicals, which appeared thrice-weekly and daily

---

[1] Frank Mott Harrison, 'Editions of *Pilgrim's Progress*', *Library*, 4th ser., XXII (1941), 73.

[2] I am indebted for these figures to Ivor W. J. Machin's unpublished doctoral dissertation, 'Popular Religious Works of the Eighteenth Century: Their Vogue and Influence' (1939, University of London, pp. 14-15, 196-218).

[3] Machin, p. 14.

[4] Introductory Letter, 'To the Rev. Mr. Jonathan Dustwich'.

respectively, contained essays on topics of general interest which reflected the aim advocated by Steele in *The Christian Hero* (1701): they tried to make the polite religious and the religious polite, and their 'wholesome project of making wit useful'[1] succeeded completely, not only with the wits, but with other parts of the reading public. The *Spectator* and the *Tatler* were much admired in Dissenting Academies[2] and among other groups where most other secular literature was frowned on: and they were often the first pieces of secular literature encountered by uneducated provincial aspirants to letters.

The periodical essay did much in forming a taste that the novel, too, could cater for. Macaulay thought that if Addison had written a novel it would have been 'superior to any that we possess';[3] while T. H. Green, alluding to this, describes the *Spectator* as 'the first and best representative of that special style of literature—the only really popular literature of our time—which consists in talking to the public about itself. Humanity is taken as reflected in the ordinary life of men . . . and . . . copied with the most minute fidelity.'[4] Nevertheless, the transition from the de Coverley Papers to the novel was by no means an immediate one, mainly because succeeding journalists were uninspired and failed to create a gallery of equally interesting characters; and this particular fictional direction was not continued in the second great journalistic innovation in eighteenth-century publishing—the foundation of the *Gentleman's Magazine* by Edward Cave, a journalist and bookseller, in 1731.

This substantial monthly periodical combined the functions of political journalism with the provision of more varied literary fare, ranging from 'An Impartial View of Various Weekly Essays' to 'Select Pieces of Poetry'. Cave tried to appeal to tastes even more various than those which the *Spectator* had catered for; in addition to much solid information he provided highly miscellaneous fare that ranged from cooking recipes to conundrums. He, too, was amazingly successful; Dr. Johnson estimated the total circulation of the *Magazine* at ten thousand and stated that it had twenty imitators; while Cave himself asserted in 1741 that it was 'read as far as the English language

[1] *Tatler*, No. 64 (1709).
[2] *Diary and Correspondence of Philip Doddridge* (London, 1829), I, 152.
[3] *Literary Essays* (London, 1923), p. 651.
[4] 'Estimate of the Value and Influence of Works of Fiction in Modern Times', *Works*, ed. Nettleship, III, 27.

extends, and . . . reprinted from several presses in Great Britain, Ireland and the Plantations'.[1]

Two of the characteristic features of the *Gentleman's Magazine* —practical information about domestic life and a combination of improvement with entertainment—were later to be embodied in the novel. Further, the transition from the *Spectator* to the *Gentleman's Magazine* demonstrates that a reading public had arisen which was largely independent of traditional literary standards, and which was therefore a potential public for a literary form unsanctified by established critical canons; the newspaper itself, as the *Grub Street Journal* remarked in a satirical obituary of Defoe, was 'an amusement altogether unknown in the age of Augustus'.[2] But, although journalism had brought many new recruits for secular literature into the reading public, that public's taste for informative, improving, entertaining and easy reading had not as yet found an appropriate fictional form.

III

The *Gentleman's Magazine* also symbolises an important change in the organisation of the reading public. The *Spectator* had been produced by the best writers of the day; it catered to middle-class taste, but by a sort of literary philanthropy; Steele and Addison were for the middle-class way of life but they were not exactly of it. Less than a generation later, however, the *Gentleman's Magazine* showed a very different social orientation: it was directed by an enterprising but ill-educated journalist and bookseller, and its contributions were mainly provided by hacks and amateurs. This change suggests a development of which Richardson—printer and brother-in-law of James Leake, a bookseller and circulating library proprietor—is himself an important representative: the new prominence in the literary scene of those engaged in the trades of manufacturing and selling the products of the printing press. The main reason for this prominence is clear: the decline of literary patronage by the court and the nobility had tended to create a vacuum between the author and his readers; and this vacuum had been quickly filled by the middlemen of the literary market-place, the publishers, or, as they were then usually called, the booksellers, who

[1] Lennart Carlson, *The First Magazine* (Providence, R.I., 1938), pp. 62-63, 77, 81.   [2] No. 90 (1731).

occupied a strategic position between author and printer, and between both of these and the public.

By the beginning of the eighteenth century, the booksellers, especially those in London, had achieved a financial standing, a social prominence, and a literary importance considerably greater than that of either their forebears or of their counterparts abroad. They had among their number several knights (Sir James Hodges, Sir Francis Gosling, Sir Charles Corbett), High Sheriffs (Henry Lintot) and Members of Parliament (William Strahan); and many of them, such as the Tonsons, Bernard Lintot, Robert Dodsley and Andrew Millar, consorted with the great figures of London life. Together with some of the printers they owned or controlled all the main channels of opinion, newspapers, magazines and critical reviews, and were thus well placed to secure advertising and favourable reviewing for their wares.[1] This virtual monopoly of the channels of opinion also brought with it a monopoly of writers. For, despite the efforts to allow independent access of authors to the public made by the Society for the Encouragement of Learning, 'The Trade' remained the only fruitful form of publication for the author.

The power of the booksellers to influence authors and audience was undoubtedly very great, and it is therefore necessary to inquire whether this power was in any way connected with the rise of the novel.

Contemporary opinion was certainly much concerned with the new influence of the booksellers, and there were frequent assertions that it had had the effect of turning literature itself into a mere market commodity. This view was expressed most succinctly by Defoe, in 1725: 'Writing . . . is become a very considerable Branch of the English Commerce. The Booksellers are the Master Manufacturers or Employers. The several Writers, Authors, Copyers, Sub-writers, and all other Operators with Pen and Ink are the workmen employed by the said Master Manufacturers.'[2] Defoe did not condemn this commercialisation, but most of the spokesmen of traditional literary standards did so in emphatic terms. Goldsmith, for example, often deplored 'that fatal revolution whereby writing is

[1] See Stanley Morison, *The English Newspaper* (Cambridge, 1932), pp. 73-75, 115, 143-146; B. C. Nangle, *The Monthly Review, 1st Series, 1749–1789* (Oxford, 1934), p. 156.
[2] *Applebee's Journal*, July 31, 1725, *cit.* William Lee, *Life and Writings of Daniel Defoe* (London, 1869), III, 410.

converted to a mechanic trade; and booksellers, instead of the great, become the patrons and paymasters of men of genius'.[1] Fielding went further, and explicitly connected this 'fatal revolution' with a disastrous decline in literary standards: he asserted that the 'paper merchants, commonly called booksellers', habitually employed 'journeymen of the trade' without 'the qualifications of any genius or learning', and suggested that their products had driven out good writing by the operation of a kind of Gresham's Law, forcing the public to 'drink cider water . . . because they can produce no other liquor'.[2]

Grub Street was but another name for this 'fatal revolution'. Saintsbury,[3] and many others, have no difficulty in showing that 'Grub Street' is, in one sense, a myth; the booksellers actually supported more authors more generously than ever patronage had. But in another sense Grub Street did exist, and for the first time: what Pope and his friends were really alarmed about was the subjection of literature to the economic laws of *laissez-faire*, a subjection which meant that the booksellers, whatever their own tastes, were forced, in a phrase which George Cheyne used in a letter to Richardson, to be 'Curls by Profession';[4] they had to procure from the Grub Street Dunces whatever the public might wish to buy.

The novel was widely regarded as a typical example of the debased kind of writing by which the booksellers pandered to the reading public. Fielding's friend and collaborator, for example, James Ralph, wrote in *The Case of Authors* (1758):

> Book-making is the manufacture the bookseller must thrive by: The Rules of Trade oblige him to buy as cheap and sell as dear as possible. . . . knowing best what Assortment of Wares will best suit the Market, he gives out his Orders accordingly; and is as absolute in prescribing the Time of Publication, as in proportioning the Pay.
>
> This will account in a good Degree for the Paroxysms of the press: The sagacious Bookseller feels the Pulse of the Times, and according to the stroke, prescribes not to cure, but flatter the Disease: As long as the Patient continues to swallow, he continues

---

[1] 'The Distresses of a Hired Writer', 1761, in *New Essays*, ed. Crane (Chicago, 1927), p. 135.   [2] *True Patriot*, No. 1, 1745.

[3] 'Literature', *Social England*, ed. H. D. Traill and J. S. Mann (London, 1904), V, 334–338.

[4] *Letters of Doctor George Cheyne to Richardson*, 1733–1743, ed. Mullett (Columbia, Missouri, 1943), pp. 48, 51-52.

to administer; and on the first Symptom of a Nausea, he changes the Dose. Hence the Cessation of all Political Carminatives, and the Introduction of Cantharides, in the shape of Tales, Novels, Romances, *etc.*[1]

In fact, however, it is very unlikely that the process was as conscious and direct as Ralph suggests. He was writing at a time when, after the great success of the novels of Richardson and Fielding, and the subsequent spread of circulating libraries, the Grub Street hacks had been set to writing novels and translating French ones on a considerable scale by such booksellers and circulating library proprietors as Francis and John Noble. Until then, however, there is very little evidence that the booksellers played a direct part in stimulating the writing of novels; on the contrary, if we examine the works which the booksellers are known to have actively promoted, we find that their bias was primarily for large works of information such as Ephraim Chambers's *Cyclopaedia* (1728), Johnson's *Dictionary* (1755) and his *Lives of the Poets* (1779–1781), and many other historical and scientific compilations, which they commissioned on a lavish scale.

It is true that it was two booksellers, Charles Rivington and John Osborne, who asked Richardson to produce a popular guide to familiar letter-writing, and thus supplied the initial impetus to the writing of *Pamela*. But *Pamela* itself was something of an accident; Richardson, closely in touch with literary demand as he was, expressed his surprise at its 'strange success' and sold two-thirds of the copyright for twenty pounds, although he was wiser with his two later novels.[2] Nor is it likely that Fielding's crucial experiment, *Joseph Andrews*, was in any way the result of encouragement from the booksellers. The tradition that Fielding was amazed when the bookseller Millar offered him two hundred pounds for the manuscript, and some shorter pieces,[3] certainly suggests that, although Millar, after the great success of *Pamela*, anticipated large sales for Fielding's first novel, neither he nor anyone else had previously encouraged Fielding to take this new literary direction by suggesting that it was likely to be lucrative.

But if the booksellers did little or nothing to promote the rise of the novel directly, there are some indications that, as an indirect result of their role in removing literature from the

[1] P. 21. [2] See McKillop, *Richardson*, pp. 16, 27, 293-294.
[3] Cross, *Fielding*, I, 315-316.

control of patronage and bringing it under the control of the laws of the market-place, they both assisted the development of one of the characteristic technical innovations of the new form—its copious particularity of description and explanation—and made possible the remarkable independence of Defoe and Richardson from the classical critical tradition which was an indispensable condition of their literary achievement.

Once the writer's primary aim was no longer to satisfy the standards of patrons and the literary élite, other considerations took on a new importance. Two of them, at least, were likely to encourage the author to prolixity: first, to write very explicitly and even tautologically might help his less educated readers to understand him easily; and secondly, since it was the bookseller, not the patron who rewarded him, speed and copiousness tended to become the supreme economic virtues.

This second tendency was pointed out by Goldsmith when he considered the relationship between the bookseller and the author in his *Enquiry into the Present State of Learning* (1759): 'There cannot perhaps be imagined a combination more prejudicial to taste than this. It is the interest of the one to allow as little for writing, and of the other to write as much, as possible.'[1] Goldsmith's view here finds some confirmation in the fact that the specific accusation that an author wrote diffusely for economic reasons became fairly common in the early eighteenth century; John Wesley, for example, suggested somewhat uncharitably that Isaac Watts's long-windedness was 'to get money'.[2] The possibility that this tendency may also have influenced the rise of the novel finds some support in the fact that somewhat similar charges were also levelled at both Defoe and Richardson.

The most obvious result of the application of primarily economic criteria to the production of literature was to favour prose as against verse. In *Amelia* (1751) Fielding's hackney author makes this connection very clear: 'A sheet is a sheet with the booksellers; and, whether it be in prose or verse, they make no difference'.[3] Consequently, finding that rhymes 'are stubborn things', the denizen of Grub Street turns away from writing poetry for the magazines and engages in the production of novels. For two reasons: because 'romance writing is the only

---

[1] *Works*, ed. Cunningham (New York, 1908), vi, 72-73.
[2] A. P. Davis, *Isaac Watts* (New York, 1943), p. 221.   [3] Bk. VIII, ch. 5.

branch of our business that is worth following'; and because 'it is certainly the easiest work in the world; you may write it almost as fast as you can set pen to paper'.

Defoe's own career had long before followed this course; after using the current medium of verse satire in his early career he turned to an almost exclusive use of prose. This prose, of course, was easy, copious, unpremeditated—the very qualities that were most consonant both with the narrative manner of his novels and with the maximum economic reward for his labours with the pen. Verbal grace, complication of structure, concentration of effect, all these take time and are likely to require a good deal of revision, whereas Defoe seems to have taken the economic implications of the writer's situation to an unexampled extreme by considering revision as something to be undertaken only if extra remuneration was offered. Such, at least, was the assertion of the anonymous editor of the 1738 edition of Defoe's *Complete English Tradesman*, who wrote of Defoe's writings that they were 'generally speaking . . . too verbose and circumlocutory', and added that 'to have a complete work come off his hands, it was necessary to give him so much per sheet to write it in his own way; and half as much afterwards to lop off its excrescences, or abstract it. . . .'[1]

There is somewhat similar evidence in the case of Richardson, although the economic motive was probably much less pressing. In 1739 his friend Dr. George Cheyne reproved him for thinking in terms of the booksellers' practice of valuing 'the Price to the Author by the Number of Sheets'.[2] Later, Shenstone wrote of *Clarissa* that Richardson had 'needlessly spun out his Book to an extravagant Prolixity . . . which he could scarce have done had he not been a *Printer* as well as an Author'; then—with an unconscious tribute to Richardson's formal realism—he continued: 'Nothing but *Fact* could authorise so much particularity, and indeed not that: but in a court of Justice'.[3]

Defoe and Richardson, of course, did not break with classical literary criteria merely in the matter of prose style; they did so in nearly every aspect of their vision of life, and of the techniques by which it was embodied. Here, too, they are the expression of the profound changes in the social context of literature,

[1] 4th ed.   [2] *Letters to Richardson*, ed. Mullett, p. 53.
[3] *Letters*, ed. Mallam (Minneapolis, 1939), p. 199.

changes which further weakened the prestige of established critical standards.

The mid-eighteenth century was well aware of how the new balance of power had revolutionised the recruitment both of critics and authors. According to Fielding the whole world of letters was becoming 'a democracy, or rather a downright anarchy'; and there was no one to enforce the old laws, since, as he wrote in the *Covent Garden Journal* (1752), even the 'offices of criticism' had been taken over by 'a large body of irregulars' who had been admitted 'into the realm of criticism without knowing one word of the ancient laws'.[1] A year later Dr. Johnson suggested in the *Adventurer* that the irregulars were equally powerfully established in the field of authorship: 'The present age', he wrote, 'may be styled, with great propriety, the Age of Authors; for, perhaps, there never was a time in which men of all degrees of ability, of every kind of education, of every profession and employment, were posting with ardour so general to the press'. Then, emphasising the contrast with the past, he added: 'The province of writing was formerly left to those who, by study or appearance of study, were supposed to have gained knowledge unattainable by the busy part of mankind'.[2]

Among the writers who could hardly have become so under the old dispensation, and who knew little or nothing of the 'ancient laws' of literature, we must certainly number those representative specimens of the busy part of eighteenth-century mankind, Defoe and Richardson. Their ideas and training were such that they could hardly have hoped to appeal to the old arbiters of literary destiny; but when we recall how adverse the classical viewpoint was to the requirements of formal realism, it becomes apparent that their very different allegiances were probably an essential condition for their literary innovations. Mrs. Chapone, indeed, drew this conclusion in Richardson's case: 'It is only from the ignorant that we can now have anything original; every master copies from those that are of established authority, and does not look at the natural object'.[3] Defoe and Richardson were certainly freer to present 'the natural object' in whatever way they wished than were writers in France, for example, where literary culture was still primarily oriented to the Court; and it is probably for this reason that it was in England that the novel was able to make an earlier and

[1] Nos. 23, 1.   [2] No. 115.   [3] *Posthumous Works* . . ., 1807, I, 176.

more complete break with the matter and manner of previous fiction.

Ultimately, however, the supersession of patronage by the booksellers, and the consequent independence of Defoe and Richardson from the literary past, are merely reflections of a larger and even more important feature of the life of their time —the great power and self-confidence of the middle class as a whole. By virtue of their multifarious contacts with printing, bookselling and journalism, Defoe and Richardson were in very direct contact with the new interests and capacities of the reading public; but it is even more important that they themselves were wholly representative of the new centre of gravity of that public. As middle-class London tradesmen they had only to consult their own standards of form and content to be sure that what they wrote would appeal to a large audience. This is probably the supremely important effect of the changed composition of the reading public and the new dominance of the booksellers upon the rise of the novel; not so much that Defoe and Richardson responded to the new needs of their audience, but that they were able to express those needs from the inside much more freely than would previously have been possible.

CHAPTER III

'Robinson Crusoe', Individualism and the Novel

THE novel's serious concern with the daily lives of ordinary people seems to depend upon two important general conditions: the society must value every individual highly enough to consider him the proper subject of its serious literature; and there must be enough variety of belief and action among ordinary people for a detailed account of them to be of interest to other ordinary people, the readers of novels. It is probable that neither of these conditions for the existence of the novel obtained very widely until fairly recently, because they both depend on the rise of a society characterised by that vast complex of interdependent factors denoted by the term 'individualism'.

Even the word is recent, dating only from the middle of the nineteenth century. In all ages, no doubt, and in all societies, some people have been 'individualists' in the sense that they were egocentric, unique or conspicuously independent of current opinions and habits; but the concept of individualism involves much more than this. It posits a whole society mainly governed by the idea of every individual's intrinsic independence both from other individuals and from that multifarious allegiance to past modes of thought and action denoted by the word 'tradition' —a force that is always social, not individual. The existence of such a society, in turn, obviously depends on a special type of economic and political organisation and on an appropriate ideology; more specifically, on an economic and political organisation which allows its members a very wide range of choices in their actions, and on an ideology primarily based, not on the tradition of the past, but on the autonomy of the individual, irrespective of his particular social status or personal capacity. It is generally agreed that modern society is uniquely individualist in these respects, and that of the many historical causes for its emergence two are of supreme importance—the rise of modern industrial capitalism and the spread of Protestantism, especially in its Calvinist or Puritan forms.

I

Capitalism brought a great increase of economic specialisation; and this, combined with a less rigid and homogeneous social structure, and a less absolutist and more democratic political system, enormously increased the individual's freedom of choice. For those fully exposed to the new economic order, the effective entity on which social arrangements were now based was no longer the family, nor the church, nor the guild, nor the township, nor any other collective unit, but the individual: he alone was primarily responsible for determining his own economic, social, political and religious roles.

It is very difficult to say when this change of orientation began to affect society as a whole—probably not until the nineteenth century. But the movement certainly began much earlier. In the sixteenth century the Reformation and the rise of national states decisively challenged the substantial social homogeneity of mediaeval Christendom, and, in the famous words of Maitland, 'for the first time, the Absolute State faced the Absolute Individual'. Outside the political and religious sphere, however, change was slow, and it is likely that it was not until the further development of industrial capitalism, especially in England and in the Low Countries, that a mainly individualist social and economic structure came into being and started to affect a considerable part, although by no means a majority, of the total population.

It is, at least, generally agreed that the foundations of the new order were laid in the period immediately following the Glorious Revolution of 1689. The commercial and industrial classes, who were the prime agents in bringing about the individualist social order, had achieved greater political and economic power; and this power was already being reflected in the domain of literature. The middle classes of the towns, we have seen, were becoming much more important in the reading public; and at the same time literature began to view trade, commerce and industry with favour. This was a rather new development. Earlier writers, Spenser, Shakespeare, Donne, Ben Jonson and Dryden, for example, had tended to support the traditional economic and social order and had attacked many of the symptoms of emergent individualism. By the beginning of the eighteenth century, however, Addison, Steele and Defoe were somewhat ostentatiously setting the seal of literary approval on the heroes of economic individualism.

The new orientation was equally evident in the philosophical domain. The great English empiricists of the seventeenth century were as vigorously individualist in their political and ethical thought as in their epistemology. Bacon hoped to make a really new start in social theory by applying his inductive method to an accumulation of factual data about a great number of particular individuals;[1] Hobbes, also feeling that he was dealing with a subject that had not been properly approached before, based his political and ethical theory on the fundamentally egocentric psychological constitution of the individual;[2] while in his *Two Treatises of Government* (1690) Locke constructed the class system of political thought based on the indefeasibility of individual rights, as against the more traditional ones of Church, Family or King. That these thinkers should have been the political and psychological vanguard of nascent individualism, as well as the pioneers of its theory of knowledge, suggests how closely linked their reorientations were both in themselves and in relation to the innovations of the novel. For, just as there is a basic congruity between the non-realist nature of the literary forms of the Greeks, their intensely social, or civic, moral outlook, and their philosophical preference for the universal, so the modern novel is closely allied on the one hand to the realist epistemology of the modern period, and on the other to the individualism of its social structure. In the literary, the philosophical and the social spheres alike the classical focus on the ideal, the universal and the corporate has shifted completely, and the modern field of vision is mainly occupied by the discrete particular, the directly apprehended sensum, and the autonomous individual.

Defoe, whose philosophical outlook has much in common with that of the English empiricists of the seventeenth century, expressed the diverse elements of individualism more completely than any previous writer, and his work offers a unique demonstration of the connection between individualism in its many forms and the rise of the novel. This connection is shown particularly clearly and comprehensively in his first novel, *Robinson Crusoe*.

[1] *Advancement of Learning*, Bk. II, especially ch. 22, sect. xvi and ch. 23, sect. xiv.
[2] *Elements of Law*, Pt. I, ch. 13, sect. iii.

II

(a)

Robinson Crusoe has been very appropriately used by many economic theorists as their illustration of *homo economicus*. Just as 'the body politic' was the symbol of the communal way of thought typical of previous societies, so 'economic man' symbolised the new outlook of individualism in its economic aspect. Adam Smith has been charged with the invention; actually, the concept is much older, but it is natural that it should have come to the fore as an abstraction expressing the individualism of the economic system as a whole only when the individualism of that system itself had reached an advanced stage of development.

That Robinson Crusoe, like Defoe's other main characters, Moll Flanders, Roxana, Colonel Jacque and Captain Singleton, is an embodiment of economic individualism hardly needs demonstration. All Defoe's heroes pursue money, which he characteristically called 'the general denominating article in the world';[1] and they pursue it very methodically according to the profit and loss book-keeping which Max Weber considered to be the distinctive technical feature of modern capitalism.[2] Defoe's heroes, we observe, have no need to learn this technique; whatever the circumstances of their birth and education, they have it in their blood, and keep us more fully informed of their present stocks of money and commodities than any other characters in fiction. Crusoe's book-keeping conscience, indeed, has established an effective priority over his other thoughts and emotions; when his Lisbon steward offers him 160 moidores to alleviate his momentary difficulties on return, Crusoe relates: 'I could hardly refrain from tears while he spoke; in short, I took 100 of the moidores, and called for a pen and ink to give him a receipt for them'.[3]

Book-keeping is but one aspect of a central theme in the modern social order. Our civilisation as a whole is based on individual contractual relationships, as opposed to the unwritten, traditional and collective relationships of previous societies; and the idea of contract played an important part in the theoretical

[1] *Review*, III (1706), No. 3.
[2] *The Theory of Social and Economic Organisation*, trans. Henderson and Parsons (New York, 1947), pp. 186-202.
[3] *The Life and Strange Surprising Adventures of Robinson Crusoe*, ed. Aitken (London, 1902), p. 316.

development of political individualism. It had featured prominently in the fight against the Stuarts, and it was enshrined in Locke's political system. Locke, indeed, thought that contractual relationships were binding even in the state of nature;[1] Crusoe, we notice, acts like a good Lockean—when others arrive on the island he forces them to accept his dominion with written contracts acknowledging his absolute power (even though we have previously been told that he has run out of ink).[2]

But the primacy of the economic motive, and an innate reverence for book-keeping and the law of contract are by no means the only matters in which Robinson Crusoe is a symbol of the processes associated with the rise of economic individualism. The hypostasis of the economic motive logically entails a devaluation of other modes of thought, feeling and action: the various forms of traditional group relationship, the family, the guild, the village, the sense of nationality—all are weakened, and so, too, are the competing claims of non-economic individual achievement and enjoyment, ranging from spiritual salvation to the pleasures of recreation.[3]

This inclusive reordering of the components of human society tends to occur wherever industrial capitalism becomes the dominant force in the economic structure,[4] and it naturally became evident particularly early in England. By the middle of the eighteenth century, indeed, it had already become something of a commonplace. Goldsmith, for instance, thus described the concomitants of England's vaunted freedom in *The Traveller* (1764):

> That independence Britons prize too high,
> Keeps man from man, and breaks the social tie;
> The self-dependent lordlings stand alone,
> All claims that bind and sweeten life unknown;
> Here by the bonds of nature feebly held,
> Minds combat minds, repelling and repell'd . . .
>   Nor this the worst. As nature's ties decay,
> As duty, love, and honour fail to sway,
> Fictitious bonds, the bonds of wealth and law,
> Still gather strength, and force unwilling awe.[5]

[1] Second treatise, 'Essay concerning . . . Civil Government,' sect. 14.
[2] *Life*, pp. 277, 147.
[3] See Max Weber, *The Protestant Ethic and the Spirit of Capitalism*, trans. Parsons (London, 1930), pp. 59-76; *Social and Economic Organisation*, pp. 341-354.
[4] See, for example, Robert Redfield, *Folk Culture of Yucatan* (Chicago, 1941), pp. 338-369.   [5] ll. 339-352.

Unlike Goldsmith, Defoe was not a professed enemy of the new order—quite the reverse; nevertheless there is much in *Robinson Crusoe* that bears out Goldsmith's picture, as can be seen in Defoe's treatment of such group relationships as the family or the nation.

For the most part, Defoe's heroes either have no family, like Moll Flanders, Colonel Jacque and Captain Singleton, or leave it at an early age never to return, like Roxana and Robinson Crusoe. Not too much importance can be attached to this fact, since adventure stories demand the absence of conventional social ties. Still, in *Robinson Crusoe* at least, the hero has a home and family, and leaves them for the classic reason of *homo economicus*—that it is necessary to better his economic condition. 'Something fatal in that propension of nature' calls him to the sea and adventure, and against 'settling to business' in the station to which he is born—'the upper station of low life'; and this despite the panegyric which his father makes of that condition. Later he sees this lack of 'confined desires', this dissatisfaction with 'the state wherein God and Nature has placed' him, as his 'original sin'.[1] At the time, however, the argument between his parents and himself is a debate, not about filial duty or religion, but about whether going or staying is likely to be the most advantageous course materially: both sides accept the economic argument as primary. And, of course, Crusoe actually gains by his 'original sin', and becomes richer than his father was.

Crusoe's 'original sin' is really the dynamic tendency of capitalism itself, whose aim is never merely to maintain the *status quo*, but to transform it incessantly. Leaving home, improving on the lot one was born to, is a vital feature of the individualist pattern of life. It may be regarded as the economic and social embodiment of the 'uneasiness' which Locke had made the centre of his system of motivation,[2] an uneasiness whose existence was, in the very opposite outlook of Pascal, the index of the enduring misery of mortal man. 'All the unhappiness of men arises from one single fact, that they cannot stay quietly in their own room' Pascal had written.[3] Defoe's hero is far from agreeing. Even when he is old, Crusoe tells us how: '. . . nothing else offering, and finding that really stirring

---

[1] *Life*, pp. 2-6, 216.
[2] *Human Understanding*, Bk. II, ch. 21, sects. xxxi-lx.   [3] *Pensées*, No. 139.

about and trading, the profit being so great, and, as I may say, certain, had more pleasure in it, and more satisfaction to the mind, than sitting still, which, to me especially, was the unhappiest part of life'.[1] So, in the *Farther Adventures*, Crusoe sets out on yet another lucrative Odyssey.

The fundamental tendency of economic individualism, then, prevents Crusoe from paying much heed to the ties of family, whether as a son or a husband. This is in direct contradiction to the great stress which Defoe lays on the social and religious importance of the family in his didactic works such as the *Family Instructor*; but his novels reflect not theory but practice, and they accord these ties a very minor, and on the whole obstructive, role.

Rational scrutiny of one's own economic interest may lead one to be as little bound by national as by family ties. Defoe certainly valued individuals and countries alike primarily on their economic merits. Thus one of his most patriotic utterances takes the characteristic form of claiming that his compatriots have a greater productive output per hour than the workmen of any other country.[2] Crusoe, we notice, whom Walter de la Mare has justly called Defoe's Elective Affinity,[3] shows xenophobia mainly where the economic virtues are absent. When they are present—as in the Spanish Governor, a French papist priest, a faithful Portuguese factor—his praise is unstinted. On the other hand, he condemns many Englishmen, such as his English settlers on the island, for their lack of industry. Crusoe, one feels, is not bound to his country by sentimental ties, any more than to his family; he is satisfied by people, whatever their nationality, who are good to do business with; and he feels, like Moll Flanders, that 'with money in the pocket one is at home anywhere'.[4]

What might at first appear to place *Robinson Crusoe* in the somewhat special category of 'Travel and Adventure' does not, then, altogether do so. The plot's reliance on travel does tend to allot *Robinson Crusoe* a somewhat peripheral position in the novel's line of development, since it removes the hero from his usual setting in a stable and cohesive pattern of social relations.

[1] *Farther Adventures of Robinson Crusoe*, ed. Aitken (London, 1902), p. 214.
[2] *A Plan of the English Commerce* (Oxford, 1928), pp. 28, 31-32.
[3] *Desert Islands and Robinson Crusoe* (London, 1930), p. 7.
[4] *Moll Flanders*, ed. Aitken (London, 1902), I, 186.

But Crusoe is not a mere footloose adventurer, and his travels, like his freedom from social ties, are merely somewhat extreme cases of tendencies that are normal in modern society as a whole, since, by making the pursuit of gain a primary motive, economic individualism has much increased the mobility of the individual. More specifically, Robinson Crusoe's career is based, as modern scholarship has shown,[1] on some of the innumerable volumes which recounted the exploits of those voyagers who had done so much in the sixteenth century to assist the development of capitalism by providing the gold, slaves and tropical products on which trade expansion depended; and who had continued the process in the seventeenth century by developing the colonies and world markets on which the future progress of capitalism depended.

Defoe's plot, then, expresses some of the most important tendencies of the life of his time, and it is this which sets his hero apart from most of the travellers in literature. Robinson Crusoe is not, like Autolycus, a commercial traveller rooted in an extended but still familiar locality; nor is he, like Ulysses, an unwilling voyager trying to get back to his family and his native land: profit is Crusoe's only vocation, and the whole world is his territory.

The primacy of individual economic advantage has tended to diminish the importance of personal as well as group relationships, and especially of those based on sex; for sex, as Weber pointed out,[2] being one of the strongest non-rational factors in human life, is one of the strongest potential menaces to the individual's rational pursuit of economic ends, and it has therefore, as we shall see, been placed under particularly strong controls in the ideology of industrial capitalism.

Romantic love has certainly had no greater antagonist among the novelists than Defoe. Even sexual satisfaction—where he speaks of it—tends to be minimised; he protested in *The Review*, for example, that 'the Trifle called Pleasure in it' was 'not worth the Repentance'.[3] As to marriage, his attitude is complicated by the fact that economic and moral virtue in the male is no guarantee of a profitable matrimonial investment: on his colony 'as

[1] See especially A. W. Secord, *Studies in the Narrative Method of Defoe* (Urbana, 1924).
[2] Weber, *Essays in Sociology*, trans. Gerth and Mills (New York, 1946), p. 350.
[3] I (1705), No. 92.

it often happens in the world (what the wise ends of God's Providence are in such a disposition of things I cannot say), the two honest fellows had the two worst wives, and the three reprobates, that were scarce worth hanging . . . had three clever, diligent, careful and ingenious wives'.[1] His puzzled parenthesis bears eloquent testimony to the seriousness with which he views this flaw in the rationality of Providence.

It is not surprising, therefore, that love plays little part in Crusoe's own life, and that even the temptations of sex are excluded from the scene of his greatest triumphs, the island. When Crusoe does notice the lack of 'society' there, he prays for the solace of company, but we observe that what he desires is a male slave.[2] Then, with Friday, he enjoys an idyll without benefit of woman—a revolutionary departure from the traditional expectations aroused by desert islands from the *Odyssey* to the *New Yorker*.

When eventually Crusoe returns to civilisation, sex is still strictly subordinated to business. Only when his financial position has been fully secured by a further voyage does he marry; and all he tells us of this supreme human adventure is that it was 'not either to my disadvantage or dissatisfaction'. This, the birth of three children, and his wife's death, however, comprise only the early part of a sentence, which ends with plans for a further voyage.[3]

Women have only one important role to play, and that is economic. When Crusoe's colonists draw lots for five women, we are gleefully informed that:

> He that drew to choose first . . . took her that was reckoned the homeliest and eldest of the five, which made mirth enough among the rest . . . but the fellow considered better than any of them, that it was application and business that they were to expect assistance in as much as anything else; and she proved the best wife of all the parcel.[4]

'The best wife of all the parcel.' The language of commerce here reminds us that Dickens once decided on the basis of Defoe's treatment of women that he must have been 'a precious dry and disagreeable article himself'.[5]

[1] *Farther Adventures*, p. 78.   [2] *Life*, pp. 208-210, 225.
[3] *Life*, p. 341.   [4] *Farther Adventures*, p. 77.
[5] John Forster, *Life of Charles Dickens*, revised Ley (London, 1928), p. 611 n.

The same devaluation of non-economic factors can be seen in Crusoe's other personal relationships. He treats them all in terms of their commodity value. The clearest case is that of Xury, the Moorish boy who helped him to escape from slavery and on another occasion offered to prove his devotion by sacrificing his own life. Crusoe very properly resolves 'to love him ever after' and promises 'to make him a great man'. But when chance leads them to the Portuguese Captain, who offers Crusoe sixty pieces of eight—twice Judas's figure—he cannot resist the bargain, and sells Xury into slavery. He has momentary scruples, it is true, but they are cheaply satisfied by securing a promise from the new owner to 'set him free in ten years if he turn Christian'. Remorse later supervenes, but only when the tasks of his island life make manpower more valuable to him than money.[1]

Crusoe's relations with Man Friday are similarly egocentric. He does not ask him his name, but gives him one. Even in language—the medium whereby human beings may achieve something more than animal relationships with each other, as Crusoe himself wrote in his *Serious Reflections*[2]—Crusoe is a strict utilitarian. 'I likewise taught him to say Yes and No',[3] he tells us; but Friday still speaks pidgin English at the end of their long association, as Defoe's contemporary critic Charles Gildon pointed out.[4]

Yet Crusoe regards the relationship as ideal. He is 'as perfectly and completely happy if any such thing as complete happiness can be found in a sublunary state'.[5] A functional silence, broken only by an occasional 'No, Friday', or an abject 'Yes, Master', is the golden music of Crusoe's *île joyeuse*. It seems that man's social nature, his need for friendship and understanding, is wholly satisfied by the righteous bestowal or grateful receipt, of benevolent but not undemanding patronage. It is true that later, as with Xury, Crusoe promises himself 'to do something considerable' for his servant, 'if he outlive me'. Fortunately, no such sacrifice is called for, as Friday dies at sea, to be rewarded only by a brief word of obituary compassion.[6]

[1] *Life*, pp. 27, 34-36, 164.
[2] *Serious Reflections during the Life and Surprising Adventures of Robinson Crusoe*, ed. Aitken (London, 1902), p. 66.   [3] *Life*, p. 229.
[4] *Robinson Crusoe Examin'd and Criticis'd*, ed. Dottin (London and Paris, 1923), pp. 70, 78, 118.   [5] *Life*, pp. 245-246.
[6] *Farther Adventures*, pp. 133, 177-180.

Emotional ties, then, and personal relationships generally, play a very minor part in *Robinson Crusoe*, except when they are focussed on economic matters. For instance, after Crusoe has left, it is only when his faithful old agent in Lisbon reveals that he is now a very rich man that we get any emotional climax: 'I turned pale and grew sick; and had not the old man run and fetched me a cordial, I believe the sudden surprise of joy had overset nature, and I had died upon the spot'.[1] Only money —fortune in its modern sense—is a proper cause of deep feeling; and friendship is accorded only to those who can safely be entrusted with Crusoe's economic interests.

Sitting still, we saw, was 'the unhappiest part of life' to Robinson Crusoe; leisure pursuits are almost as bad. In this he resembles his author, who seems to have made as few concessions to such distractions as anyone. The fewness of Defoe's literary friendships has been commented on, and he is perhaps a unique example of a great writer who was very little interested in litera-ture, and says nothing of interest about it as literature.[2]

In his blindness to aesthetic experience Crusoe is Defoe's peer. We can say of him as Marx said of his archetypal capitalist: 'enjoyment is subordinated to capital, and the individual who enjoys to the individual who capitalises'.[3] Some of the French versions of *Robinson Crusoe* make him address hymns of praise to nature, beginning 'Oh Nature!'[4] Defoe did not. The natural scene on the island appeals not for adoration, but for exploita-tion; wherever Crusoe looks his acres cry out so loud for improve-ment that he has no leisure to observe that they also compose a landscape.

Of course, in a wintry way, Crusoe has his pleasures. If he does not, like Selkirk,[5] dance with his goats, he at least plays with them, and with his parrot and his cats; but his deepest satisfactions come from surveying his stock of goods: 'I had everything so ready at my hand,' he says, 'that it was a great

---

[1] *Life*, p. 318.
[2] See James R. Sutherland, *Defoe* (London, 1937), p. 25; W. Gückel and E. Günther, 'D. Defoes und J. Swifts Belesenheit und literarische Kritik', *Palaestra*, CIL (1925).
[3] My translation from *Notes on Philosophy and Political Economy*, in *Oeuvres Philosophiques*, ed. Molitor (Paris, 1937), VI, 69.
[4] See William-Edward Mann, *Robinson Crusoë en France* (Paris, 1916), p. 102.
[5] See Appendix, *Serious Reflections*, ed. Aitken, p. 322.

pleasure to me to see all my goods in such order, and especially to find my stock of all necessaries so great.'[1]

(b)

If Robinson Crusoe's character depends very largely on the psychological and social orientations of economic individualism, the appeal of his adventures to the reader seems mainly to derive from the effects of another important concomitant of modern capitalism, economic specialisation.

The division of labour has done much to make the novel possible: partly because the more specialised the social and economic structure, the greater the number of significant differences of character, attitude and experience in contemporary life which the novelist can portray, and which are of interest to his readers; partly because, by increasing the amount of leisure, economic specialisation provides the kind of mass audience with which the novel is associated; and partly because this specialisation creates particular needs in that audience which the novel satisfies. Such, at least, was the general view of T. H. Green: 'In the progressive division of labour, while we become more useful as citizens, we seem to lose our completeness as men . . . the perfect organisation of modern society removes the excitement of adventure and the occasion for independent effort. There is less of human interest to touch us within our calling. . . .' 'The alleviation' of this situation, Green concluded, 'is to be found in the newspaper and the novel.'[2]

It is very likely that the lack of variety and stimulation in the daily task as a result of economic specialisation is largely responsible for the unique dependence of the individual in our culture upon the substitute experiences provided by the printing press, particularly in the forms of journalism and the novel. *Robinson Crusoe*, however, is a much more direct illustration of Green's thesis, since much of its appeal obviously depends on the quality of the 'occasions for independent effort' in the economic realm which it offers Defoe's hero, efforts which the reader can share vicariously. The appeal of these efforts is surely a measure of the depth of the deprivations involved by economic specialisation, deprivations whose far-reaching nature is

[1] *Life*, p. 75.
[2] 'Estimate of the Value and Influence of Works of Fiction in Modern Times', *Works*, ed. Nettleship, III, 40.

suggested by the way our civilisation has reintroduced some of the basic economic processes as therapeutic recreations: in gardening, home-weaving, pottery, camping, woodwork and keeping pets, we can all participate in the character-forming satisfactions which circumstances force on Defoe's hero; and like him, demonstrate what we would not otherwise know, that 'by making the most rational judgement of things, every man may be in time master of every mechanic art'.[1]

Defoe was certainly aware of how the increasing economic specialisation which was a feature of the life of his time had made most of the 'mechanic arts' alien to the experience of his readers. When Crusoe makes bread, for instance, he reflects that ''Tis a little wonderful and what I believe few people have thought much upon, viz., the strange multitude of little things necessary in the providing, procuring, curing, dressing, making and finishing this one article of bread'.[2] Defoe's description goes on for seven pages, pages that would have been of little interest to people in mediaeval or Tudor society, who saw this and other basic economic processes going on daily in their own households. But by the early eighteenth century, as Kalm reported, most women did not 'bake, because there is a baker in every parish or village',[3] and Defoe could therefore expect his readers to be interested in the very detailed descriptions of the economic life which comprise such an important and memorable part of his narrative.

Robinson Crusoe, of course, does not deal with the actual economic life of Defoe's own time and place. It would be somewhat contrary to the facts of economic life under the division of labour to show the average individual's manual labour as interesting or inspiring; to take Adam Smith's famous example of the division of labour in *The Wealth of Nations*,[4] the man who performs one of the many separate operations in the manufacture of a pin is unlikely to find his task as absorbing and interesting as Crusoe does. So Defoe sets back the economic clock, and takes his hero to a primitive environment, where labour can be presented as varied and inspiring, and where it has the further significant difference from the pin-maker's at home that there is an absolute equivalence between individual effort and individual reward. This was the final change from contemporary

---

[1] *Life*, p. 74.   [2] *Life*, p. 130.
[3] *Account of His Visit to England*, p. 326.   [4] Bk. I, ch. 1.

economic conditions which was necessary to enable Defoe to give narrative expression to the ideological counterpart of the Division of Labour, the Dignity of Labour.

The creed of the dignity of labour is not wholly modern: in classical times the Cynics and Stoics had opposed the denigration of manual labour which is a necessary part of a slave-owning society's scale of values; and later, Christianity, originally associated mainly with slaves and the poor, had done much to remove the odium on manual labour. The idea, however, was only fully developed in the modern period, presumably because its compensatory affirmation became the more necessary as the development of economic specialisation made manual labour more stultifying; and the creed itself is closely associated with the advent of Protestantism. Calvinism in particular tended to make its adherents forget the idea that labour was God's punishment for Adam's disobedience, by emphasising the very different idea that untiring stewardship of the material gifts of God was a paramount religious and ethical obligation.[1]

The quality of Crusoe's stewardship cannot be doubted; he allows himself little time for rest, and even the advent of new manpower—Friday's—is a signal, not for relaxation, but for expanded production. Defoe clearly belongs to the tradition of Ascetic Protestantism. He had written much that sounds like the formulations of Weber, Troeltsch and Tawney; in Dickory Cronke's aphorism, for example: 'When you find yourself sleepy in a morning, rouse yourself, and consider that you are born to business, and that in doing good in your generation, you answer your character and act like a man'.[2] He had even— with a certain sophistic obtuseness—propounded the view that the pursuit of economic utility was quite literally an imitation of Christ: 'Usefulness being the great pleasure, and justly deem'd by all good men the truest and noblest end of life, in which men come nearest to the character of our B. Saviour, who went about doing good'.[3]

Defoe's attitude here exhibits a confusion of religious and material values to which the Puritan gospel of the dignity of

[1] See Ernst Troeltsch, *Social Teaching of the Christian Churches*, trans. Wyon (London, 1931), I, 119; II, 589; Tawney, *Religion and the Rise of Capitalism* (London, 1948), pp. 197-270.
[2] *The Dumb Philosopher* (1719), ed. Scott (London, 1841), p. 21.
[3] *The Case of Protestant Dissenters in Carolina*, 1706, p. 5.

labour was peculiarly liable: once the highest spiritual values had been attached to the performance of the daily task, the next step was for the autonomous individual to regard his achievements as a quasi-divine mastering of the environment. It is likely that this secularisation of the Calvinist conception of stewardship was of considerable importance for the rise of the novel. *Robinson Crusoe* is certainly the first novel in the sense that it is the first fictional narrative in which an ordinary person's daily activities are the centre of continuous literary attention. These activities, it is true, are not seen in a wholly secular light; but later novelists could continue Defoe's serious concern with man's worldly doings without placing them in a religious framework. It is therefore likely that the Puritan conception of the dignity of labour helped to bring into being the novel's general premise that the individual's daily life is of sufficient importance and interest to be the proper subject of literature.

III

Economic individualism explains much of Crusoe's character; economic specialisation and its associated ideology help to account for the appeal of his adventures; but it is Puritan individualism which controls his spiritual being.

Troeltsch has claimed that 'the really permanent attainment of individualism was due to a religious, and not a secular movement, to the Reformation and not the Renaissance'.[1] It is neither feasible nor profitable to attempt to establish priorities in such matters, but it is certainly true that if there is one element which all forms of Protestantism have in common it is the replacement of the rule of the Church as the mediator between man and God by another view of religion in which it is the individual who is entrusted with the primary responsibility for his own spiritual direction. Two aspects of this new Protestant emphasis—the tendency to increase consciousness of the self as a spiritual entity, and the tendency to a kind of democratisation of the moral and social outlook—are particularly important both to *Robinson Crusoe* and to the development of the presuppositions on which the formal realism of the novel is based.

The idea of religious self-scrutiny as an important duty for each individual is, of course, much older than Protestantism;

[1] *Social Teaching*, I, 328.

it derives from the individualist and subjective emphasis of primitive Christianity, and finds its supreme expression in St. Augustine's *Confessions*. But it is generally agreed that it was Calvin, in the sixteenth century, who re-established and systematised this earlier pattern of purposive spiritual introspection, and made it the supreme religious ritual for the layman as well as for the priest: every good Puritan conducted a continual scrutiny of his inner man for evidence of his own place in the divine plot of election and reprobation.

This 'internalisation of conscience' is everywhere manifested in Calvinism. In New England, it has been said, 'almost every literate Puritan kept some sort of journal';[1] and, in England, *Grace Abounding* is the great monument of a way of life which Bunyan shared with the other members of his sect,[2] the Baptists, who were, with one or two minor additions and subtractions, orthodox Calvinists. In later generations the introspective habit remained even where religious conviction weakened, and there resulted the three greatest autobiographical confessions of the modern period, those of Pepys, Rousseau and Boswell, all of whom were brought up under the Calvinist discipline; their fascination with self-analysis, and indeed their extreme egocentricity, are character traits which they shared both with later Calvinism in general[3] and with Defoe's heroes.

(a)

The importance of this subjective and individualist spiritual pattern to Defoe's work, and to the rise of the novel, is very evident. *Robinson Crusoe* initiates that aspect of the novel's treatment of experience which rivals the confessional autobiography and outdoes other literary forms in bringing us close to the inward moral being of the individual; and it achieves this closeness to the inner life of the protagonist by using as formal basis the autobiographical memoir which was the most immediate and widespread literary expression of the introspective tendency of Puritanism in general.

Defoe himself, of course, was born and bred a Puritan. His father was a Dissenter, perhaps a Baptist, more probably a Presbyterian, in any case a Calvinist; and he sent his son to a

---

[1] Perry Miller and Thomas H. Johnson, *The Puritans* (New York, 1938), p. 461.
[2] See William York Tindall, *John Bunyan: Mechanick Preacher* (New York, 1934), pp. 23-41. [3] Troeltsch, *Social Teaching*, II, 590.

dissenting academy, probably intending him for the ministry. Defoe's own religious beliefs changed a good deal, and he expressed in his writings the whole gamut of doctrines, from intransigent predestinarianism to rational deism, which Puritanism held during its varied course of development; nevertheless, there is no doubt that Defoe remained and was generally considered to be a Dissenter, and that much of the outlook revealed in his novels is distinctively Puritan.

There is nothing to suggest that Robinson Crusoe was intended to be a Dissenter. On the other hand, the note of his religious reflections is often Puritan in character—their tenor has been seen by one theologian as very close to the Presbyterian Shorter Catechism of the 1648 Westminster Assembly.[1] Crusoe certainly exhibits frequent signs of Bibliolatry: he quotes some twenty verses of the Bible in the first part of *Robinson Crusoe* alone, besides making many briefer references; and he sometimes seeks divine guidance by opening the Bible at random. But the most significant aspect of his spiritual life is his tendency to rigorous moral and religious self-examination. Each of his actions is followed by a passage of reflection in which Crusoe ponders over the problem of how it reveals the intentions of divine providence. If the corn sprouts, it is surely a divine miracle 'so directed for my sustenance'; if he has a bout of fever 'a leisurely review of the miseries of death'[2] eventually convinces him that he deserves reprobation for neglecting to show his gratitude for God's mercies to him. The modern reader no doubt tends to pay little attention to these parts of the narrative; but Crusoe and his author showed their point of view very clearly by allotting the spiritual realm as much importance as the practical, both in space and emphasis. It would therefore appear that what are probably the vestigial remnants of the Calvinist introspective discipline helped to provide us for the first time in the history of fiction with a hero whose day-by-day mental and moral life is fully shared by the reader.

This crucial literary advance was not, of course, brought about by the introspective tendency of Puritanism alone. As we have seen, the gospel of work had a similar effect in giving the individual's daily economic task almost as much importance as his daily spiritual self-examination; and the parallel effects of

[1] James Moffat, 'The Religion of Robinson Crusoe', *Contemporary Review*, CXV (1919), 669.　　　　[2] *Life*, I, 85, 99.

both these tendencies were supplemented by another closely related tendency in Puritanism.

If God had given the individual prime responsibility for his own spiritual destiny, it followed that he must have made this possible by signifying his intentions to the individual in the events of his daily life. The Puritan therefore tended to see every item in his personal experience as potentially rich in moral and spiritual meaning; and Defoe's hero is acting according to this tradition when he tries to interpret so many of the mundane events of the narrative as divine pointers which may help him to find his own place in the eternal scheme of redemption and reprobation.

In that scheme, of course, all souls had equal chances, and it therefore followed that the individual had as full an opportunity of showing his spiritual qualities in the ordinary conduct of life as in its rarer and more dramatic exigencies. This was one reason for the general Puritan tendency towards the democratisation of the moral and social scale, and it was assisted by several other factors. There were, for instance, many social, moral and political reasons why the Puritans should be hostile to the aristocratic scale of values; nor could they fail to disapprove of its literary expression in the traditional heroes of romance, extrovert conquerors whose victories are won, not in the spirit or in the counting-house but on the battlefield and in the boudoir. It is at all events clear that Puritanism brought about a fundamental and in a sense democratic orientation in the social and literary outlook of its adherents, an orientation which was described by Milton's lines in *Paradise Lost*: 'To know / That which before us lies in daily life / Is the prime wisdom',[1] and which evoked one of Defoe's most eloquent pieces of writing, an essay in *Applebee's Journal* (1722) on the funeral of Marlborough. The essay's peroration begins:

What then is the work of life? What the business of great men, that pass the stage of the world in seeming triumph as these men, we call heroes, have done? Is it to grow great in the mouth of fame, and take up many pages in history? Alas! that is no more than making a tale for the reading of posterity, till it turns into fable and romance. Is it to furnish subject to the poets, and live in their immortal rhymes, as they call them? That is, in short, no more than to be hereafter turned into ballad and song, and be sung by

[1] VIII, 192-194.

old women to quiet children; or, at the corner of a street, to gather crowds in aid of the pickpocket and the whore. Or is their business rather to add virtue and piety to their glory, which alone will pass them into Eternity, and make them truly immortal? What is glory without virtue? A great man without religion is no more than a great beast without a soul.

Then Defoe modulates into something more like the narrowly ethical evaluation of merit which was to be one of the legacies of Puritanism to the middle-class code: 'What is honour without merit? And what can be called true merit, but that which makes a person a good man, as well as a great man'.[1]

Neither Crusoe, nor indeed any of Defoe's heroes, it must be admitted, are conspicuous by these standards of virtue, religion, merit and goodness; and, of course, Defoe did not intend them to be so. But these standards do represent the moral plane on which Defoe's novels exist, and by which his heroes must be judged: the ethical scale has been so internalised and democratised that, unlike the scale of achievement common in epic or romance, it is relevant to the lives and actions of ordinary people. In this Defoe's heroes are typical of the later characters of the novel: Robinson Crusoe, Moll Flanders and even Colonel Jacque never think of glory or honour; they have their being on the moral plane of day-to-day living more completely than those of previous narratives, and their thoughts and actions only exhibit an ordinary, a democratic goodness and badness. Robinson Crusoe, for instance, is Defoe's most heroic character, but there is nothing unusual about his personality or the way he faces his strange experiences; as Coleridge pointed out, he is essentially 'the universal representative, the person, for whom every reader could substitute himself . . . nothing is done, thought, suffered, or desired, but what every man can imagine himself doing, thinking, feeling, or wishing for'.[2]

Defoe's presentation of Robinson Crusoe as the 'universal representative' is intimately connected with the egalitarian tendency of Puritanism in yet another way. For not only did this tendency make the way the individual faced every problem of everyday life a matter of deep and continuing spiritual concern; it also encouraged a literary outlook which was suited to describing such problems with the most detailed fidelity.

[1] *Cit.* W. Lee, *Daniel Defoe* (London, 1869), III, 29-30.
[2] *Works*, ed. Potter, p. 419.

In *Mimesis*, a brilliant panorama of realistic representation in literature from Homer to Virginia Woolf, Erich Auerbach has demonstrated the general connection between the Christian view of man and the serious literary portrayal of ordinary people and of common life. The classical theory of genres had reflected the social and philosophical orientation of Greece and Rome: tragedy described the heroic vicissitudes of people better than ourselves in appropriately elevated language, whereas the domain of everyday reality belonged to comedy which was supposed to portray people 'inferior to ourselves' in an appropriately 'low' style. Christian literature, however, reflecting a very different social and philosophical outlook, had no place for this *Stiltrennung* or segregation of styles according to the class status of the subject-matter. The gospel narratives treated the doings of humble people with the utmost seriousness and on occasion, indeed, with sublimity; later, this tradition was continued in many of the mediaeval literary forms, from the lives of the saints to the miracle plays; and it eventually found its greatest expression in Dante's *Divina Commedia*.[1]

The classicising tendencies of the Renaissance and the Counter-Reformation, however, re-established the old doctrine of genre, and indeed elaborated it to an extent that would certainly have surprised Aristotle. The supreme example of this elaboration is found in French literature of the seventeenth century, and especially in tragedy; not only was the unremitting use of a fully codified *style noble* prescribed, but even the objects and actions of everyday life were banished from the stage.

In Protestant countries, however, the *Stiltrennung* never achieved such authority, especially in England where neo-classicism was confronted by the example of Shakespeare and that characteristic mingling of the tragic and comic modes which was part of his legacy from the Middle Ages. Nevertheless, in one important respect even Shakespeare followed the *Stiltrennung*: his treatment of low and rustic characters is very similar to that of the protagonists of the neo-classical tradition from Ben Jonson to Dryden, and there is nothing egalitarian about it. It

---

[1] *Mimesis: The Representation of Reality in Western Literature*, trans. Trask (Princeton, 1953), especially pp. 41-49, 72-73, 148-173, 184-202, 312-320, 387, 431-433, 466, 491. I translate *stil-trennung*, from the German edition (Bern, 1946), 'segregation of styles', as slightly more specific than Mr. Trask's 'separation of styles'. The two succeeding paragraphs continue to summarise from *Mimesis*, except for what is said about Puritanism.

is very significant that the main exceptions to this derogatory attitude are found in the works of Puritan writers. In Adam, Milton created the first epic hero who is essentially a 'universal representative'; Bunyan, seeing all souls as equal before God, accorded the humble and their lives a much more serious and sympathetic attention than they received in the other literature of his period; while the works of Defoe are the supreme illustration in the novel of the connection between the democratic individualism of Puritanism and the objective representation of the world of everyday reality and all those who inhabit it.

(b)

There is a great difference, however, between Bunyan and Defoe, a difference which suggests why it is Defoe, rather than Bunyan, who is often considered to be our first novelist. In the earlier fiction of the Puritan movement—in such works as Arthur Dent's *Plain Man's Pathway to Heaven*, or the stories of Bunyan and his Baptist *confrère* Benjamin Keach—we have many elements of the novel: simple language, realistic descriptions of persons and places, and a serious presentation of the moral problems of ordinary individuals. But the significance of the characters and their actions largely depends upon a transcendental scheme of things: to say that the persons are allegorical is to say that their earthly reality is not the main object of the writer, but rather that he hopes to make us see through them a larger and unseen reality beyond time and place.

In Defoe's novels, on the other hand, although religious concerns are present they have no such priority of status: indeed the heritage of Puritanism is demonstrably too weak to supply a continuous and controlling pattern for the hero's experience. If, for example, we turn to the actual effect of Crusoe's religion on his behaviour, we find that it has curiously little. Defoe often suggests that an incident is an act of Divine providence or retribution, but this interpretation is rarely supported by the facts of the story. To take the crucial instance: if Crusoe's original sin was filial disobedience—leaving home in the first place—it is certain that no real retribution follows, since he does very well out of it; and later he often sets out for further journeys without any fear that he may be flouting Providence. This indeed comes very near to the 'neglect' of the 'Cautions, warning and instruction . . . Providence' which Crusoe called a 'kind of

Practical Atheism' in his *Serious Reflections*.[1] Where Providence is bringing blessings—as, for instance, when he finds the grains of corn and rice—things are different: Crusoe need only accept. But the trilogy as a whole certainly suggests that any of the less co-operative interventions of Providence can safely be neglected.

Marx sourly noted this somewhat gratuitous character of Crusoe's religious life. 'Of his prayers we take no account, since they are a source of pleasure to him, and he looks on them as so much recreation.'[2] He would have been pleased to find that Gildon thought that the 'religious and useful reflections' were 'in reality . . . put in . . . to swell the bulk of Defoe's treatise to a five-shilling book'.[3] Both Marx and Gildon were right in drawing attention to the discontinuity between the religious aspects of the book and its action: but their explanations do Defoe some injustice. His spiritual intentions were probably quite sincere, but they have the weakness of all 'Sunday religion' and manifest themselves in somewhat unconvincing periodical tributes to the transcendent at times when a respite from real action and practical intellectual effort is allowed or enforced. Such, certainly, is Crusoe's religion, and we feel that it is in the last analysis the result of an unresolved and probably uncon-scious conflict in Defoe himself. He lived fully in the sphere of practical and utilitarian action, and could be wholly true to his being when he described this aspect of Robinson Crusoe's life. But his religious upbringing forced him from time to time to hand over a brilliant piece of narrative by a star-reporter to a distant colleague on the religious page who could be relied on to supply suitable spiritual commentaries quickly out of stock. Puritanism made the editorial policy unalterable; but it was usually satisfied by a purely formal adherence. In this, too, Defoe is typical of the development of Puritanism; in the phrase of H. W. Schneider, 'beliefs seldom become doubts; they become ritual'.[4] Otherworldly concerns do not provide the essential themes of Defoe's novels: but they do punctuate the narrative with comminatory codas that demonstrate a lifetime of somewhat mechanical practice.

[1] P. 191.　　　[2] *Capital* (New York, 1906), p. 88.
[3] *Robinson Crusoe Examin'd*, ed. Dottin, pp. 110-111.
[4] *The Puritan Mind* (New York, 1930), p. 98. A close analogy to Crusoe's gloomy spiritual self-accusations which have so little effect upon his actions, is provided by the rituals described in Perry Miller, 'Declension in a Bible Commonwealth', *Proc. Amer. Antiquarian Soc.*, LI (1941), 37-94.

The relative impotence of religion in Defoe's novels, then, suggests not insincerity but the profound secularisation of his outlook, a secularisation which was a marked feature of his age —the word itself in its modern sense dates from the first decades of the eighteenth century. Defoe himself had been born at a time when the Puritan Commonwealth had just collapsed at the Restoration, while *Robinson Crusoe* was written in the year of the Salters' Hall controversy, when, after the last hopes of Dissent in a compromise with the Anglican Church had been given up, even their effort to unite among themselves proved impossible. In the *Serious Reflections of Robinson Crusoe* Defoe's hero meditates on the ebbing of the Christian religion throughout the world; it is a bitterly divided minority force in a largely pagan world, and God's final intervention seems remoter than ever. Such, at least, is the conclusion to which Robinson Crusoe is forced by his own experience in the last words of the book:

> . . . no such zeal for the Christian religion will be found in our days, or perhaps in any age of the world, till Heaven beats the drums itself, and the glorious legions from above come down on purpose to propagate the work, and reduce the whole world to the obedience of King Jesus—a time which some tell us is not far off, but of which I heard nothing in all my travels and illuminations, no, not one word.[1]

'No, not one word': the dying fall leaves Crusoe to his despair. What he was told to expect and what he has experienced do not agree. Until heaven beats the drums itself he must reconcile himself to a pilgrim's progress through an effectively secular world, make his own way along a path no longer clearly illumined by God's particular providences.

The causes of secularisation in the period are many, but one of the most important, especially as far as Puritanism is concerned, was economic and social progress. In New England, for instance, the Pilgrim Fathers soon forgot that they had originally founded 'a plantation of religion, not a plantation of Trades'; and it has been said that Governor Bradford, in his *History of Plymouth Plantation*, shows how a Puritan saint came to write 'less and less like a Puritan preacher and more and more like the author of *Robinson Crusoe*'.[2] In England, by Defoe's

---

[1] P. 235.
[2] William Haller, *The Rise of Puritanism* (New York, 1938), p. 191.

time, the more respectable dissenting sects at least were dominated by wealthy and somewhat time-serving merchants and financiers; and opportunities for further gain drove many prosperous Dissenters not only to occasional conformity, but into the Anglican Church.[1] In his early years Defoe had violently denounced occasional conformity, but Robinson Crusoe, we notice, is an occasional conformist with a vengeance—he even passes as a Papist when it is economically expedient to do so.

The conflict between spiritual and material values is an old one, but it was perhaps more obvious in the eighteenth century than at any other time; more obvious because so many people thought, apparently in perfectly good faith, that it did not really exist. Bishop Warburton, for example, argued that 'to provide for utility is, at the same time, to provide for truth, its inseparable associate'.[2] The reluctance to consider the extent to which spiritual and material values may be opposed is very marked in Defoe's novels, and it can even be argued that the crucial critical problem which they raise is whether they do not in fact confuse the whole issue. But, whatever our decision on this point, it is at least clear that the mere possibility of such a confusion only exists because Defoe presents us with a narrative in which both 'high' and 'low' motives are treated with equal seriousness: the moral continuum of his novels is much closer than was that of any previous fiction to the complex combination of spiritual and material issues which moral choices in daily life customarily involve.

It would seem, then, that Defoe's importance in the history of the novel is directly connected with the way his narrative structure embodied the struggle between Puritanism and the tendency to secularisation which was rooted in material progress. At the same time it is also apparent that the secular and economic viewpoint is the dominant partner, and that it is this which explains why it is Defoe, rather than Bunyan, who is usually considered to be the first key figure in the rise of the novel.

De Vogüé, the Catholic opponent of the French Realists, found an atheistic presumption in the novel's exclusion of the

---

[1] See A. L. Barbauld, *Works* (London, 1825), II, 314; Weber, *Protestant Ethic*, p. 175.
[2] *Cit.* A. W. Evans, *Warburton and the Warburtonians* (Oxford, 1932), p. 44.

non-natural;[1] and it is certain that the novel's usual means —formal realism—tends to exclude whatever is not vouched for by the senses: the jury does not normally allow divine intervention as an explanation of human actions. It is therefore likely that a measure of secularisation was an indispensable condition for the rise of the new genre. The novel could only concentrate on personal relations once most writers and readers believed that individual human beings, and not collectivities such as the Church, or transcendent actors, such as the Persons of the Trinity, were allotted the supreme role on the earthly stage. The novel, Georg Lukács has written, is the epic of a world forsaken by God;[2] it presents, in de Sade's phrase, 'le tableau des mœurs séculaires'.[3]

This, of course, is not to say that the novelist himself or his novel cannot be religious, but only that whatever the ends of the novelist may be, his means should be rigidly restricted to terrestrial characters and actions: the realm of the spirit should be presented only through the subjective experiences of the characters. Thus Dostoevsky's novels, for example, in no sense depend for their verisimilitude or their significance on his religious views; divine intervention is not a necessary construct for an adequate and complete explanation of the causes and meanings of each action, as it is in Bunyan. Alyosha and Father Zossima are portrayed very objectively: indeed, the very brilliance of Dostoevsky's presentation shows that he cannot assume, but must prove, the reality of the spirit: and *The Brothers Karamazov* as a whole does not depend upon any non-naturalistic causation or significance to be effective and complete.

To sum up, we can say that the novel requires a world view which is centred on the social relationships between individual persons; and this involves secularisation as well as individualism, because until the end of the seventeenth century the individual was not conceived as wholly autonomous, but as an element in a picture which depended on divine persons for its meaning, as well as on traditional institutions such as Church and Kingship for its secular pattern.

At the same time the positive contribution of Puritanism, not only to the development of modern individualism but to the rise

---

[1] See F. W. J. Hemmings, *The Russian Novel in France, 1884–1914* (London, 1950), pp. 31-32.   [2] *Die Theorie des Romans* (Berlin, 1920), p. 84.
[3] *Idée sur les romans* (Paris, 4th ed., n.d.), p. 42.

of the novel, and to its later tradition in England, must not be underestimated. It was through Puritanism that Defoe brought into the novel a treatment of the individual's psychological concerns that was a tremendous advance in the kind of forensic ratiocination which had previously passed for psychological description in even the best of the romances, such as those of Madame de La Fayette. Nor does the fact that, in the words of Rudolph Stamm, who has given the most complete account of Defoe's religious position, Defoe's writings show that his 'own experience of reality had nothing in common with that of a believing Calvinist'[1] disprove the positive importance of Defoe's dissenting background. For we can say of him, as of later novelists in the same tradition, such as Samuel Richardson, George Eliot or D. H. Lawrence, that they have inherited of Puritanism everything except its religious faith. They all have an intensely active conception of life as a continuous moral and social struggle; they all see every event in ordinary life as proposing an intrinsically moral issue on which reason and conscience must be exerted to the full before right action is possible; they all seek by introspection and observation to build their own personal scheme of moral certainty; and in different ways they all manifest the self-righteous and somewhat angular individualism of the earlier Puritan character.

IV

We have until now been primarily concerned with the light which Defoe's first work of fiction sheds on the nature of the connections between economic and religious individualism and the rise of the novel; but since the primary reason for our interest in *Robinson Crusoe* is its literary greatness, the relation between that greatness and the way it reflects the deepest aspirations and dilemmas of individualism also requires brief consideration.

Robinson Crusoe falls most naturally into place, not with other novels, but with the great myths of Western civilisation, with *Faust*, *Don Juan* and *Don Quixote*. All these have as their basic plots, their enduring images, a single-minded pursuit by the

[1] 'Daniel Defoe: An Artist in the Puritan Tradition', *PQ*, XV (1936), 227. On the very difficult problem of Defoe's religion, see especially Stamm's *Der aufgeklärte Puritanismus Daniel Defoes* (Zürich and Leipzig, 1936); John R. Moore, 'Defoe's Religious Sect', *RES*, XVII (1941), 461-467; Arthur Secord, 'Defoe in Stoke Newington', *PMLA*, LXXVI (1951), 217.

protagonist of one of the characteristic desires of Western man. Each of their heroes embodies an *arete* and a *hubris*, an exceptional prowess and a vitiating excess, in spheres of action that are particularly important in our culture. Don Quixote, the impetuous generosity and the limiting blindness of chivalric idealism; Don Juan, pursuing and at the same time tormented by the idea of boundless experience of women; Faustus, the great knower, his curiosity always unsatisfied, and therefore damned. Crusoe, of course, seems to insist that he is not of their company; *they* are very exceptional people, whereas anyone would do what *he* did, in the circumstances. Yet he too has an exceptional prowess; he can manage quite on his own. And he has an excess: his inordinate egocentricity condemns him to isolation wherever he is.

The egocentricity, one might say, is forced on him, because he is cast away on an island. But it is also true that his character is throughout courting its fate and it merely happens that the island offers the fullest opportunity for him to realise three associated tendencies of modern civilisation—absolute economic, social and intellectual freedom for the individual.

It was Crusoe's realisation of intellectual freedom which made Rousseau propose the book as 'the one book that teaches all that books can teach' for the education of Émile; he argued that 'the surest way to raise oneself above prejudices, and order one's judgement on the real relationship between things, is to put oneself in the place of an isolated man, and to judge of everything as that man would judge of them according to their actual usefulness'.[1]

On his island Crusoe also enjoys the absolute freedom from social restrictions for which Rousseau yearned—there are no family ties or civil authorities to interfere with his individual autonomy. Even when he is no longer alone his personal autarchy remains—indeed it is increased: the parrot cries out his master's name; unprompted Friday swears to be his slave for ever; Crusoe toys with the fancy that he is an absolute monarch; and one of his visitors even wonders if he is a god.[2]

Lastly, Crusoe's island gives him the complete *laissez-faire* which economic man needs to realise his aims. At home market conditions, taxation and problems of the labour supply make it

[1] *Émile, ou De l'éducation* (Paris, 1939), pp. 210, 214.
[2] *Life*, pp. 226, 164, 300, 284.

impossible for the individual to control every aspect of production, distribution and exchange. The conclusion is obvious. Follow the call of the wide open places, discover an island that is desert only because it is barren of owners or competitors, and there build your personal Empire with the help of a Man Friday who needs no wages and makes it much easier to support the white man's burden.

Such is the positive and prophetic side of Defoe's story, the side which makes Crusoe an inspiration to economists and educators, and a symbol both for the displaced persons of urban capitalism, such as Rousseau, and for its more practical heroes, the empire builders. Crusoe realises all these ideal freedoms, and in doing so he is undoubtedly a distinctively modern culture-hero. Aristotle, for example, who thought that the man 'who is unable to live in society, or who has no need because he is sufficient for himself, must be either a beast or a god',[1] would surely have found Crusoe a very strange hero. Perhaps with reason; for it is surely true that the ideal freedoms he achieves are both quite impracticable in the real world and in so far as they can be applied, disastrous for human happiness.

It may be objected that Robinson Crusoe's achievements are credible and wholly convincing. This is so, but only because in his narrative—perhaps as an unconscious victim of what Karl Mannheim has called the 'Utopian mentality' which is dominated by its will to action and consequently 'turns its back on everything which would shake its belief'[2]—Defoe disregarded two important facts: the social nature of all human economies, and the actual psychological effects of solitude.

The basis for Robinson Crusoe's prosperity, of course, is the original stock of tools which he loots from the shipwreck; they comprise, we are told, 'the biggest magazine of all kinds . . . that was ever laid up for one man'.[3] So Defoe's hero is not really a primitive nor a proletarian but a capitalist. In the island he owns the freehold of a rich though unimproved estate. Its possession, combined with the stock from the ship, are the miracles which fortify the faith of the supporters of the new economic creed. But only that of the true believers: to the sceptic the classic idyll of free enterprise does not in fact sustain the view that anyone has ever attained comfort and security only by his

[1] *Politics*, Bk. I, ch. 2.
[2] *Ideology and Utopia* (London, 1936), p. 36.   [3] *Life*, p. 60.

own efforts. Crusoe is in fact the lucky heir to the labours of countless other individuals; his solitude is the measure, and the price of his luck, since it involves the fortunate decease of all the other potential stockholders; and the shipwreck, far from being a tragic peripety, is the *deus ex machina* which makes it possible for Defoe to present solitary labour, not as an alternative to a death sentence, but as a solution to the perplexities of economic and social reality.

The psychological objection to *Robinson Crusoe* as a pattern of action is also obvious. Just as society has made every individual what he is, so the prolonged lack of society actually tends to make the individual relapse into a straightened primitivism of thought and feeling. In Defoe's sources for *Robinson Crusoe* what actually happened to the castaways was at best uninspiring. At worst, harassed by fear and dogged by ecological degradation, they sank more and more to the level of animals, lost the use of speech, went mad, or died of inanition. One book which Defoe had almost certainly read, *The Voyages and Travels of J. Albert de Mandelslo*, tells of two such cases; of a Frenchman who, after only two years of solitude on Mauritius, tore his clothing to pieces in a fit of madness brought on by a diet of raw tortoise; and of a Dutch seaman on St. Helena who disinterred the body of a buried comrade and set out to sea in the coffin.[1]

These realities of absolute solitude were in keeping with the traditional view of its effects, as expressed by Dr. Johnson: the 'solitary mortal', he averred, was 'certainly luxurious, probably superstitious, and possibly mad: the mind stagnates for want of employment; grows morbid, and is extinguished like a candle in foul air'.[2]

In the story just the opposite happens: Crusoe turns his forsaken estate into a triumph. Defoe departs from psychological probability in order to redeem his picture of man's inexorable solitariness, and it is for this reason that he appeals very strongly to all who feel isolated—and who at times does not? An inner voice continually suggests to us that the human isolation which individualism has fostered is painful and tends ultimately to a life of apathetic animality and mental derangement; Defoe answers confidently that it can be made the arduous prelude to the fuller realisation of every individual's potentialities; and

[1] See Secord, *Narrative Method of Defoe*, pp. 28-29.
[2] *Thraliana*, ed. Balderston (Oxford, 1951), I, 180.

the solitary readers of two centuries of individualism cannot but applaud so convincing an example of making a virtue out of a necessity, so cheering a colouring to that universal image of individualist experience, solitude.

That it is universal—the word that is always to be found inscribed on the other side of the coin of individualism—can hardly be doubted. We have already seen how, although Defoe himself was an optimistic spokesman of the new economic and social order, the unreflecting veracity of his vision as a novelist led him to report many of the less inspiring phenomena associated with economic individualism which tended to isolate man from his family and his country. Modern sociologists have attributed very similar consequences to the other two major trends which are reflected in *Robinson Crusoe*. Max Weber, for example, has shown how the religious individualism of Calvin created among its adherents a historically unprecedented 'inner isolation';[1] while Émile Durkheim derived from the division of labour and its associated changes many of the endless conflicts and complexities of the norms of modern society, the *anomie*[2] which sets the individual on his own and, incidentally, provides the novelists with a rich mine of individual and social problems when he portrays the life of his time.

Defoe himself seems to have been much more aware of the larger representativeness of his epic of solitude than is commonly assumed. Not wholly aware, since, as we have seen, he departed from its actual economic and psychological effects to make his hero's struggles more cheering than they might otherwise have been; nevertheless Crusoe's most eloquent utterances are concerned with solitude as the universal state of man.

The *Serious Reflections of Robinson Crusoe* (1720) are actually a miscellaneous compilation of religious, moral and thaumaturgic material, and cannot, as a whole, be taken seriously as a part of the story: the volume was primarily put together to cash in on the great success of the first part of the trilogy, *The Life and Strange Surprising Adventures*, and the smaller one of the *Further Adventures*. There are, however, in the prefaces, and the first essay, 'On Solitude', a number of valuable clues as to what, on second thoughts at least, Defoe saw as the meaning of his hero's experiences.

[1] *Protestant Ethic*, p. 108.
[2] *De la division du travail social*, Bk. II, chs. 1 and 3.

In 'Robinson Crusoe's Preface' he suggests that the story 'though allegorical, is also historical': it is based on the life of 'a man alive, and well known too, the actions of whose life are the just subject of these volumes, and to whom all or most part of the story most directly alludes'; and Defoe hints that he is himself the 'original' of which Robinson Crusoe is the 'emblem'; that it is his own life which he is portraying allegorically.

Many critics have denied, and even derided the claim. *Robinson Crusoe* had apparently been attacked as fictitious, and it is argued that Defoe was merely using the allegorical argument very largely to controvert this criticism, and also to alleviate the popular Puritan aversion to fiction which he largely shared. Still, the claim to some autobiographical relevance cannot be wholly rejected: *Robinson Crusoe* is the only book for which he made the claim; and it fits in very well with much of what we know of Defoe's outlook and aspirations.

Defoe was himself an isolated and solitary figure in his time; witness the summary of his own life which he wrote in the preface to a 1706 pamphlet, *A Reply to a Pamphlet, Entitled ' The Lord Haversham's Vindication of His Speech . . .'* where he complains:

> how I stand alone in the world, abandoned by those very people that own I have done them service; . . . how, with . . . no helps but my own industry, I have forced misfortune, and reduced them, exclusive of composition, from seventeen to less than five thousand pounds; how, in gaols, in retreats, in all manner of extremities, I have supported myself without the assistance of friends or relations.

'Forcing his way with undiscouraged diligence' is surely the heroism which Crusoe shares with his creator: and in 'Robinson Crusoe's Preface' it is this quality which he mentions as the inspiring theme of his book: 'Here is invincible patience recommended under the worst of misery, indefatigable application and undaunted resolution under the greatest and most discouraging circumstances'.

Having asserted an autobiographical meaning for his story, Defoe goes on to consider the problem of solitude. His discussion is an interesting illustration of Weber's view of the effects of Calvinism. Most of the argument is concerned with the Puritan insistence on the need for the individual to overcome the world in his own soul, to achieve a spiritual solitude without recourse to monasticism. 'The business is to get a retired soul', he says, and goes on: 'All the parts of a complete solitude are to be as effectually enjoyed, if we please, and sufficient grace assisting, even in the most populous cities, among the hurries of conversation and gallantry of a court, or the noise and business of a camp, as in the deserts of Arabia and Lybia, or in the desolate life of an uninhabited island'.

This note, however, occasionally relapses into a more general statement of solitude as an enduring psychological fact: 'All reflection is carried home, and our dear self is, in one respect, the end of living. Hence man may be properly said to be alone in the midst of crowds and the hurry of men and business. All the reflections which he makes are to himself; all that is pleasant he embraces for himself; all that is irksome and grievous is tasted but by his own palate.'[1] Here the Puritan insistence on possessing one's soul intact from a sinful world is couched in terms which suggest a more absolute, secular and personal alienation from society. Later this echo of the redefined aloneness of Descartes's *solus ipse* modulates into an anguished sense of personal loneliness whose overpowering reality moves Defoe to his most urgent and moving eloquence:

> What are the sorrows of other men to us, and what their joy? Something we may be touched indeed with by the power of sympathy, and a secret turn of the affections; but all the solid reflection is directed to ourselves. Our meditations are all solitude in perfection; our passions are all exercised in retirement; we love, we hate, we covet, we enjoy, all in privacy and solitude. All that we communicate of those things to any other is but for their assistance in the pursuit of our desires; the end is at home; the enjoyment, the contemplation, is all solitude and retirement; it is for ourselves we enjoy, and for ourselves we suffer.

'We covet, we enjoy, all in privacy and solitude': what really occupies man is something that makes him solitary wherever he is, and too aware of the interested nature of any relationship with other human beings to find any consolation there. 'All that we communicate . . . to any other is but for their assistance in the pursuit of our desires': a rationally conceived self-interest makes a mockery of speech; and the scene of Crusoe's silent life is not least a Utopia because its functional silence, broken only

---

[1] Pp. 7, 15, 2, 2-3.

by an occasional 'Poor Robinson Crusoe' from the parrot, does not impose upon man's ontological egocentricity the need to assume a false façade of social intercourse, or to indulge in the mockery of communication with his fellows.

· *Robinson Crusoe*, then, presents a monitory image of the ultimate consequences of absolute individualism. But this tendency, like all extreme tendencies, soon provoked a reaction. As soon as man's aloneness was forced on the attention of mankind, the close and complex nature of the individual's dependence on society, which had been taken for granted until it was challenged by individualism, began to receive much more detailed analysis. Man's essentially social nature, for instance, became one of the main topics of the eighteenth-century philosophers; and the greatest of them, David Hume, wrote in the *Treatise of Human Nature* (1739) a passage which might almost have been a refutation of *Robinson Crusoe*:

> We can form no wish which has not a reference to society. . . . Let all the powers and elements of nature conspire to serve and obey one man; let the sun rise and set at his command; the sea and rivers roll as he pleases, and the earth still furnish spontaneously whatever may be useful or agreeable to him; he will still be miserable, till you give him one person at least with whom he may share his happiness, and whose esteem and friendship he may enjoy.[1]

Just as the modern study of society only began once individualism had focussed attention on man's apparent disjunctions from his fellows, so the novel could only begin its study of personal relationships once *Robinson Crusoe* had revealed a solitude that cried aloud for them. Defoe's story is perhaps not a novel in the usual sense since it deals so little with personal relations. But it is appropriate that the tradition of the novel should begin with a work that annihilated the relationships of the traditional social order, and thus drew attention to the opportunity and the need of building up a network of personal relationships on a new and conscious pattern; the terms of the problem of the novel and of modern thought alike were established when the old order of moral and social relationships was shipwrecked, with Robinson Crusoe, by the rising tide of individualism.

[1] Bk. II, pt. 2, sect. v.

CHAPTER IV

Defoe as Novelist: 'Moll Flanders'

THERE has been much more disagreement among critics about Defoe's achievement than about that of the two later claimants to the paternity of the novel, Richardson and Fielding. On the one hand, Leslie Stephen, commended by F. R. Leavis as having said 'all that need be said' about Defoe as a novelist,[1] remarks that 'the merit of De Foe's narratives bears a direct proportion to the intrinsic merit of a plain statement of the facts',[2] and thus expresses the common nineteenth-century view that, as William Minto put it, Defoe was 'a great, a truly great liar, perhaps the greatest that ever lived'[3]—but little else. More recently Mark Schorer, after an analysis of the connection in *Moll Flanders* between moral inadequacy and primitive novelistic technique, concludes that the book is 'our classic revelation of the mercantile mind: the morality of measurement which Defoe has apparently neglected to measure'.[4] These critics—and many more—are unconvinced of Defoe's claim to be considered a major novelist. On the other hand, there are the many admirers who rate Defoe very high, from Coleridge (speaking, it is true, only of *Robinson Crusoe*) to Virginia Woolf, who writes that '*Moll Flanders* and *Roxana* . . . stand among the few great English novels which we can call indisputably great'.[5]

The previous chapter on *Robinson Crusoe* suggested some of the ultimate historical reasons for the importance of Defoe in the tradition of the novel; but it was not primarily concerned with the issues on which the critical disagreement is based. Nor is *Robinson Crusoe* the best example for such a purpose: although it is probably Defoe's most powerful and enduring work, and certainly his most popular one, Clara Reeve was surely right in her early survey of fiction, *The Progress of Romance* (1785),[6] to

---

[1] *The Great Tradition* (London, 1948), p. 2, n. 2.
[2] 'Defoe's Novels', *Hours in a Library* (London, 1899), I, 31.
[3] *Daniel Defoe* (London, 1887), p. 169.
[4] 'Introduction', *Moll Flanders* (Modern Library College Edition, New York, 1950), p. xiii.
[5] 'Defoe', *The Common Reader*, 1st Series (London, 1938), p. 97.   [6] I, 127.

class it among 'works singular and original'. Since E. M. Forster's *Aspects of the Novel* (1927) at least, *Moll Flanders* has been widely taken as representative of what Defoe could achieve in the way of the novel proper, and—although *Colonel Jacque*, *Roxana* and *A Journal of Plague Year* all have some excellencies unrivalled elsewhere—it imposes itself as the best single work for the purpose of investigating Defoe's methods as a novelist and his place in the tradition of the novel.

The pre-eminence of *Moll Flanders* among Defoe's novels is in no way the result of its being fundamentally different in subject and attitude from *Robinson Crusoe*. The heroine, it is true, is a criminal; but the high incidence of crime in our civilisation is itself mainly due to the wide diffusion of an individualist ideology in a society where success is not easily or equally attainable to all its members.[1] Moll Flanders, like Rastignac and Julien Sorel, is a characteristic product of modern individualism in assuming that she owes it to herself to achieve the highest economic and social rewards, and in using every available method to carry out her resolve.

It is because her crimes, like the travels of Robinson Crusoe, are rooted in the dynamics of economic individualism that Moll Flanders is essentially different from the protagonists of the picaresque novel. The *picaro* happens to have a real historical basis—the breakdown of the feudal social order—but this is not the point of his adventures; he is not so much a complete individual personality whose actual life experiences are significant in themselves as a literary convention for the presentation of a variety of satiric observations and comic episodes. Defoe, on the other hand, presents his whores, pirates, highwaymen, shoplifters and adventurers as ordinary people who are normal products of their environment, victims of circumstances which anyone might have experienced and which provoke exactly the same moral conflicts between means and ends as those faced by other members of society. Some of Moll Flanders's actions may be very similar to those of the *picaro*, but the feeling evoked by them is of a much more complete sympathy and identification: author and reader alike cannot but take her and her problems much more seriously.

[1] See Edwin H. Sutherland, *Principles of Criminology*, 4th ed. (New York, 1947), pp. 3-9, 69-81; Robert K. Merton, 'Social Structure and Anomie', *American Sociological Review*, III (1938), 680.

This seriousness extends to the dangers which she runs as a result of her criminal activities; her exposure to the sanctions of the law is much more continuous and rigorous than anything in picaresque novels—punishment is a reality, not a convention. This is in part a literary matter: the *picaro* enjoys that charmed immunity from the deeper stings of pain and death which is accorded to all those fortunate enough to inhabit the world of comedy, whereas it is the essence of Defoe's fictional world that its pains, like its pleasures, are as solid as those of the real world. But the difference between *Moll Flanders* and the picaresque novel is also the result of a specific social change closely related to the rise of individualism, a change whereby one of the characteristic institutions of modern urban civilisation had come into existence by the early eighteenth century: a well-defined criminal class, and a complex system for handling it, with law-courts, informers and even crime reporters like Defoe.

In the Middle Ages the examples of Christ and St. Francis gave sanction to the view that poverty, far from being a disgrace, might well enhance the individual's prospects of salvation. In the sixteenth century, however, as a result of a new emphasis on economic achievement, the opposite viewpoint came to be widely accepted:[1] indigence was both shameful in itself and presumptive evidence of present wickedness and future damnation. This view is shared by Defoe's heroes; they would rather steal than beg, and they would lose their own self-respect—and the reader's—if they did not exhibit this characteristic *hubris* of economic man.

The acceptance of the aims of economic individualism also involved a new attitude to society and its law. The very distinction between criminal and non-criminal only becomes paramount when the individual's orientation to life is determined, not by his acceptance of the positive standards of the community, but by his own personal aims which are restrained only by the legal power of authority. This process is very evident in *Moll Flanders*: the law, in Goldsmith's words, merely 'forces unwilling awe'; the *polis* has become the police.

The more immediate social background of *Moll Flanders* is provided by the efforts of the state to deal with the growth of crime, especially in London. As theft increased, and the golden age of the highwayman was signalised by *The Beggar's Opera*

[1] See A. V. Judges, *The Elizabethan Underworld* (London, 1930), pp. xii-xxvi.

(1728), punishments for offences against property became much more severe: Moll Flanders is liable to hanging and is actually transported for stealing 'two pieces of brocaded silk', while her mother suffered the same fate for 'three pieces of fine Holland'.[1] The actual form of their punishment brings us back to the world of *Robinson Crusoe*, and the connection between economic individualism and colonial development. Some ten thousand metropolitan criminals were transported from the Old Bailey to the North American Plantations between 1717 and 1775;[2] many of them, like Moll Flanders and Colonel Jacque, were able to find legitimate expression there for the impulse which had made them criminals at home.

Although *Moll Flanders* has a criminal background, then, it is essentially an expression of forces and attitudes very closely related to those analysed in *Robinson Crusoe*: similarly, although the literary form in which these forces and attitudes are embodied in *Moll Flanders* is in some respects more successful or at least more novelistic than elsewhere, it is not essentially different in kind; most of what is said here, therefore, on Defoe's treatment of plot, character and total literary structure, holds good for all his novels, and for their general relationship to the forces of individualism.

I

Here is an episode from the later life of Moll Flanders as a thief:

> The next thing of moment was an attempt at a gentlewoman's gold watch. It happened in a crowd, at a meeting house, where I was in very great danger of being taken. I had full hold of her watch, but giving a great jostle as if somebody had thrust me against her, and in the juncture giving the watch a fair pull, I found it would not come, so I let it go that moment, and cried as if I had been killed, that somebody had trod upon my foot, and that there was certainly pickpockets there, for somebody or other had given a pull at my watch; for you are to observe that on these adventures we always went very well dressed, and I had very good clothes on, and a gold watch by my side, as like a lady as other folks.
>
> I had no sooner said so but the other gentlewoman cried out,

[1] *Moll Flanders*, ed. Aitken (London, 1902), II, 101; I, 2.
[2]. J D. Butler, 'British Convicts Shipped to American Colonies', *American Historical Review*, II (1896), 25.

'A Pickpocket,' too, for somebody, she said, had tried to pull her watch away.

When I touched her watch I was close to her, but when I cried out I stopped as it were short, and the crowd bearing her forward a little, she made a noise too, but it was at some distance from me, so that she did not in the least suspect me; but when she cried out, 'A Pickpocket,' somebody cried out, 'Ay, and here has been another; this gentlewoman has been attempted too.'

At that very instant, a little farther in the crowd, and very luckily too, they cried out, 'A Pickpocket,' again, and really seized a young fellow in the very fact. This, though unhappy for the wretch, was very opportunely for my case, though I had carried it handsomely enough before; but now it was out of doubt, and all the loose part of the crowd ran that way, and the poor boy was delivered up to the rage of the street, which is a cruelty I need not describe, and which however, they are always glad of, rather than be sent to Newgate, where they lie often a long time and sometimes they are hanged, and the best they can look for, if they are convicted is to be transported.[1]

It is very convincing. The gold watch is a real object, and it won't come, even with 'a fair pull'. The crowd is composed of solid bodies, pushing forwards and backwards, and lynching another pickpocket in the street outside. All this happens in a real, particular place. It is true that, as is his custom, Defoe makes no attempt to describe it in detail, but the little glimpses that emerge win us over completely to its reality. A dissenting meeting-house is a piquant choice for these activities, to be sure, but Defoe does not arouse suspicion that he is a literary man by drawing attention to its ironic inappropriateness.

If we have any doubts, they are concerned, not with the authenticity of the episode, but with its literary status. The vividness of the scene itself is curiously incidental. Defoe gets into the middle of the action, with 'I had full hold of her watch', and then suddenly changes from laconic reminiscent summary to a more detailed and immediate presentation, as though only to back up the truth of his initial statement. Nor has the scene been planned as a coherent whole: we are soon interrupted in the middle of the scene by an aside explaining something that might have been explained before, the important fact that Moll Flanders was dressed like a gentlewoman herself: this transition

[1] II, 19-20.

adds to our trust that no ghost-writer has been imposing order on Moll Flanders's somewhat rambling reminiscences, but if we had seen Moll dressed 'as like a lady as other folks' from the beginning, the action would have run more strongly, because uninterruptedly, into the next incident of the scene—the raising of the alarm.

Defoe goes on to stress the practical moral, which is that the gentlewoman should have 'seized the next body that was behind her', instead of crying out. In so doing, Defoe lives up to the didactic purpose professed in the 'Author's Preface', but at the same time he directs our attention to the important problem of what the point of view of the narrator is supposed to be. We presume that it is a repentant Moll, speaking towards the end of her life: it is therefore surprising that in the next paragraph she should gaily describe her 'governess's' procuring activities as 'pranks'. Then a further confusion about the point of view becomes apparent: we notice that to Moll Flanders other pickpockets, and the criminal fraternity in general, are a 'they', not a 'we'. She speaks as though she were not implicated in the common lot of criminals; or is it, perhaps, Defoe who has unconsciously dropped into the 'they' he himself would naturally use for them? And earlier, when we are told that 'the other gentlewoman' cried out, we wonder why the word 'other'? Is Moll Flanders being ironical about the fact that she too was dressed like a gentlewoman, or has Defoe forgotten that, actually, she is not?

Nor are these doubts about the completeness of Defoe's control over his narrative dispelled by the relationship, or rather lack of relationship, between this passage and the rest of the book. The transition to the next episode is somewhat confusing. It is effected, first by the address to the reader explaining how to deal with pickpockets, and then by a somewhat confusing *résumé* of the governess's life which is introduced by the words: 'I had another adventure, which puts this matter out of doubt, and which may be an instruction for posterity in the case of a pickpocket'. We and posterity, however, remain uninstructed, since the ensuing adventure turns out to be concerned with shoplifting: it seems likely that Defoe did not have the end of his paragraph in mind when he began it, and improvised an expository transition to mark time until some other incident suggested itself.

The connection between the meeting-house scene and the

narrative as a whole confirms the impression that Defoe paid little attention to the internal consistency of his story. When she is transported to Virginia Moll Flanders gives her son a gold watch as a memento of their reunion; she relates how she 'desired he would now and then kiss it for my sake', and then adds sardonically that she did not tell him 'that I stole it from a gentlewoman's side, at a meeting house in London'.[1] Since there is no other episode in *Moll Flanders* dealing with watches, gentlewomen and meeting-houses, we must surely infer that Defoe had a faint recollection of what he had written a hundred pages earlier about the attempt on the gentlewoman's gold watch, but forgot that it had failed.

These discontinuities strongly suggest that Defoe did not plan his novel as a coherent whole, but worked piecemeal, very rapidly, and without any subsequent revision. This is indeed very likely on other grounds. His main aim as a writer was certainly to achieve a large and effective output—over fifteen hundred pages of print in the year that saw *Moll Flanders*; and this output was not primarily intended for a careful and critical audience. That Defoe had very little of the author's usual fastidious attitude to his work, or even of the author's sensitiveness to adverse criticism, is very evident from the terms of his prefatory apology for the poetic imperfections of the work of which he was perhaps most proud, *The True-Born Englishman*: '. . . without being taken for a conjuror, I may venture to foretell, that I shall be cavilled at about my mean style, rough verse, and incorrect language, things I indeed might have taken more care in. But the book is printed; and though I see some faults, it is too late to mend them. And this is all I think needful to say . . .' If Defoe was as nonchalant as this about an early work, and a poem at that, it is surely unlikely that he gave a second thought to the possible inconsistencies in a work of popular fiction such as *Moll Flanders*; especially as, for such an ill-regarded and ephemeral kind of writing, his publisher would probably not have offered the extra payment which Defoe would apparently have required for revising his manuscript.

Defoe's very casual attitude to his writing goes far to explain the inconsistencies in matters of detail which are very common in all his works; the same lack of coherent initial plan or of later revision can be surmised in the nature of his narrative method.

[1] II, 158.

Nearly all novels employ a combination of two different methods of reporting: relatively full scenic presentation where, at a definite time and place, the doings of the characters are reported more or less fully; and passages of barer and less detailed summary which set the stage and provide a necessary connective framework. The tendency of most novelists is to reduce these latter synopses to a minimum and to focus as much attention as possible on a few fully realised scenes; but this is not the case with Defoe. His story is told in over a hundred realised scenes whose average length is less than two pages, and an equally large number of passages containing rapid and often perfunctory connective synopses.

The effect is obvious: almost every page offers evidence of the fall in tension as we switch from episode to summary—for a minute Moll Flanders will appear brilliantly illumined, only to fall back into the semi-darkness of confused recollection. It is certain that it is the fully presented episodes which include all that is vivid and memorable in *Moll Flanders*, and which are rightly quoted by enthusiasts as evidence of Defoe's narrative genius; but they surely forget how large a proportion of the book is occupied by uninspired summary, plaster over an inordinate number of cracks. Defoe, certainly, makes no effort to reduce the amount of patchwork required by consolidating the episodes into as large units as possible. The first main group of episodes, for example, when Moll is seduced by the Elder Brother, is divided into a very large number of separate encounters between the characters concerned, each of whose effectiveness is largely dissipated as the narrative relapses into bare summary. Similarly Moll's reaction to the discovery of the incestuous nature of her marriage to her half-brother is split up into so many separate scenes that the emotional force of the episode as a whole is much weakened.

This somewhat primitive aspect of Defoe's narrative technique is partly a reflection of the nature of his basic literary purpose —to produce a convincing likeness to the autobiographical memoir of a real person; and it will therefore require further examination in this larger context. First, however, the present analysis of the meeting-house passage must be concluded by a brief consideration of what is surely its most strikingly successful aspect—its prose.

Defoe's prose is not in the ordinary sense well-written, but it

is remarkably effective in keeping us very close to the consciousness of Moll Flanders as she struggles to make her recollection
clear: as we read we feel that nothing but an exclusive concentration on this single aim could account for such complete
disregard of normal stylistic considerations—the repetitions
and parentheses, the unpremeditated and sometimes stumbling
rhythm, the long and involved sequences of co-ordinate clauses.
The length of the sentences might at first sight seem to interfere
with the effect of spontaneous authenticity; but in fact the lack
of marked pauses within the sentences, and the frequent re-
capitulations, tend to heighten the effect.

The most remarkable thing about the prose of the passage is
perhaps the fact that it is Defoe's usual style. No previous
author's normal way of writing could so credibly have passed
for the characteristic utterance of such an uneducated person
as Moll Flanders; that Defoe's prose could do so quite naturally
is partly the result of the changes in the situation of authors
described in the second chapter, and partly of many other con-
verging forces which, in the last few decades of the seventeenth
century, had already done much to bring the language of literature much closer to the speech habits and the comprehension
of the ordinary reader.

The first of these forces was the attempt of the Royal Society
to develop a more factual prose. This cannot be considered of
primary importance in the formation of Defoe's style, although
there may have been some influence through the scientific and
modern bias of the curriculum of the dissenting academy at
Newington Green which he attended. Certainly Defoe's prose
fully exemplifies the celebrated programme of Bishop Sprat: 'a
close, naked, natural way of speaking; positive expressions; clear
senses; a native easiness; bringing all things as near the mathematical plainness as they can: and preferring the language of
artisans, countrymen and merchants before that of wits or
scholars'.[1] Defoe naturally preferred such language since he was
a merchant himself. His vocabulary is certainly that of 'artisans
and countrymen' in the sense that it contains a higher proportion of words of Anglo-Saxon origin than that of any other
well-known writer, with the significant exception of Bunyan;[2]

---

[1] *History of the Royal Society*, 1667, p. 113.
[2] Gustaf Lannert, *Investigation of the Language of 'Robinson Crusoe'* (Uppsala, 1910),
p. 13.

at the same time it has a certain 'mathematical plainness', a positive and wholly referential quality very well suited to carrying out the purpose of language as Locke had defined it, 'to convey the knowledge of things'. Indeed Defoe's style reflects the Lockean philosophy in one very significant detail: he is usually content with denoting only the primary qualities of the objects he describes—their solidity, extension, figure, motion and number—especially number: there is very little attention to the secondary qualities of objects, to their colours, sounds or tastes.[1]

The simple and positive quality of Defoe's prose, then, embodies the new values of the scientific and rational outlook of the late seventeenth century; but this was also the tendency of certain new styles of preaching. Richard Baxter, for example, whom Defoe had read and whose religious position was very similar to his own, made plainness his supreme aim; and it was plainness of a quasi-scientific kind, since his purpose was to bring home to his audience what he described as 'Soul Experiments', 'Heart Occurrences' and 'God's Operations'.[2] Even Baxter's mode of emphasis, his technique of persuasion, depended almost entirely on the simplest of rhetorical devices, repetition. In this, and in his whole theory and practice, indeed, he was very close to Defoe: how close is suggested by Baxter's account of the considerations that had swayed him when forming his style as a preacher:

> The more I have to do with ignorant sort of people the more I find that we cannot possibly speak too plainly to them. If we do not use their own vulgar dialect, they understand us not. Nay, if we do so, yet if we compose those very words into a handsomeness of sentence, or if we speak anything briefly, they feel not what we say. Nay, I find if we do not purposely dress out the matter into such a length of words, and use some repetition of it, that they may hear it inculcated on them again, we do but overrun their understandings, and they presently lose us. That very style and way that is apt to be a little offensive to the exact and that is tedious and loathsome to the curious ear . . . must be it that must do most good upon the ignorant.[3]

[1] *Human Understanding*, Bk. III, ch. 10, sect. xxiii; Bk. II, ch. 8, sects. ix, x.
[2] *Reliquiae Baxterianae*, ed. Sylvester, 1696, p. 124.
[3] *Cit.* F. J. Powicke, *Life of the Reverend Richard Baxter, 1615–1691* (London, 1924), pp. 283–284. Among the evidence for Defoe's interest in Baxter may be mentioned the fact that he quotes at least two of his works (Gückel and Günther, *Belesenheit*, p. 8).

Defoe's prose is probably a good deal closer to 'vulgar dialect' and understanding than anything envisaged by Sprat or Baxter; mainly for the reason suggested by Defoe's own statement that 'Preaching of sermons is speaking to a few of mankind: printing of books is talking to the whole world'.[1] Defoe, as a journalist, wrote for the largest audience of all, and his concessions to its capacities were therefore much greater. He told his readers in the *Review* that he had 'chosen a down-right plainness, and to speak home both in fact and style' because it was 'more generally instructing and clear to the understanding of the people I am speaking to';[2] he was fully aware that as a result the more educated readers might consider him clumsy and repetitive, but urged that he 'must be borne with in that tautology, for the sake of evident and public utility'.[3]

The direct connection between Defoe's early years as a journalist and pamphleteer and the verisimilitude of his novels is suggested by the case of his first famous piece of narrative, *The True Relation of the Apparition of Mrs. Veal* (1706). Leslie Stephen used it to illustrate Defoe's fictional methods as a novelist;[4] actually Defoe was reporting what he heard when he went down to Canterbury to interview a Mrs. Bargrave who had seen the apparition in question. It cannot be denied, however, that what Stephen says about 'the manufacturing of corroborative evidence' and the 'deflection of interest' from the weak links in the chain of argument applies perfectly to the novels, if not to *Mrs. Veal*; and some part of Defoe's notable success in the art of enlisting our belief in his fictions may, therefore, be attributed, without undue cynicism, to his training in the hard school of journalism.

The nature of Defoe's journalistic experience had been particularly well adapted to further his later career as a novelist because, in the course of writing his thrice-weekly newspaper, *The Review*, almost single-handed for a period of some nine years—from 1704 to 1713, he had developed himself as an editorial character, 'Mr. Review', with a markedly personal manner of writing. His voice—that of a garrulous, pugnacious, homespun, but at times equivocating man of the people—

[1] *The Storm* . . . 1704, sig. A²ʳ.
[2] *Review*, VII (1710), No. 39 (*cit.* William L. Payne, *Mr. Review* (New York, 1947, p. 31).
[3] *Review*, V (1709), No. 139.   [4] 'Defoe's Novels', pp. 4-8.

needed little change when he assumed the role of Moll Flanders.

To journalism we can also attribute much of the responsibility for what is probably Defoe's supreme gift—his readability. His works invite, more justly than most, the familiar encomium that 'once taken up they cannot easily be laid down'. Indeed Defoe had the indelicate prescience to advance the claim on his own behalf, for he concluded his preface to the *Memoirs of a Cavalier*, with more than his wonted syntactical inelegance, '. . . nothing more can invite than the story itself, which, when the reader enters into, he will find it very hard to get out of, until he has gone through it'.

II

Defoe's novels are landmarks in the history of fiction largely because they are the first considerable narratives which embody all the elements of formal realism. But although formal realism helps to define the uniqueness of the novel, it obviously does not by any means exhaust our critical desiderata about it; the novel may have a distinctive representational technique, but if it is to be considered a valuable literary form it must also have, like any other literary form, a structure which is a coherent expression of all its parts. Our preliminary examination has suggested several doubts about the coherence of *Moll Flanders*; and this, combined with the extent of the critical disagreement about Defoe's status as a novelist, makes necessary a fuller analysis of its total structure, and particularly of the relationship between three of its main components, plot, character and moral theme.

A brief recapitulation of the plot of *Moll Flanders* will make clear its episodic nature. The story falls into two main parts; the first and longer one devoted to the heroine's career as a wife, and the second to her criminal activities and their consequences. The first part is composed of five main episodes, each of them ended by the death or departure of a husband; and there are two main sub-episodes, one of them concerning the abortive affair with a married man at Bath, and the other with the stratagems whereby her friend the Redriff widow secures a mate.

It is true that three of the main episodes are not wholly independent. The first marriage, closely related as it is both with Moll's first efforts to improve her condition and her seduction by the Elder Brother, forms a satisfactory and indeed symbolic prelude to the novel as a whole, although it has no later connection with the plot. The third marriage, with her half-brother, leads to the discovery of the secret of her birth, and thus has links both with the beginning of Moll's life and with the final scenes in Virginia where she finds him and her son again. While the fourth marriage, to James or Jemmy, the Irish, Lancashire or highwayman husband (it is typical of Defoe's onomastic nonchalance that such copious alternative identifications should seem desirable); is connected to the later part of the book from Moll's trial at the Old Bailey onwards. On the other hand, although some of the plot components in the first part are related to each other, the interlocking remains rudimentary, and during long intervals it is wholly submerged in the details of Moll's other activities.

The second, and for many readers the most interesting, part of the book is mainly devoted to Moll's career as a thief; its only connection with the rest of the plot is that it finally leads first to her arrest, then to the reunion with James in prison, to her later transportation, and eventually to her return to Virginia and her family there. Ultimately, therefore, Moll's criminal adventures end in a renewal of our contact with the two main episodes of the earlier half of the plot, and thus make possible a fairly neat conclusion to the novel as a whole.

This degree of continuity, based on the relationships between the heroine, her mother, half-brother, favourite husband and only significant child, gives *Moll Flanders* a degree of structural coherence which makes it unique among Defoe's novels. The only comparable plot is that of *Roxana*, and there the unifying mechanism, though simpler, is somewhat similar: a child grown to maturity, relic of the seamy past, haunts the present and the heroine's possibilities of prosperous retirement. In neither novel, however, does Defoe show any clear intention of winding up his plot with any sense of completeness or finality. In *Roxana*, after taking the mother-daughter relationship with a seriousness which seems to be tending to a tragic *dénouement*, he ends the novel with the whole matter in the air; while *Moll Flanders* closes in some confusion with the heroine and later her husband coming back to England. Even when a resolution of the plot would seem to be both easy and logical, Defoe apparently prefers and certainly achieves the inconsequential and the incomplete.

These inconclusive endings are typical of Defoe, and in one sense they are undeniably effective; they serve as a final reminder that the order of the narrative is determined only by the sequence of actual events in the lives of the protagonists. Defoe flouts the orderliness of literature to demonstrate his total devotion to the disorderliness of life.

This unqualified allegiance to the pseudo-biographical mode goes far to explain the type of plot Defoe used. We do not know how far he was indebted to any particular formal model in writing *Moll Flanders*, and the actual prototype of the heroine, if any, has not been established. It is, however, quite clear that the only likely analogues of Defoe's fiction are provided by some biographical form of writing, that all these forms consist of a loose stringing together of incidents in chronological sequence, and that they derive whatever unity they possess from the fact that all these incidents happen to the same person.

The closest analogy in point of subject-matter to *Moll Flanders* is provided by the rogue biographies, a native tradition which was much more exclusively devoted to realistic social documentation than were the picaresque novels. The genre had begun in completely factual compilations, such as Thomas Harman's *Caveat for Common Cursitors* (1566), and had developed into a partly fictional form influenced by picaresque tales and jest-books. The rogue biographies are certainly episodic, but they are unlike *Moll Flanders* as a whole in that the norms of daily life tend to be lost in a welter of anecdotes concerning trickery and deception which are not particularly plausible. A similar unreality, however, is usually to be found in those very episodes in *Moll Flanders* which offer the closest parallel to the staple materials of the rogue biographies [1]—episodes such as the mutual deception of the heroine and her Lancashire husband, her turning the tables on the mercer and getting damages for false arrest, or her rhyming courtship with her half-brother,[2] a poetical *tour de force* which is surely not very much at home in the life history of a lady who shows few other signs of familiarity with the Muses.

The mere fact, however, that these few incidents stand out

[1] For a study of the closest seventeenth-century analogue to *Moll Flanders*, see Ernest Bernbaum, *The Mary Carleton Narratives, 1663–1673* (Cambridge, Mass., 1914), especially pp. 85–90.

[2] I, 145–158; II, 52–65; I, 77–78.

from the rest of Defoe's narrative indicates how great the difference is between most of *Moll Flanders* and the rogue biographies. These incidents, like those typical of the rogue biographies, all have a contrived air: in this they resemble the traditional conception of plot in fiction, where the author chose his story because it was in some way so neat, so amusing or so striking that it stood out from the common run of experience and asked to be told and retold. The novel, however, has characteristically used a plot of a very different type, based on an action which belongs wholly to ordinary experience; and it is on this kind of action that *Moll Flanders* is in the main based.

It would appear, then, that Defoe's plot in *Moll Flanders* is closer to authentic biography, whether of criminals, travellers or other persons, than to the semi-fictional rogue biography. It is interesting, in this connection, to note that, two years before writing *Moll Flanders*, Defoe compiled a more or less genuine Memoir, the *Life of Mr. Duncan Campbell*, a well-known fortune-teller, and that there he stated: 'Of all the writings delivered in an historical manner to the world, none certainly were ever held in greater esteem than those which give us the lives of distinguished private men at full length; and, as I may say, to the life'.[1] Defoe's high regard for genuine biography is reflected in the way his own novels always pass themselves off as authentic autobiography. This alone would involve the type of narrative structure he used: he had only to absorb himself completely in his own make-believe that *Moll Flanders* was the life of a real person, and an episodic but life-like plot sequence was inevitable. It is unlikely that Defoe ever reflected on the other literary consequences of such a plot; if he did, he was probably quite content to sacrifice whatever formal disabilities might ensue in exchange for the absolute authenticity which they made possible, and indeed relatively easy.

The disabilities are obvious and serious. Aristotle thought that the episodic plot whose unity depends only on its being the history of one character was the worst kind of plot, because 'there are many actions of one man which cannot be made to form one action; and also because history is concerned with what actually happened, as opposed to poetry which deals with the probable or necessary'.[2] It may be that in the novel these objections are not final, but there is much to be said for the

[1] 'The Introduction.'   [2] *Poetics*, 8, 9.

view that, on the contrary, Defoe's concentration on producing pseudo-history, although a crucial step in the development of the kind of plot suited to the novel's formal realism, was so exclusive that the other ends of fiction, the ends of poetry in Aristotle's sense, were inevitably crowded out of the picture. Inevitably, because the disabilities that ensue from an episodic plot do not end there, but deny Defoe the advantages of a structure which will give coherence and larger implication to the thoughts and acts of his characters.

Moll Flanders is certainly, as E. M. Forster says, a novel of character;[1] the plot throws the whole burden of interest on the heroine, and many readers have felt that she supports it triumphantly. On the other hand, Leslie Stephen has reproached Defoe with a lack of 'all that goes by the name of psychological analysis in modern fiction',[2] and not altogether without justification, at least if our emphasis is on the word analysis. There is probably no episode in *Moll Flanders* where the motivation is unconvincing, but for somewhat damaging reasons—few of the situations confronting Defoe's heroine call for any more complex discriminations than those of Pavlov's dog: Defoe makes us admire the speed and resolution of Moll's reactions to profit or danger; and if there are no detailed psychological analyses, it is because they would be wholly superfluous.

There are two main ways in which later novelists have manifested their powers of psychological understanding: indirectly, by revealing the character's personality through his actions; or directly, by specific analysis of the character's various states of mind. Both these methods, of course, can be and usually are combined; and they are usually found in conjunction with a narrative structure designed to embody the character's development, and to present him with crucial moral choices which bring his whole personality into play. There is very little of these things in *Moll Flanders*. Defoe does not so much portray his heroine's character as assume its reality in every action, and carry his reader with him—if we accede to the reality of the deed, it is difficult to challenge the reality of the doer. It is only when we attempt to fit all her acts together, and see them as an expression of a single personality, that doubts arise; nor are

[1] *Aspects of the Novel*, p. 61.   [2] 'Defoe's Novels', p. 17.

these doubts allayed when we discover how little we are told about some of the things we should need to know for a full picture of her personality, and how some of the things we are told seem contradictory.

These deficiencies are especially apparent in Defoe's treatment of personal relationships. We are told very little, for example, about the quality of Moll Flanders's loves, and even our information about their quantity is suspiciously meagre. When she accuses herself of having 'lain with thirteen men', we cannot but resent the fact that some six lovers have been hidden not only from her fifth husband, but, much more unforgiveably, from us. Even among those lovers we know, we cannot be sure which Moll preferred. We have a strong impression that James is her favourite, and that she leaves him for the fifth or banking one only out of dire economic necessity; yet she tells us that on her honeymoon with the latter she 'never lived four pleasanter days together', and that five years of an 'uninterrupted course of ease and content' ensued. When James later reappears, however, our earlier impression recurs with renewed force:

> He turned pale, and stood speechless, like one thunderstruck, and, not able to conquer the surprise, said no more but this, 'Let me sit down'; and sitting down by a table, he laid his elbow on the table, and leaning his head on his hand, fixed his eyes on the ground as one stupid. I cried so vehemently, on the other hand, that it was a good while ere I could speak any more; but after I had given some vent to my passion by tears, I repeated the same words, 'My dear, do you not know me?' At which he answered, Yes, and said no more a good while.[1]

Defoe's laconic narrative manner could be supremely evocative when it was focussed on personal relationships, but this happened rather rarely, probably because neither Defoe nor Moll Flanders conceived of such intangible concerns as important and continuing elements in human life. We are certainly given very little help in understanding Moll's conflicting feelings during her marriage with the banker. Like the first two husbands, he is individualised only to the extent of being given an ordinal number; and Moll's life with him is treated as a brief and wholly self-contained episode whose emotional premise

[1] I, 190, 196, 197; II, 113-114.

does not have to be reconciled with other features of her life and character. Defoe, indeed, emphasises this discontinuity by telling us that James wrote three times to Moll at this time suggesting that they go off to Virginia as she had earlier proposed,[1] but only after the fifth husband has been long dead: another novelist would have made such pleas an opportunity for clarifying his heroine's conflicting feelings towards the two men, but Defoe gives us only the bare facts, long after they have lost their potential power for psychological illumination.

If we attempt to draw any conclusion from Defoe's treatment of these particular personal relationships it must surely be that Moll Flanders was unaffectedly happy with both husbands, and that although her love of one of them was deeper, she did not allow this sentiment to interfere with the solid comforts which the other was able to provide. She is, obviously, affectionate but no sentimentalist. We get a somewhat different picture, however, when we come to consider her character, not as a wife, but as a mother. On the one hand, she can behave with complete sentimental abandon, as when she kisses the ground her long-separated son Humphry has been standing on; on the other hand, although she shows some fondness for two or three of her children, she is by normal standards somewhat callous in her treatment of most of them—the majority are mentioned only to be forgotten, and, once left in the care of relatives or foster-mothers, are neither redeemed subsequently nor even inquired after when opportunity permits. Here the conclusion about her character must surely be that, although there are extenuating circumstances, she is often a heartless mother. It is difficult to see how this can be reconciled either with her kissing the ground that Humphry has trodden, or with the fact that she herself loudly condemns unnatural mothers,[2] but never makes any such accusation against herself even in her deepest moments of penitent self-reprobation.

One explanation of this apparent contradiction would make it a matter, not of psychological understanding but of literary technique: briefly that in reading Defoe we must posit a kind of limited liability for the narrative, accepting whatever is specifically stated, but drawing no inferences from omissions, however significant they may seem. If Moll Flanders does not seem to

[1] II, 117.   [2] I, 180-183.

regret James during her fifth marital career, this is only because Defoe did not conceive of the attitudes of characters to each other as enduring realities on which his narrative technique should focus. If Moll Flanders is silent about the eventual fate of all her children except Humphry and the four reported dead, we must not infer that she is without proper maternal feeling, but only that Defoe did not keep his characters in mind when they were off the stage. In both cases, in fact, our interpretation should not be allowed to go beyond what is positively stated by Defoe or Moll Flanders.

There is also another explanation for the lack of full evidence from which to deduce Moll Flanders's personality through her conduct of personal relations: the fact that the criminal individualism which Moll pursues in her later days tends to minimise the importance of personal relationships. Like the other inhabitants of the criminal milieu, she has to assume false names and false identities, and much of her life is devoted to maintaining these pretences. Nearly all her personal contacts, therefore, are coloured by this role; they can never be deep or unreserved, and they are necessarily transitory in a sense, therefore Defoe is being realistic when he portrays the personal relationships of Moll Flanders as a series of essentially casual encounters, very like those of the real vagrants and criminals described by Mayhew in the next century. Here is one such report:

> In the morning I was turned out [from a union], and after I had left I picked up with a young woman who had slept in the union overnight. I said I was going on the road across country to Birmingham, and I axed her to go with me. I had never seen her before. She consented and we went along together begging our way. . . . I lost the young woman when I was put in prison in Manchester. She never came to see me in quod. She cared nothing for me. She only kept company with me to have someone on the road along with her; and I didn't care for her, not I.[1]

The laconic authenticity of this passage is very similar to that of Defoe, and it typifies the desultory nature of personal relations in the criminal milieu. This milieu, indeed, has effects on personal relations not unlike those which economic individualism produces in *Robinson Crusoe*; Mayhew's vagrant, Moll

[1] *Mayhew's Characters*, ed. Quennell (London, 1951), pp. 294-296.

Flanders, and most of Defoe's other characters all belong on Crusoe's island; essentially solitary, they take a severely functional view of their fellows.

Neither Defoe's narrative focus, then, nor the nature of his subject, is such as to reveal Moll's personality through the part she plays in personal relationships. This does not in itself undermine the plausibility of Defoe's presentation of his heroine's psychology: some of the apparent discrepancies noted above are mainly negative—the result of lack of information: while the basic difficulty might reasonably be resolved by assuming that Moll Flanders is naturally warm-hearted but that circumstances often force her to play a lone hand. The very fact that Moll Flanders has no stable setting in personal relationships, however, presents considerable difficulties in determining whether this is so. Usually when we attempt to make up our minds about anyone's total personality we take into account as many views about the person as possible, and by comparing them with our own are able to achieve a kind of stereoscopic effect.

No such enlightenment is forthcoming on Defoe's heroine. The episodic nature of the plot means that, although there are some two hundred characters in *Moll Flanders*, no one of them knows the heroine for more than a fraction of her career; while the autobiographical mode of presentation means that their attitudes to Moll Flanders are only given to us if and how she wishes. Their evidence actually reveals a unanimity of a very suspect kind—Defoe's heroine apparently excites in those best qualified to judge her—James, the Governess, Humphry, for instance—the most unqualified and selfless devotion. On the other hand, the reader, observing that Moll Flanders herself is never wholly honest and disinterested in her dealings with them, or indeed with anyone else, may well feel inclined to interpret their apparent adoration as evidence of a paranoid delusion on Moll Flanders's part rather than as an accurate appraisal of her character on theirs. Everyone seems to exist only for her, and no one seems to resent it. One might have expected the Governess, for example, to regret Moll's reformation since it deprives her of a prize source of stolen goods; instead, she becomes 'a true penitent'[1] as soon as the heroine has no further use for her services.

[1] II, 102.

If none of those close to Moll Flanders seem at all aware of her true character, and if we continue to suspect that her own account of herself may be partial, our only remaining resource for an objective view of her personality is Defoe himself. Here again, however, we at once encounter difficulties. For Moll Flanders is suspiciously like her author, even in matters where we would expect striking and obvious differences. The facts show that she is a woman and a criminal, for example; but neither of these roles determines her personality as Defoe has drawn it.

Moll Flanders, of course, has many feminine traits; she has a keen eye for fine clothes and clean linen, and shows a wifely concern for the creature comforts of her males. Further, the early pages of the book undoubtedly present a young girl with a lifelike clarity, and later there are many touches of a rough cockney humour that is undeniably feminine in tone. But these are relatively external and minor matters, and the essence of her character and actions is, to one reader at least, essentially masculine. This is a personal impression, and would be difficult, if not impossible, to establish: but it is at least certain that Moll accepts none of the disabilities of her sex, and indeed one cannot but feel that Virginia Woolf's admiration for her was largely due to admiration of a heroine who so fully realised one of the ideals of feminism: freedom from any involuntary involvement in the feminine role.

Moll Flanders is also similar to her author in another respect: she seems fundamentally untouched by her criminal background, and, on the contrary, displays many of the attitudes of a virtuous and public-minded citizen. Here, again, there is no glaring inconsistency, but there is a marked pattern of attitudes which distinguishes Moll from other members of her class: in the passage quoted above she showed no fellow-feeling for the boy pickpocket; later she is full of virtuous indignation at the 'hardened wretches' of Newgate, and they repay in kind by hooting at her derisively; and when finally she is transported she has the satisfaction of observing, from her privileged comfort in the captain's quarters, that the 'old fraternity' are 'kept under hatches'.[1] Moll Flanders obviously places criminals into two classes: most of them are vicious reprobates who richly deserve their fate; but she and a few of her friends are essentially

[1] II, 90, 112, 90; I, 62-63; II, 134.

113

virtuous and deserving people who have been unfortunate—she is even morally pure in her whoring since it is, as she assures us, by necessity and not 'for the sake of the vice'.[1] Like Defoe, in fact, she is a good Puritan who, despite a few necessary and regrettable compromises, has, in the main and in defiance of illustrious precedent, lived in a world of pitch and not been defiled.

It is this freedom from the probable psychological and social consequences of everything she does which is the central implausibility of her character as Defoe has drawn it. It applies, not only to her crimes, but to everything she does. If we take the incest theme, for example, we find that although her half-brother becomes incapable in body and mind mainly because Moll Flanders has left him, after revealing her terrible secret, she herself is quite unaffected by the circumstance, once she has left Virginia. Nor are her son's feelings towards her influenced, apparently, by the fact that he is the offspring of an incestuous marriage; nor even by the fact that his mother, after deserting him for some twenty years, only returns because, having been transported back to his vicinity, she thinks that she may now have an estate to inherit, an estate which he would otherwise enjoy.

Moll Flanders's character, then, is not noticeably affected either by her sex, by her criminal pursuits, or indeed by any of the objective factors which might have been expected to set her apart from her author; on the other hand, she shares with Defoe and most of his heroes many of the character traits that are usually regarded as middle-class. She is obsessed with gentility and keeping up appearances; her pride is much involved in knowing how to get good service and proper accommodation; and she is in her heart a rentier, for whom life has no greater terror than when her 'main stock wastes apace'.[2] More specifically it is apparent that, like Robinson Crusoe, she has, by some process of osmosis, picked up the vocabulary and attitudes of a tradesman. Indeed her most positive qualities are the same as Crusoe's, a restless, amoral and strenuous individualism. It is, no doubt, possible to argue that these qualities might be found in a character of her sex, station and personal vicissitudes; but it is not likely, and it is surely more reasonable to assume that all these contradictions are the consequence of a process to

[1] I, 131, 139.   [2] I, 131.

which first-person narration is peculiarly prone; that Defoe's identification with Moll Flanders was so complete that, despite a few feminine traits, he created a personality that was in essence his own.

The hypothesis of the unconscious identification between Defoe and his heroine seems equally valid when we come to analyse the third aspect of the total structure of *Moll Flanders*—its larger moral significance.

The 'Author's Preface' states that 'there is not a wicked action in any part of it, but is first or last rendered unhappy or unfortunate'. This moral claim for *Moll Flanders* amounts only to the assertion that it teaches a somewhat narrow kind of ethical lesson—vice must be paid for and crime does not pay. Even this, however, is not substantiated by the narrative itself. What seems to have happened is that Defoe succumbed to the eternal danger of the crime story: to be interesting the author has to project himself as completely as possible into the mind of the crook, but, having once donned the colours of crime, he plays to win. Defoe cannot bear to let Moll Flanders come on evil days. Her fortunes vary, it is true; but she never falls so low as to be forced to break her early resolve never to 'work housework',[1] and she retains her middle-class status even in prison. For the most part, whether as wife, mistress or thief, she is exceptionally successful, and when the crash comes she saves enough of her ill-gotten gains to stock a plantation and yet retain a considerable balance in England.

Moll's penitent prosperity, then, is based on her criminal career, and the sincerity of her reformation is never put to the acid test of sacrificing material for moral good. The plot, in fact, flatly contradicts Defoe's purported moral theme.

It remains conceivable, however, that some other kinds of moral significance could have been embodied in the narrative, presumably by other means than those of the implications of the plot. Defoe, for example, might have used direct editorial commentary to force the reader to see his protagonist from the proper viewpoint by drawing attention to her inveterate selfishness and the superficiality of her repentance. Such editorial intrusion, however, would have interfered with Defoe's primary purpose, that of giving the impression that *Moll Flanders* is a

---

[1] I, 4-6.

literal and authentic autobiography, and the method was therefore unacceptable.

Whatever moral significance Defoe wished to attach to his
story, therefore, had to spring directly from the moral consciousness of his heroine. This meant that she had to function both as
a character and as an editorial mouthpiece and she therefore
had to recount the story from the perspective of her later penitence. This also involved difficulties; partly because Moll's loves
and larcenies would obviously lose most of their attraction for
the reader if they were too heavily sprinkled with the ashes of
repentance; and partly because such a perspective called for a
very rigorous separation in time between the consciousness that
had performed the evil deeds and the reformed consciousness
that was responsible for their redaction.

Defoe's unawareness of these problems is suggested by the
way his 'Author's Preface' evades the crucial issue of the relation of the novel to Moll's 'own memorandums', which it was
allegedly 'written from'. The 'pen employed in finishing her
story' mentions a 'copy which first came to hand' and which
needed much bowdlerising to 'make it speak language fit to be
read'; but the existence is also inferred of later, and presumably
chaster, documents which showed Moll 'grown humble and
penitent, as she afterwards pretends to be'. On these, however,
Defoe is silent, and we therefore cannot tell which—if any—of
the moral and religious reflections in the text were actually
made by the heroine, nor at what period in her life.

This irresolution about the time scale is sometimes apparent
even in the wording of the penitent reflections. It is evident, for
instance, that one of Moll's earliest and not altogether venial
sins is that of bigamy: she is not divorced from her second husband and there is no report of his death; her later amorous
career, therefore, is one of cumulative bigamy interspersed with
adultery. The problem, however, only enters her moral consciousness once, when she is conscience-stricken by her Bath
gallant's determination not to continue their 'unhappy correspondence'. She writes: 'But I never once reflected that I was
all this while a married woman, a wife to Mr. B——, the linen
draper, who, though he had left me by the necessity of his circumstances, had no power to discharge me from the marriage
contract which was between us, or to give me a legal liberty to
marry again; so that I had been no less a whore and adultress

all this while. I then reproached myself with the liberties I had taken, and how I had been a snare to this gentleman. . . .'[1]

At first sight this passage appears to be the reflection made by a penitent Moll looking back on her former heedlessness; if so, one cannot but doubt the rigour of her spiritual scrutiny, since there are no such reflections about the two later—and equally bigamous—marriages. If, however, we look at the passage again it becomes evident that the point cannot be pursued because there is a real confusion about the time at which the reflection is supposed to be made. In writing 'I then reproached myself', 'then' surely implies that Moll Flanders reproached herself at the time the event occurred; if this is so, she or her author have surely forgotten that the original time status of the paragraph, which begins 'I never once reflected', implied that the moral reflections were made long after the event when remorse had finally supervened.

Defoe, then, failed to locate his didactic commentary convincingly in any particular period of his heroine's moral development; and this may stand as an example of his general failure to resolve the formal problems to which his moral purpose and his autobiographical narrative mode committed him. One reason for this is no doubt that Defoe did not give either his art or his conscience the searching attention which his moral aims involved; on the other hand, we must remember that he was in fact faced with a problem which was then new and has since remained the central problem of the novel: how to impose a coherent moral structure on narrative without detracting from its air of literal authenticity.

Formal realism is only a mode of presentation, and it is therefore ethically neutral: all Defoe's novels are also ethically neutral because they make formal realism an end rather than a means, subordinating any coherent ulterior significance to the illusion that the text represents the authentic lucubrations of an historical person. But the individual case-book is an arid study except in the hands of a skilled interrogator who can elicit the things we want to know, which are often the very things the person concerned does not know or is unwilling to admit: the problem of the novel was to discover and reveal these deeper meanings without any breach of formal realism.

Later novelists were to see that although formal realism

[1] I, 126-127.

imposed a more absolute and impersonal optical accuracy upon the manner in which literature performed its ancient task of holding the mirror up to nature, there were nevertheless ways in which a moral pattern could be conveyed, although they were perhaps more difficult and indirect than those of previous literary forms. For, in place of direct comment, or the power of tone and imagery, the pattern had to depend upon the manipulation of the mirror in time, in place, in closeness, in brilliance. 'Point of view' was to become the crucial instrument whereby the writer expressed his moral sensibility, and pattern came to be the result of the hidden skill whereby the angles at which the mirror was held were made to reflect reality as the novelist saw it. No such pattern emerges from Defoe's treatment of plot and characterisation in *Moll Flanders*; as for the moral consciousness of his heroine, it continues to elude us in the infinite regress produced by the lack of co-ordination between the different aspects of his narrative purpose.

III

Those who, like John Peale Bishop, see *Moll Flanders* as 'one of the great English novels, perhaps the greatest',[1] can hardly fail to notice this lack of co-ordination, but they discern behind it a firm grasp on the realities of human behaviour. As to the moralising, they assume that Defoe cannot have meant it seriously, and that the story belongs to that class of novel where the discrepancy between the apparent moral tenor and any intelligent understanding of it by the reader is a literary device by which the author tells us that his work must be interpreted ironically: the method may be called that of the conspicuous absence of authorial endorsement from first-person narration, and it has certainly been used successfully in such modern analogues of *Moll Flanders* as Anita Loos's *Gentlemen Prefer Blondes* and Joyce Cary's *Herself Surprised*.

To read *Moll Flanders* in this way would imply that Defoe was quite separate from his creation, that he did not even intend the moral asseverations of the preface seriously, and that on the contrary he was unrepentantly delighted with his depiction of the subversive and ironic counterpoint between material and moral considerations which is the most conspicuous feature of

[1] *Collected Essays*, ed. Wilson (New York, 1948), p. 388.

the novel to the modern reader. This interpretation, though consistent with a good deal of the present analysis, is in essence diametrically opposed to it: nevertheless it has received wide enough recent support to demand further examination.

Perhaps the most famous claim made for Defoe as an artist was made by Coleridge, in a marginal note on the passage in *Robinson Crusoe* where the hero comes across some gold in the cabin of the wreck:

> I smil'd to my self at the Sight of this Money, O Drug! Said I aloud, what are thou good for, Thou are not worth to me, no not the taking off of the Ground, one of those Knives is worth all this Heap, I have no Manner of use for thee, e'en remain where thou art, and go to the Bottom as a Creature whose Life is not worth saving. However, upon Second Thoughts, I took it away;* and wrapping all this in a Piece of Canvas . . .

So Defoe, and at the asterisk Coleridge commented:

> Worthy of Shakespeare;—and yet the simple semi-colon after it, the instant passing on without the least pause of reflex consciousness is more exquisite and masterlike than the touch itself. A meaner writer, a Marmontel, would have put an '!' after 'away', and have commenced a new paragraph.[1]

We smile at the phrase 'on second thoughts', with its casual deflation of Crusoe's rhetorical paradox about the worthlessness of gold, and are tempted to see a fine literary decorum in Defoe's avoidance of any further explanation of the compulsive irrationality of economic man. Yet, can we be sure that the irony is not accidental? Is this paradoxical monologue really suited to Crusoe's character or his present situation? Isn't it more typical of Defoe the economic publicist ever on the alert to enforce the useful truth that goods alone constitute real wealth? And if so —isn't the apparent irony merely the result of the extreme insouciance with which Defoe the publicist jerks himself back to his role as novelist, and hastens to tell us what he knows Crusoe, and indeed anyone else, would actually do in the circumstances?

We certainly cannot allow Coleridge's praise to pass as it stands. He used the 1812 edition of the book, which—like most later editions—had put a good deal of order into Defoe's

[1] *Miscellaneous Criticism*, ed. Raysor (London, 1936), p. 294.

haphazard punctuation: the early editions actually give a comma, not a semi-colon, after 'I took it away'. Further—Coleridge's case for Defoe's literary mastery depends a great deal on Defoe's having first combined the two components of the irony—the uselessness of gold in the circumstances, and the decision to take it nevertheless—into a single unit of meaning, and on his having then refused to give any obvious signal to the reader, such as an exclamation mark. In fact, however, not only is there a comma for Coleridge's semi-colon, but there are lots of others as the sentence rambles on for some fifteen lines, during which Crusoe swims ashore and a storm blows up. This seems to be hiding the effect a little too much: and suggests that the real reason for the semblance of irony here and elsewhere in Defoe may well be the amount of heterogeneous matter which he habitually aggregates into one syntactical unit, together with the extreme casualness by which the transitions between the disparate items are effected.

Coleridge's enthusiasm may in any case serve to remind us of the danger to which, it has been alleged, the wise are especially prone: that of seeing too much. This seems to be what happens in Virginia Woolf's two essays in the *Common Reader*. Do not the texts of *Robinson Crusoe* and *Moll Flanders* provide her with an occasion for being wise, for seeing more than is really there? She writes, for instance, of 'a plain earthenware pot stands in the foreground . . . [which] . . . persuades us to see remote islands and the solitudes of the human soul'.[1] In view of the essay 'On Solitude' in the last part of *Robinson Crusoe* it is surely more likely that Defoe's technique was not subtle or conscious enough to be able to evoke the theme of human solitude and to instruct us in elementary pottery at the same time and in the same narrative.

So when Virginia Woolf writes of Defoe subduing 'every other element to his design'[2] I remain sceptical. Is there—either in *Robinson Crusoe* or in *Moll Flanders*—any design whatsoever in the usual sense of the term? Isn't such an interpretation really a kind of indirect critical repayment for the feeling of superiority which Defoe enables us to derive from his humble and unpondered prose, a feeling of superiority which enables us to convert the extreme cases of his narrative *gaucherie* into irony?

[1] 'Robinson Crusoe', *The Common Reader, Second Series* (London, 1948), p. 58.
[2] *Ibid.*

Moll Flanders has a few examples of patent and conscious irony. There is, first of all, a good deal of dramatic irony of a simple kind: for example in Virginia, where a woman relates the story of Moll's incestuous marriage, not knowing that she is addressing its chief figure.[1] There are also some examples of much more pointed irony, as in the passage when, as a little girl, Moll Flanders vows that she will become a gentlewoman when she grows up, like one of her leisured but scandalous neighbours:

> 'Poor child,' says my good old nurse, 'you may soon be such a gentlewoman as that, for she is a person of ill fame, and has had two bastards.'
> I did not understand anything of that; but I answered, 'I am sure they call her madam, and she does not go to service nor do housework'; and therefore I insisted that she was a gentlewoman, and I would be such a gentlewoman as that.[2]

It is good dramatic irony to point this prophetic episode with the phrase 'such a gentlewoman as that', where the verbal emphasis also drives home the difference between virtue and class, and the moral dangers of being taken in by external evidences of gentility. We can be certain that the irony is conscious because its tenor is supported by Defoe's other writings, which often show a somewhat rancorous spirit towards the failure of the gentry to provide proper models of conduct: there is a similar tendency, for example, in Moll's later ironical description of the eldest brother as 'a gay gentleman who . . . had levity enough to do an ill-natured thing, yet had too much judgment of things to pay too dear for his pleasures'. Here, the combination of stylistic elegance and demonstrable consonance with Defoe's own point of view makes us sure that Moll Flanders's reflection after she has been duped by James is also ironical: ''Tis something of relief even to be undone by a man of honour, rather than by a scoundrel'.[3] The verbal hyperbole drives home the contrast between overt and actual moral norms: 'undone' is a calculated exaggeration, Moll Flanders being what she is already; and the ambiguity of 'a man of honour' seems to be used with full consciousness of its subversive effect.

These examples of conscious irony in *Moll Flanders*, however,

[1] II, 142.   [2] I, 8.   [3] I, 14, 155.

fall far short of the larger, structural irony which would suggest that Defoe viewed either his central character or his purported moral theme ironically. There is certainly nothing in *Moll Flanders* which clearly indicates that Defoe sees the story differently from the heroine. There are, it is true, a few cases where such an intention seems possible: but on examination they are seen to have none of the hallmarks of the conscious examples of irony given above; instead, they are much closer to the passage in *Robinson Crusoe*.

A particularly close parallel to Crusoe's bathetic fall from his rhetorical climax occurs after Moll Flanders has revealed the terrible truth of her birth to her husband and half-brother:

> I saw him turn pale and look wild; and I said, 'Now remember your promise, and receive it with presence of mind; for who could have said more to prepare you for it than I have done?' However, I called a servant, and got him a little glass of rum (which is the usual dram of the country), for he was fainting away.[1]

The insistence on credibility—leading to the fussy parenthesis explaining why rum and not brandy—creates a violent contrast between the great stress of the emotion and its very humdrum cure. Life, one might agree, is like that; but any writer who wanted to insist on the intensity of the emotion would not suggest that a glass of rum would meet the case. Especially a little one—'little' is a good example of how a 'realistic' attention to minute but somehow inappropriate detail can help to create irony.

Formally, we notice, the passage is similar to the gold one; the transition between the incongruous elements uses the adversative 'however' which insists on the logical connection in the narrator's mind. If Defoe had merely begun a new paragraph, the irony would have been much diminished, since it depends on the apparent insistence that the two juxtaposed items—in each case an emotional or abstract extreme followed by a more practical consideration—really belong to the same universe of discourse.

The passage is also typical in content, because the suspicion of irony is aroused by a bathetic transition from sentiment to action which is very common in Defoe's novels, although it is never certain that he intends it ironically. There is the occasion,

[1] I, 103.

for instance, when Moll, in her unwonted transport of feeling, kisses the ground her son has trodden on, but desists as soon as it is urged upon her that the ground is 'damp and dangerous'.[1] It is perhaps possible that Defoe was laughing at his heroine's unabashed mixture of sentimentality and common sense; but it is surely more likely that he had to get Moll off her knees before he could get on with the story, and that he did not ponder the means of doing so very carefully.

The lack of insulation between incongruous attitudes seems particularly ironical if we are already predisposed to regard one of them as false. This happens with many of the moralising passages, and Defoe certainly does nothing to obviate our incredulity by the way he introduces them. One glaringly improbable case occurs when an as yet impenitent Moll relates to the governess how she was picked up by a drunken man whom she later robbed, and goes on to improve the occasion by quoting Solomon in the course of a lay sermon against drunkenness. The governess is much moved, Moll tells us:

> . . . it so affected her that she was hardly able to forbear tears, to think how such a gentleman ran a daily risk of being undone, every time a glass of wine got into his head.
>
> But as to the purchase I got, and how entirely I stripped him, she told me it pleased her wonderfully. 'Nay, child,' says she, 'the usage may, for aught I know, do more to reform him than all the sermons that ever he will hear in his life.' And if the remainder of the story be true, so it did.[2]

The two women then combine to anticipate divine retribution, and to milk the poor gentleman of his cash, in order to drive their lesson home. The episode is certainly a travesty of piety and morality; and yet it is very unlikely that Defoe is being ironical; any more than he is later when, by some very human obliquity, Moll Flanders excuses herself from the prison chaplain's appeal that she confess her sins on the grounds of his addiction to the bottle.[3] Both episodes are plausible enough psychologically: the devotees of one vice are often less charitable than the virtuous about the other ones they happen not to favour. The problem, however, is whether Defoe himself overlooked, and expected his readers to overlook, the very damaging nature of the context in which his homilies against alcohol occur.

[1] II, 141.   [2] II, 37-38.   [3] II, 93.

There is every reason to believe that he did: the lesson itself must have been intended seriously, and not ironically; as for its context, we have already seen that there was no way in which Defoe could make good his didactic professions except by making Moll double as chorus for his own honest beliefs; and there is therefore good reason to believe that the moral imperceptiveness which is so laughably clear to us is in fact a reflection of one of the psychological characteristics of Puritanism which Defoe shared with his heroine.

Svend Ranulf, in his *Moral Indignation and Middle Class Psychology*, has shown, mainly from Commonwealth pamphlets, how the Puritans were much more addicted to outbursts of moral indignation than were the Royalists.[1] One of the strengths of Puritanism, he suggests, lay in its tendency to convert its demand for righteousness into a somewhat uncharitable aggressiveness against the sins of others: and this, of course, carried with it a complementary tendency for the individual to be mercifully blind to his own faults. Moll Flanders frequently exemplifies this tendency. One famous instance is the passage when she consoles herself for having stolen a child's gold necklace with the reflection: 'I only thought I had given the parents a just reproof for their negligence, in leaving the poor lamb to come home by itself, and it would teach them to take more care another time'.[2] There is no doubt about the psychological veracity of the reflection: the conscience is a great casuist. There is, however, some doubt about Defoe's intention: is it meant to be an ironical touch about his heroine's moral duplicities, her tendency to be blind to the beam in her own eye? or did Defoe forget Moll as he raged inwardly at the thought of how careless parents are, and how richly they deserve to be punished?

If Defoe intended the passage to be an ironical portrayal of spiritual self-deception, it becomes necessary to assume that he saw Moll Flanders's character as a whole in this light, for the incident is typical of her general blindness to her own spiritual and mental dishonesty. She always lies about her financial position, for instance, even to those she loves. Thus when the mutual trickery with James is revealed, she conceals a thirty-pound bank-bill 'and that made freer of the rest, in consideration of his circumstances, for I really pitied him heartily'. Then she goes

---

[1] Copenhagen, 1938, especially pp. 94, 198.   [2] I, 204.

on, 'But to return to this question, I told him I never willingly deceived him and I never would'. Later, after his departure, she says: 'Nothing that ever befell me in my life sank so deep into my heart as this farewell. I reproached him a thousand times in my thoughts for leaving me, for I would have gone with him through the world, if I had begged my bread. I felt in my pocket, and there I found ten guineas, his gold watch, and two little rings. . . .'[1] She cannot even in theory attest the reality of her devotion by expressing her willingness to beg her bread, without immediately proving that it was only a rhetorical hyperbole by reassuring herself that she has enough in her pocket to keep her in bread for a lifetime. There is surely no conscious irony here: for Defoe and his heroine generous sentiments are good, and concealed cash reserves are good too, perhaps better; but there is no feeling that they conflict, or that one attitude undermines the other.

Defoe had accused the occasional conformists of 'playing Bo-Peep with God Almighty'.[2] The term admirably describes the politic equivocations about common honesty and moral truth so common in *Moll Flanders*. Defoe there 'plays Bo-Peep' at various levels: from the sentence and the incident to the fundamental ethical structure of the whole book, his moral attitude to his creation is as shallow and devious and easily deflected as his heroine's on the occasion when her married gallant writes to her to terminate the affair, and urges her to change her ways, she writes: 'I was struck with this letter, as with a thousand wounds; the reproaches of my own conscience were such as I cannot express, for I was not blind to my own crime; and I reflected that I might with less offence have continued with my brother, since there was no crime in our marriage on that score, neither of us knowing it.'[3]

No writer who had allowed himself to contemplate either his heroine's conscience, or the actual moral implications of her career, in a spirit of irony, could have written this seriously. Nor could he have written the account of James's moral reformation, in which Moll Flanders tells us how she brought him the riches given by her son, not forgetting 'the horses, hogs, and cows, and other stores for our plantation' and concludes 'from this time forward I believe he was as sincere a penitent and as thoroughly a reformed man as ever God's goodness brought

[1] I, 154, 158.   [2] *True Collection* . . ., p. 315.   [3] I, 126.

back from a profligate, a highwayman, and a robber'.[1] We, not Defoe, are ironically aware of the juxtaposition of the powers of God and Mammon; we, not Defoe, laugh at the concept of reformation through hogs and cows.

Whatever disagreement there may be about particular instances, it is surely certain that there is no consistently ironical attitude present in *Moll Flanders*. Irony in its extended sense expresses a deep awareness of the contradictions and incongruities that beset man in this vale of tears, an awareness which is manifested in the text's purposeful susceptibility to contradictory interpretations. As soon as we have become aware of the author's ulterior purpose, we can see all the apparent contradictions as indications of the coherent attitude underlying the whole work. Such a way of writing obviously makes severe demands upon the attention of the author and the reader: the implication of every word, the juxtaposition of every episode, the relation of every part to the whole, all must exclude any interpretation except the intended one. It is, as we have seen, very unlikely that Defoe wrote in this way, or that he had such readers; indeed, all the evidence points the other way.

It may be objected that Defoe wrote at least one avowedly ironical work, *The Shortest Way with Dissenters* (1702). And it is true that there he very successfully imitated the style, the temper and the basic strategy of the exasperated High Churchmen who at last saw an opportunity under Anne for crushing the Dissenters. Actually, however, as is well known, many readers took the pamphlet as a genuine expression of extreme Tory churchmanship; and the reason for this is made clear by a study of the work: as in *Moll Flanders*, Defoe's vicarious identification with the supposed speaker was so complete that it obscured his original intention; his only conscious exercise in irony, in fact, was indeed a masterpiece, but a masterpiece not of irony but of impersonation.

There is not time here to demonstrate this at length, but the contemporary reception of *The Shortest Way* at least shows that it does not constitute irrefutable evidence that irony was a weapon which Defoe could handle effectively. Nor, indeed, is this view held by all those who see *Moll Flanders* as a work of irony. Bonamy Dobrée, for example, in a persuasive commentary

[1] II, 160.

finds the novel 'full of delicious irony so long as we keep outside Moll'. But since, as he admits and as has been argued above, it is very difficult to believe that Defoe was objective enough to be able to keep outside his heroine, Dobrée's claim that *Moll Flanders* is 'an astonishing incomparable masterpiece'[1] seems to depend on the view that its irony is unintentional and unconscious.

Our crucial problem, therefore, would seem to be how we can explain the fact that a novel which was not intended ironically should be seen in such a light by so many modern readers. The answer would seem to be a matter not of literary criticism but of social history. We cannot today believe that so intelligent a man as Defoe should have viewed either his heroine's economic attitudes or her pious protestations with anything other than derision. Defoe's other writings, however, do not support this belief, and it may be surmised that the course of history has brought about in us powerful and often unconscious predispositions to regard certain matters ironically which Defoe and his age treated quite seriously.

Among these predispositions, these ironigenic attitudes, two at least are strongly aroused by *Moll Flanders*: the guilt feelings which are now fairly widely attached to economic gain as a motive; and the view that protestations of piety are suspect anyway, especially when combined with a great attention to one's own economic interest. But, as we have seen, Defoe was innocent of either attitude. He was not ashamed to make economic self-interest his major premise about human life; he did not think such a premise conflicted either with social or religious values; and nor did his age. It is likely, therefore, that one group of apparent ironies in *Moll Flanders* can be explained as products of an unresolved and largely unconscious conflict in Defoe's own outlook, a conflict which is typical of the late Puritan disengagement of economic matters from religious and moral sanctions.

Most of the other ironies in *Moll Flanders* can be explained on similar lines. One group of apparent ironies, we noted, centred round the deflation of emotional considerations by practical ones: here, surely, we have the rational and sceptical instincts of Defoe unconsciously rebelling against the sentimental scenes and speeches which the genre and its readers

[1] 'Some Aspects of Defoe's Prose', *Pope and His Contemporaries, Essays Presented to George Sherburn*, ed. Clifford and Landa (Oxford, 1949), p. 176.

required. Another group of possible ironies centres round the amorous adventures of the heroine; we find it difficult to believe that these were told only for purposes of moral edification. Yet the ambivalence here is typical of the secularised Puritan. John Dunton, for example, an eccentric Dissenter and an acquaintance of Defoe's, wrote a monthly paper exposing prostitution, *The Night Walker: or, Evening Rambles in Search after Lewd Women* (1696–97), in which a virtuous purpose is avowed as strongly and as unconvincingly as it is today by sensational journalists engaged in similar appeals to public lubricity. An even closer analogy is supplied by Pepys: he bought a pornographic work and read it in his office on Sundays, commenting 'a mighty lewd book, but not amiss for a sober man to read once over to inform himself in the villainy of the world.'[1]

There are other areas of conflict in Defoe's outlook which explain two further important difficulties in the critical interpretation of *Moll Flanders*. One reason for the feeling that Defoe cannot be serious about Moll's spiritual reformation is that her remorse and penitence are not supported by the action or even by any sense of real psychological change: as in *Robinson Crusoe*, the spiritual dimension is presented as a series of somewhat inexplicable religious breakdowns in the psychic mechanism, breakdowns, however, which do not permanently impair her healthy amorality. But this dissociation of religion from ordinary life was a natural consequence of secularisation, and the same feature of the life of Defoe's time is probably also the cause of the central confusion in Moll Flanders's moral consciousness— her tendency to confuse penitence for her sins with chagrin at the punishment of her crimes. The secularisation of individual morality obviously tended to emphasise the distinction which Hobbes made when he wrote that 'every crime is a sin, but not every sin a crime';[2] it is surely because Moll Flanders's genuine fears only extend to the probable results of the discovery of her crimes that we feel, to quote Reed Whittemore, that in her moral consciousness 'Hell is almost bound by Newgate's wall'.[3]

Many of the apparent discrepancies in *Moll Flanders*, then, are concerned with areas of individual morality where the last two centuries have taught us to make careful distinctions, but where the early eighteenth century tended to be a good deal

---

[1] *Diary*, ed. Wheatley (London, 1896), VII, 279.
[2] *Leviathan*, Pt. II, ch. 27.   [3] *Heroes and Heroines* (New York, 1946), p. 47.

less sensitive. It is natural, therefore, that we should be prone to see irony where there is more probably only a confusion —a confusion which our century is much better prepared to discern than was Defoe or his age. It is probably significant in this connection that the most ardent admirers of *Moll Flanders* are unhistorical in their outlook and interests. E. M. Forster, for instance, in *Aspects of the Novel* specifically excludes period considerations from his inquiry; while John Peale Bishop, perhaps accepting but misreading Defoe's concluding assertion 'Written in the year 1683', dates the novel itself in 1668.[1]

There is another historical explanation of a somewhat different kind for the modern tendency to read *Moll Flanders* ironically: the rise of the novel. We place Defoe's novels in a very different context from that of their own time; we take novels much more seriously now, and we judge his by the more exacting literary standards of today. This presumption, combined with Defoe's actual mode of writing, forces us to explain a great deal as ironical. We believe, for example, that a sentence should have unity; if we must invent one for sentences which are really a random accumulation of clauses containing many disparate or incongruous items, we can impose unity only by an ironical subordination of some items to others. Similarly with the larger units of composition, from the paragraph to the total structure: if we assume on *a priori* grounds that a coherent plan must be present, we find one, and thereby produce a complex pattern out of what are actually incongruities.

Life itself, of course, is a suitable enough object for ironical contemplation, and so the tendency to regard *Moll Flanders* as ironic is in a sense a tribute to Defoe's vitality as a writer—it is partly because what he creates seems so real that we feel we must define our attitude to it. But, of course, such an attitude on the reader's part is excluded by genuinely ironical writing more than by any other: every way of looking at the events has been anticipated and either organised into the whole work, or made impossible. There is no evidence of such an exclusion in *Moll Flanders*, much less of a comprehensive control operating over every aspect of the work. If they are ironies, they are surely the ironies of social and moral and literary disorder. Perhaps, however, they are better regarded not as the achievements of an ironist, but as accidents produced by the random application

---

[1] *Collected Essays*, p. 47; the actual date was 1722.

of narrative authenticity to conflicts in Defoe's social and moral and religious world, accidents which unwittingly reveal to us the serious discrepancies in his system of values.

That these discrepancies are revealed at all, incidentally, is a tribute to the searching power of formal realism, which permits and indeed encourages the presentation of literary objects and attitudes which had not hitherto jostled each other in the same work but had been segregated in separate ones such as tragedy, comedy, history, picaresque, journalism and homily. Later novelists such as Jane Austen and Flaubert were to incorporate such conflicts and incongruities into the very structure of their works: they created irony, and made novel readers sensitive to its effects. We cannot but approach Defoe's novels through the literary expectations which later masters of the form made possible, and these expectations seem to find some justification as a result of our acute awareness of the conflicting nature of the two main forces in Defoe's philosophy of life—rational economic individualism and concern for spiritual redemption—which together held his divided but not, apparently, uneasy allegiance. Nevertheless, if we are primarily concerned with Defoe's actual intentions, we must conclude that although he reveals the sophistries whereby these dual allegiances are preserved intact, he does not, strictly speaking, portray them; consequently *Moll Flanders* is undoubtedly an ironic object, but it is not a work of irony.

IV

The preceding sections are not intended as a denial of the importance of Defoe as a novelist, but only as a demonstration of a fact that might perhaps have been taken for granted if it had not been challenged or overlooked by many recent critics: the fact that Defoe's novels lack both the consistency in matters of detail of which many lesser writers are capable, and the larger coherences found in the greatest literature. Defoe's forte was the brilliant episode. Once his imagination seized on a situation he could report it with a comprehensive fidelity which was much in advance of any previous fiction, and which, indeed, has never been surpassed. These episodes are irresistible in quotation; and the pre-eminence of *Moll Flanders* is perhaps mainly due to its strong claim to be not so much a great novel as Defoe's richest anthology.

How far we should allow Defoe's gift for the perfect episode to outweigh his patent shortcomings—weaknesses of construction, inattention to detail, lack of moral or formal pattern—is a very difficult critical problem. There is something about Defoe's genius which is as confident and indestructible as the resilient selfhood of his heroine, and which all but persuades us to accept the notorious critical heresy that the single talent well employed can make up for all the others.

The talent, of course, is the supreme one in the novel: Defoe is the master illusionist, and this almost makes him the founder of the new form. Almost, but not quite: the novel could be considered established only when realistic narrative was organised into a plot which, while retaining Defoe's lifelikeness, also had an intrinsic coherence; when the novelist's eye was focussed on character and personal relationships as essential elements in the total structure, and not merely as subordinate instruments for furthering the verisimilitude of the actions described; and when all these were related to a controlling moral intention. It was Richardson who took these further steps, and it is primarily for this reason that he, rather than Defoe, is usually regarded as the founder of the English novel.

Defoe created his own personal genre, which stands wholly alone in the history of literature, as befits the creator of Robinson Crusoe: and this solitary position is directly related to the role of individualism in his works, as is suggested by the curiously close parallel between his fiction and the plays of an earlier individualist and literary innovator, Christopher Marlowe.

Both men were lowly born, poor, well educated, restless, energetic; both found it difficult to find a satisfactory place in the society of their day, and both eventually achieved contact with the mysteries of power through the seamier side of government, as informers and secret agents. Their lives are reflected in their writings. Both expressed themselves most fully through characters who are radically alienated from society, and who appear to be unconscious autobiographical projections; certainly, despite their vastly different circumstances they have a strong family resemblance—Tamburlaine to Barabas and Faustus, Robinson Crusoe to Moll Flanders and Colonel Jacque. The presence of such central characters is associated both in Marlowe and Defoe with similar structural and thematic difficulties. The plots tend to be episodic, and the basic conflict is not fully embodied in terms of relationships between the characters—all tends to resolve itself into an *ego contra mundum*. The issue of the conflict is similarly ambiguous: the moral, social and religious norms which are eventually brought in to punish the hero for his defiant self-assertion are less convincingly presented than his breaches of them, so that their triumph seems at best perfunctory, and leaves us in some doubt as to how fully it is endorsed by the author.

The most positive value that emerges from the works of Defoe and Marlowe is certainly not that of the traditional moral order; as in the case of Stendhal, the supreme expression of individualism in French literature, the vision of life presented is remarkable not for its wisdom but for its energy. This duality, perhaps, poses the central problem both for the moral evaluation of individualism in general, and of the figure of Moll Flanders. Her wisdom is not impressive; it is at best of a low atavistic kind wholly directed to the problems of survival; but nothing could be more impressive than her energy, and it too has a moral premise, a kind of inarticulate and yet fortifying stoicism. Everything happens to Moll Flanders and nothing leaves scars; the very tone of her reminiscences assures us that no vicissitude can ever impair her comfortable vitality; our grossest crimes and our most contemptible moral weaknesses, apparently, will never deprive us of the love of others or even of our own self-respect; the whole book, indeed, is a series of variations on individualism's eternal challenge to the orthodoxy of the present and the wisdom of the past, a sequence in which the heroine, an unabashed Parolles, asserts defiantly, 'Simply the thing I am shall make me live'.

These words epitomise the claim which both the form and the content of Defoe's novels make on posterity; and it is very appropriate that the claim should have been fully allowed only when, after the passing of nearly two centuries which had accorded them only a somewhat sub-literary fame,[1] they found a new resonance in the last few decades, decades when the novel, and its associated way of life, individualism, seem to have come full circle.

At a time when the technique of the novel had reached an unexampled complication, Defoe's formal artlessness seemed

[1] See Charles E. Burch, 'British Criticism of Defoe as a Novelist, 1719–1860', *Englische Studien*, LXVIII (1932), 178-198.

more piquant than ever before. It was easy to see the cumbrous-
ness of Richardson or the artificiality of Fielding, because the
novel had gone far beyond their solutions of its formal problems.
But Defoe did not compete, and it was refreshing to acclaim a
writer who still spoke vividly to us although he had not, apparently, given a moment's reflection as to the technical problems
involved in so doing: and, in the novel form at least, artless
authenticity seemed preferable to all but the highest art. So
Virginia Woolf and E. M. Forster gave us a Defoe of the
'twenties, an ally in the onslaught on the mechanical craftsman-
ship of Arnold Bennett and Galsworthy.

At the same time, and in the succeeding decades, the intellectual and social bases of individualism were being challenged
as never before, and this also bestowed an ironical topicality on
the work of an early recorder of its triumphs and degradations.
The Second World War, especially, brought us closer to the
prophetic nature of Defoe's picture of individualism. Camus
used Defoe's allegorical claim for *Robinson Crusoe* as epigraph to
his own allegory, *La Peste* (1948): 'It is as reasonable to represent
one kind of imprisonment by another, as it is to represent anything that really exists by that which exists not'. At the same
time André Malraux wrote that only three books, *Robinson
Crusoe, Don Quixote* and *The Idiot*, retained their truth for those
who had seen prisons and concentration camps.[1]

Defoe's concentration on isolated individuals, it would seem,
is closer to the view of life held by many writers today than to
those held in the intervening centuries. It is likely that these
writers read more into Defoe than he seriously intended, and
that the modern alienation is much more complex and less
voluntary than that of Robinson Crusoe and Moll Flanders.
But whatever Defoe's consciousness of the symbolic quality of
his novels may have been, it is certain that, at the end of the
long tradition of the European novel, and of the society whose
individualism, leisure and unexampled security allowed it to
make personal relations the major theme of its literature, Defoe
is a welcome and portentous figure. Welcome because he seems
long ago to have called the great bluff of the novel—its suggestion that personal relations really are the be-all and end-all of
life; portentous because he, and only he, among the great
writers of the past, has presented the struggle for survival in the

[1] *Les Noyers de l'Altenburg* (Paris, 1948), pp. 119-121.

bleak perspectives which recent history has brought back to a commanding position on the human stage.

The accidents of history, then, treated Defoe fortunately, although he courted them as no other writer has done, and deserves his reward. They impelled him to a step which was decisive in the history of the novel. His blind and almost purposeless concentration on the actions of his heroes and heroines, and his unconscious and unreflective mingling of their thoughts and his about the inglorious world in which they both exist, made possible the expression of many motives and themes which could not, perhaps, have come into the tradition of the novel without Defoe's shock tactics: motives such as economic egoism and social alienation; and themes such as the conflicts between old and new sets of values as they are manifested in daily life. Very few writers have created for themselves both a new subject and a new literary form to embody it. Defoe did both. In his somewhat monocular concentration on making his matter seem absolutely convincing, there was much he did not see. But what is left out is probably the price for what is so memorably and unprecedentedly put in.

CHAPTER V

Love and the Novel: 'Pamela'

THE importance of Richardson's position in the tradition of the novel was largely due to his success in dealing with several of the major formal problems which Defoe had left unsolved. The most important of them was probably that of plot, and here Richardson's solution was remarkably simple: he avoided an episodic plot by basing his novels on a single action, a courtship. It is no doubt odd that so fateful a literary revolution should have been brought about with so ancient a literary weapon; but—and this is the theme of the present chapter—in Richardson's hands it revealed new powers.

I

Madame de Staël linked the fact that the Ancients had no novels with the fact that, largely as a result of the inferior social position of women, the classical world attached relatively little importance to the emotional relationships between men and women.[1] It is certainly true that classical Greece and Rome knew little of romantic love in our sense, and the erotic life in general was not given anything like the importance and approbation it has received in modern life and literature. Even in Euripides sexual passion is clearly considered as a violation of the human norm; while not exactly a vice, it is certainly not a virtue; and, for the man especially, to allow it much scope is an indication of weakness rather than strength. As for Latin literature, its similarly derogatory attitude is suggested by a passage in the commentary of Servius on the *Aeneid*: he explains that Dido's love was not a serious enough subject for epic dignity, but that Virgil had redeemed himself by treating it in an almost comic style—*paene comicus stilus est: nec mirum, ubi de amore tractatur.*[2]

The idea that love between the sexes is to be regarded as the supreme value of life on earth is generally agreed to have had its

---

[1] *De la littérature, considérée dans ses rapports avec les institutions sociales*, in *Œuvres complètes* (Paris, 1820), IV, 215-217.   [2] Bk. IV, n. 1.

origin in the rise of *amour courtois* in eleventh-century Provence. Courtly love is in essence the result of the transfer of an attitude of religious adoration from a divine to a secular object—from the Virgin Mary to the lady worshipped by the troubadour. Like modern individualism, therefore, the rise of romantic love has deep roots in the Christian tradition, and so it is very appropriate that it should be the basis of the ideal pattern of sexual behaviour in our society. The most universal religion of the West, according to Vilfredo Pareto,[1] at least, is the sex religion; the novel supplies it with its doctrine and its rituals, just as the mediaeval romances had done for courtly love.

Courtly love, however, could not itself provide the kind of connective or structural theme which the novel required. It was primarily a leisure fantasy invented to gratify the noble lady whose actual social and economic future had already been decided by her marriage to a feudal lord; it belonged to an a-moral world, a social vacuum where only the individual existed and where the external world, with its drastic legal and religious sanctions against adultery,[2] was completely forgotten. Consequently the forms of mediaeval literature which dealt with everyday life paid no attention to courtly love, and presented womankind as a species characterised by an insatiate fleshly cupidity; while, on the other hand, the verse and prose romances which dealt with courtly love presented their heroines as angelic beings, and this idealisation was usually extended to the psychology, the background and the language of the story. Not only so: from the point of view of plot, heroic chastity is subject to exactly the same literary defects as inveterate promiscuity; both are poor in the qualities of development and surprise. In the romances, therefore, while courtly love provided the conventional beginning and end, the main interest of the narrative lay in the adventures which the knight achieved for his lady, and not in the development of the love relationship itself.

Gradually, however, the code of romantic love began to accommodate itself to religious, social and psychological reality, notably to marriage and the family. This process seems to have occurred particularly early in England, and the new ideology

---

[1] *The Mind and Society*, trans. Livingstone (New York, 1935), II, 1129; but see translator's note 1 to p. 1396.

[2] See F. Carl Riedel, *Crime and Punishment in the Old French Romances* (New York, 1938), pp. 42, 101.

which eventually came into being there does much to explain both the rise of the novel and the distinctive difference between the English and French traditions in fiction. Denis de Rougemont, in his study of the development of romantic love, writes of the French novel that 'to judge by its literature, adultery would seem to be one of the most characteristic occupations of Western man'.[1] Not so in England, where the break with the originally adulterous character of courtly love was so complete that George Moore was almost justified in claiming to have 'invented adultery, which didn't exist in the English novel till I began writing'.[2]

There are signs of the reconciliation between courtly love and the institution of marriage at least as early as Chaucer's *Franklin's Tale*, and it is very evident in Spenser's *Faerie Queene*. Later the Puritanism that is already strong in Spenser finds its supreme expression in *Paradise Lost* which is, among other things, the greatest and indeed the only epic of married life. In the next two centuries the Puritan conception of marriage and sexual relations generally became the accepted code of Anglo-Saxon society to a degree unknown elsewhere; in the words of Frieda Lawrence, who must be allowed considerable *expertise* in the matter, 'only the English have this special brand of marriage . . . the God-given unity of marriage . . . that is part of Puritanism'.[3]

Richardson played an important part in establishing this new code. He wrote at a time when a variety of economic and social changes, some of them temporary and local, but most of them characteristic of modern English and American civilisation, were combining to make marriage much more important for women than before, and at the same time much more difficult to achieve. These changes gave Richardson the enormous advantage over the writers of romance that, without recourse to any extraneous elements of complication, he could reflect the actual life of his time and yet be able to expand a single intrigue into the proportions of a novel considerably longer than any by Defoe. In *Pamela* the relationship of the lovers has all the absolute quality of romantic love; and yet it can realistically be made to involve many of the basic problems

---

[1] *L'Amour et l'Occident* (Paris, 1939), p. 2.
[2] *Cit.* Joseph Hone, *Life of George Moore* (London, 1936), p. 373.
[3] 'Foreword', *The First Lady Chatterley* (New York, 1944).

of everyday life—conflicts between social classes and their different outlooks, for example, and conflicts between the sexual instinct and the moral code. The relationship between Pamela and Mr. B., in fact, can carry the whole weight of the literary structure in a way that was impossible in the romances.

II

The values of courtly love could not be combined with those of marriage until marriage was primarily the result of a free choice by the individuals concerned. This freedom of choice has until recently been the exception rather than the rule in the history of human society, especially as far as women have been concerned. The rise of the novel, then, would seem to be connected with the much greater freedom of women in modern society, a freedom which, especially as regards marriage, was achieved earlier and more completely in England than elsewhere.

In eighteenth-century France, for example, daughters were customarily secluded from young men until their parents had arranged a marriage for them. The extent of women's freedom in England was very striking in comparison, as Montesquieu[1] and many other contemporaries pointed out. In Germany the position of women was considered to be even more disadvantageous,[2] while Lady Mary Wortley Montagu criticised *Sir Charles Grandison* on the grounds that Richardson should have known enough about the restrictions on feminine rights in Italy to realise that his hero could never have begun his amour with Clementina in her father's house.[3]

The relatively great freedom of women in England had existed at least as far back as the Elizabethan period, but it was reinforced in the eighteenth century by some aspects of the rise of individualism. Economic individualism, we have seen, tended to weaken the ties between parents and children: and its spread was associated with the development of a new kind of family system which has since become the standard one in most modern societies.

[1] *L'Esprit des lois*, Bk. XXIII, ch. 8. I am much indebted to the late Daniel Mornet for allowing me to read his notes towards a study of 'Le Mariage au 17e et 18e siècle'.

[2] Thomas Salmon, *Critical Essay Concerning Marriage*, 1724, p. 263.

[3] *Letters and Works*, II, 285.

This system can be described as the 'elementary' family, to use A. R. Radcliffe-Brown's term,[1] or as the 'conjugal' family, to use Émile Durkheim's.[2] In nearly all countries, of course, the family unit includes the 'elementary' or 'conjugal' group consisting of husband, wife and their children, but it also includes a whole complex of other less closely related kinsfolk: the use of the terms here, therefore, has a real defining force because it indicates that this elementary or conjugal group alone is what constitutes the family in our society; it is an entity formed by the voluntary union of two individuals.

This kind of family, for which we will here use Durkheim's term 'conjugal' as somewhat more descriptive and perhaps less invidious than Radcliffe-Brown's term 'elementary', is different from those of other societies and other periods in many respects, among which may be mentioned the following: on marriage the couple immediately sets up as a new family, wholly separate from their own parents and often far away from them; there is no established priority between the male and female lines of descent as regards property or authority, but instead both lineages are of equal relative unimportance; extended kinship ties in general, to grandparents, aunts and uncles, cousins, etc., have no compelling significance; and once set up, the conjugal family typically becomes an autonomous unit in economic as well as in social affairs.

These arrangements seem obvious enough to us today, but they are in fact historically new, and they all increase the importance of the marriage choice. This choice is especially fateful for the woman, because, as a result of masculine dominance in the economic field, and of the social, residential and occupational mobility brought about by capitalism, it determines, not only her most important personal relationship, but also her social, economic and even geographical future. It is natural, therefore, that modern sociologists should see romantic love as a necessary correlative of the conjugal family system;[3] a strengthening of the intrinsic bonds between man and wife being absolutely necessary to replace the greater security and continuity of the woman's lot afforded by more cohesive and

---

[1] 'Introduction', *African Systems of Kinship and Marriage*, ed. Radcliffe-Brown and Forde (London, 1950), pp. 4-5, 43-46, 60-63.

[2] 'La Famille conjugale', *Revue philosophique*, XCI (1921), 1-14.

[3] See Talcott Parsons, 'The Kinship System of the United States', *Essays in Sociological Theory Pure and Applied* (Glencoe, 1949), p. 241.

extended family systems, and to provide the isolated conjugal unit, and especially the wife, with a strong supporting ideology.

How thoroughly and how extensively the conjugal family system was established in early eighteenth-century England is difficult to say—systematised information on the subject is very hard to come by. It certainly seems likely that in the seventeenth century the traditional and patriarchal family pattern was by far the commonest. The term family, in Gregory King as in Shakespeare, refers to a whole household and often includes grandparents, cousins and even remoter kin, as well as servants and other employees, as the modern term has it. The family in this larger sense was the primary legal, religious and economic unit, under control of the paterfamilias. In economic affairs, for example, much of the food and clothing was manufactured in the home, and even the goods produced for the market were mainly produced by domestic industry; consequently it was the income of the family group as a whole which mattered, and not personal cash wages.

Economically, then, the patriarchal family stood in the way of individualism, and it is probably for this reason that the con- jugal family system has established itself most strongly in indi- vidualist and Protestant societies, and that it is essentially urban and middle class in nature.

One of the earliest indications of the transition from the patriarchal family and domestic industry is the Jacobean outcry against the decay of 'housekeeping',[1] a decay which contempor- aries attributed to the rise in power and numbers of the trading and commercial classes. It is fairly generally agreed that this section of the community first showed its strength in the Civil War, and it is significant, therefore, that Sir Robert Filmer, the chief theorist on the Royalist side, should have showed in his *Patriarcha*, published posthumously in 1680, that for him at least the new political and social movement challenged nothing less than the time-honoured basis of society and religion, the author- ity of the father over his family which was the emblem of every other kind of authority and order.[2] It is equally significant that

[1] See L. C. Knights, *Drama and Society in the Age of Jonson* (London, 1937), pp. 112-117.
[2] See T. P. R. Laslett's Introduction to Filmer's *Patriarcha* (Oxford, 1949), especially pp. 24-28, 38-41; I also owe much to personal discussions with him on these issues.

Locke, the philosopher of Whig individualism, opposed all forms of paternalism, including some aspects of the patriarchal family. His political and economic theory led him to regard the family as primarily a secular and contractual institution existing for the rational function of looking after children until they could do so for themselves. Once they could do so, he believed, 'the bonds of subjection' should 'drop quite off, and leave a man at his own free disposal'.[1] Locke is thus in one important respect a theoretician of the conjugal family.

On the whole, however, the picture of the family in the early eighteenth century is still one of slow and confused transition. Such, certainly, is the suggestion of the works of Defoe and Richardson, who, as middle-class Londoners, belonged to the social milieu where the transition was likely to be most advanced. They themselves are strongly on the traditional side as regards the authority of the father and the vital importance of the family group as a moral and religious entity; on the other hand, the tendency of their novels seems to be towards the assertion of individual freedom from family ties.

This assertion, however, was very difficult for the heroines of Defoe and Richardson to achieve, for a variety of reasons.

To begin with, the legal position of women in the eighteenth century was very largely governed by the patriarchal concepts of Roman law. The only person in the household who was *sui juris*, who was a legal entity, was its head, usually the father. A woman's property, for instance, became her husband's absolutely on marriage, although it was customary to arrange a jointure for her when the marriage articles were drawn up; the children were in law the husband's; only the husband could sue for divorce; and he had the right to punish his wife by beating or imprisoning her.

It is true that this legal position was not thought by contemporaries to represent the realities of the situation. The 1729 edition of *Magnae Britanniae Notitia*, conceding that married women 'with all their movable goods . . . are wholly *in potestate viri*', continued that 'notwithstanding all which, their condition *de facto* is the best of the world'.[2] The legal position, however, certainly emphasised the need for women to make the

---

[1] *Two Treatises of Government*, (1690), 'Essay concerning Civil Government,' sect. 55.   [2] P. 174.

right marriage and thus ensure that 'their condition *de facto*' should not be merely the expression of their abject legal status.

The opposition between patriarchal and individualist attitudes is shown very clearly by the fact that the patriarchal legal situation of married women made it impossible for them to realise the aims of economic individualism. As we should expect, Defoe saw this side of the question very clearly, and dramatised the gravity of the problem in the morally desperate expedient which Roxana is forced to adopt to overcome the legal disabilities of women. As a 'she-merchant' she realises that the pursuit of money cannot be combined with marriage, since 'the very nature of the marriage contract was . . . nothing but giving up liberty, estate, authority, and everything to the man, and the woman was indeed a mere woman ever after—that is to say, a slave'. So she refuses marriage, even with a nobleman, because 'I was as well without the titles as long as I had the estate, and while I had £2,000 a year of my own I was happier than I could be in being prisoner of state to a nobleman, for I took the ladies of that rank to be little better'.[1] Indeed Defoe's economic enthusiasm takes him perilously close to proving that, given a knowledge of banking and investment, Roxana's scandalous specialty could be developed into the most lucrative career then open to women.

To those without Roxana's peculiar combination of qualities, however, the achievement of economic independence outside marriage was becoming increasingly difficult in the eighteenth century. The decay of domestic industry affected women very adversely. A large surplus of women was created in the labour market, and this had the result of bringing down their wages to an average of something like 2s. 6d. a week, about a quarter of the average wage for men.[2]

At the same time women found it much more difficult to find a husband unless they could bring him a dowry. There is much evidence to suggest that marriage became a much more commercial matter in the eighteenth century than had previously been the case. Newspapers carried on marriage marts, with advertisements offering or demanding specified dowries and jointures; and young girls were driven into flagrantly unsuitable

[1] *Roxana*, ed. Aitken (London, 1902), I, 167-168, 58, 189.
[2] Alice Clark, *Working Life of Women in the Seventeenth Century* (London, 1919), pp. 235, 296.

marriages on grounds of economic advantage: Mrs. Delany, for instance, was married at the age of seventeen to a man nearly sixty years old, while Sterne's beloved Eliza became the wife of a middle-aged husband when she was only fourteen. According to Sir William Temple, writing at the end of the seventeenth century, the custom of making marriages 'just like other common bargains and sales, by the mere consideration of interest or gain, without any of love or esteem' was 'of no ancient date'.[1] Economic factors, of course, had in fact always been important in arranging marriages; but it is likely that the traditional power of the paterfamilias was exercised with less attention to non-material considerations as the old family system became subject to the pressures of economic individualism.

At lower social levels there is also ample evidence to support the view of Moll Flanders that the marriage market had become 'unfavourable to our sex'.[2] The hardships of poorer women were most dramatically expressed by the sale of wives, at prices ranging, apparently, from sixpence to three and a half guineas.[3] They are suggested in another way by the increase in illicit relations as more males adopted the philosophy of Bunyan's Mr. Badman—'Who would keep a cow of their own that can have a quart of milk for a penny?';[4] the extent of this increase is shown by the fact that provision for illegitimate children became one of the main problems for those concerned with poor-relief.[5] Women were also adversely affected by an increasing masculine tendency towards marrying late on economic grounds. Defoe, for example, in the *Complete English Tradesman* (1726) urged the maxim 'Do not wed till you have sped';[6] and the considerable effects of this attitude are suggested by the fact that the Society for the Propagation of Christian Knowledge was led to oppose the trend because it fostered sexual immorality.[7]

The outlook for servant girls was particularly bad. There were, it is true, some glorious catches, although none of them provide an exact parallel to the supreme one made by Pamela. But the normal fate of domestic servants was much less happy: they were usually bound to stay with their employers either

---

[1] *Works*, 1770, I, 268. See also *Tatler*, No. 199 (1710), and H. J. Habakkuk, 'Marriage Settlements in the Eighteenth Century', *Transactions of the Royal Historical Society*, 4th ser., XXXII (1950), 15-30.
[2] I, 65.   [3] J. H. Whiteley, *Wesley's England* (London, 1938), p. 300.
[4] Everyman Edition, p. 279.   [5] See Marshall, *English Poor*, pp. 207-224.
[6] Ch. 12.   [7] See Lowther Clarke, *Eighteenth Century Piety* (London, 1944), p. 16.

until they were twenty-one, or until they married; many employers forbade their servants to marry under any circumstances;[1] and in fact the number of unmarried servants in London was said to be 10,000 out of a total of 25,000 in 1760.[2] Pamela's only chance of escaping servitude until her majority might well therefore have been the marriage to her employer which she actually made, an employer, incidentally, whose marriage was a supreme act of individual choice which set at naught the traditions of his family and his class.

III

How large a proportion of the population was affected by the crisis in marriage is obviously impossible to say. For our purposes, however, it is probably sufficient to know that the matter excited great and increasing public concern: whether statisticians would have confirmed them or not, many people certainly believed that the situation was grave, and called for drastic measures.

The development which most clearly reveals how widely the crisis affected public attitudes is the change in the status of unmarried women. The idea that the 'old maid' was a ridiculous if not obnoxious type seems to have arisen in the late seventeenth century. In 1673 Richard Allestree stated in *The Ladies' Calling* that 'an old maid is now thought such a curse as no poetic Fury can exceed . . . [and as] the most calamitous creature in Nature'.[3] Later, Defoe talked a good deal about the 'set of despicable creatures, called Old Maids',[4] and there are innumerable literary caricatures of the type in eighteenth-century literature, from Mistress Tipkin in Steele's *The Tender Husband* (1705) to Fielding's Bridget Allworthy in *Tom Jones* and Smollett's Tabitha Bramble in *Humphrey Clinker*. 'Tabby', incidentally, was apparently a dyslogistic type-name for an old maid before it was applied to a humble species of cat.[5]

[1] See David Hume, 'On the Populousness of Ancient Nations', *Essays and Treatises* (Edinburgh, 1817), I, 381.

[2] John H. Hutchins, *Jonas Hanway* (London, 1940), p. 150.

[3] *Cit.* Myra Reynolds, *The Learned Lady in England, 1650–1760* (Boston, 1920), p. 318.   [4] See Lee, *Defoe*, II, 115-117, 143-144; III, 125-128, 323-325.

[5] See R. P. Utter and G. B. Needham, *Pamela's Daughters* (London, 1937), p. 217. I am much indebted to this work, and to G. B. Needham's doctoral dissertation, 'The Old Maid in the Life and Fiction of Eighteenth-Century England', Berkeley, 1938.

The major cause of the decline in status of unmarried women
is suggested by the word 'spinster'. The first usage of the term
recorded by the *Oxford English Dictionary* with the sense of 'an
unmarried woman beyond the usual age for marriage' is dated
1719, and occurs in the first number of a newspaper called *The
Spinster*. There Steele, under the name of Rachel Woolpack,
recalls that the word was not originally opprobrious, but referred
to the laudable 'industry of female manufacturers'. In the eighteenth century, however, unmarried women were no longer positive economic assets to the household because there was less need
for their labour in spinning, weaving and other economic tasks;
as a result many unmarried women were faced with the unpleasant choice between working for very low wages, or becoming largely superfluous dependents on someone else.

The second alternative was the only one as far as those of
gentle birth were concerned; for, as Jane Collier, dependent of
Fielding and friend of Richardson, wrote: 'There are many
methods for young men . . . to acquire a genteel maintenance;
but for a girl I know not one way of support that does not by
the esteem of the world, throw her below the rank of gentlewoman'.[1] A few unmarried women, it is true, such as Mistress
Elizabeth Carter, to whom William Hayley dedicated his
Philosophical, Historical and Moral Essay on Old Maids (1785), or
Jane Austen a generation later, were able to pursue successful
literary careers; and many other spinsters followed less conspicuously in their train and provided novels for the circulating
libraries. But there is no recorded case in the century of a woman
who supported herself entirely by her pen, and in any case the
career of authorship could be open only to a very small minority.

What was most needed, it was generally thought, was a substitute for the convents which had offered a haven and a vocation for gentlewomen until they were closed at the Reformation,
and which still performed the service in Catholic countries.
Mary Astell, in *A Serious Proposal to the Ladies* (1694), had urged
the establishment of a 'monastery or religious retirement';
Defoe had put forward a similar idea in his *Essay upon Projects*
(1697); while in 1739 the *Gentleman's Magazine* was very explicit
in proposing a 'New Method of making women as useful and as
capable of maintaining themselves as men are, and consequently preventing their becoming old maids or taking ill

[1] *Essay on the Art of Ingeniously Tormenting*, 1753, p. 38.

courses'.[1] Richardson had the idea much at heart; Clarissa laments the fact that she cannot take shelter in a nunnery,[2] while Sir Charles Grandison strongly advocates 'Protestant Nunneries' where 'numbers of young women, joining their small fortunes, might . . . maintain themselves genteelly on their own income; though each singly in the world would be distressed'.[3] His proposal, incidentally, was the only part of the book which Lady Mary Wortley Montagu found to praise.[4]

None of these plans were carried out, however, and the tragic dependence of unmarried gentlewomen continued. It is noticeable that many of the literary figures of the period were surrounded by a voluble cluster of spinsters—Swift, Pope, Richardson, Fielding, Johnson, Horace Walpole, for example. Many of these were total or partial dependents; not, as they might have been earlier, economically useful members of a large family household by right of birth, but recipients of voluntary individual charity.

Bachelors did not excite so much commiseration as did spinsters, but the increase of their number was widely regarded as socially deplorable and morally dangerous. At the end of the seventeenth century such political economists as Petty, Davenant and Grew had suggested that bachelors should be taxed more heavily than married men; Petty, for example, argued that whoever refused to procreate ought to 'repair unto the state the misse of another pair of hands'.[5] There were also strong moral objections to bachelorhood, especially among the Puritans: in New England celibates were not allowed to live alone.[6] Richardson manifests the same distrust in his novels, although his chief concern, however, was not so much for the morals of the bachelors as for the interests of their potential spouses, as we can see from Harriet Byron's lament that 'there are more bachelors now in England, by many thousands, than there were a few years ago: and, probably, the numbers of them (and of single women, of course) will every year increase'.[7]

Miss Byron's alarm was probably well grounded. The proportion of bachelors among the literary men of the period is

[1] *Cit. Pamela's Daughters*, p. 229.   [2] *Clarissa*, Everyman Edition, I, 62.
[3] *Grandison* (London, 1812), IV, 155.   [4] *Letters and Works*, II, 291.
[5] See E. A. J. Johnson, *Predecessors of Adam Smith* (London, 1937), p. 253.
[6] Edmund S. Morgan, *The Puritan Family* (Boston, 1944), p. 86.   [7] *Grandison*, II, 11.

certainly very high: Pope, Swift, Isaac Watts, James Thomson, Horace Walpole, Shenstone, Hume, Gray and Cowper, for example, remained unmarried; and there seems in general to have been an unprecedented topicality in a burlesque poem of the period, *The Bachelor's Soliloquy* (1744), which began, 'To wed or not to wed, that is the question'.

Richardson's solution was apparently that of Grandison's forthright 'I am for having everybody marry'.[1] Actually, even if all the men had complied, the problem of marriage for women would still have remained fairly grave, since the large surplus of women in England, and especially in London, which was revealed by the 1801 census[2] was very probably in existence during the whole of the century; such certainly was the common belief.[3] The only solution, therefore, would have been polygyny, or polygamy, to use the usual eighteenth-century term; and the fact that there was indeed a good deal of interest in the topic during the period suggests how serious and widespread the crisis in marriage was thought to be.

The details of the controversy about polygamy do not concern us here, since it cannot be said that plurality of wives is common in the English novel,[4] except possibly in the decorous variant practised in Thomas Amory's *John Buncle* (1756), where the old love is hurriedly dispatched to the grave before the new is donned. Briefly, polygamy, whose legitimacy had been argued by some extreme Protestant bibliolators in the seventeenth century, attracted both the Deists,[5] who could attack the orthodox Christian view of marriage by pointing out that polygamy was approved by the Mosaic Law, and the political economists, from Isaac Vossius to David Hume,[6] who saw in polygamy a possible solution of the problem of depopulation, which they assumed (quite wrongly) to be menacing society as a result of increasing celibacy.[7]

[1] *Grandison*, II, 330.

[2] J. B. Botsford, *English Society in the Eighteenth Century* . . . (New York, 1924), p. 280.

[3] See Goldsmith, 'Essay on Female Warriors' (*Miscellaneous Works*, ed. Prior, New York, 1857, I, 254).

[4] Although see A. O. Aldridge, 'Polygamy in Early Fiction . . .', *PMLA*, LXV (1950), 464-472.

[5] See A. O. Aldridge, 'Polygamy and Deism', *JEGP*, XLVIII (1949), 343-360.

[6] See, for example, David Hume's essay 'Of Polygamy and Divorces'.

[7] See James Bonar, *Theories of Population from Raleigh to Arthur Young* (New York, 1931), p. 77.

Orthodox Christians and moralists, of course, attacked the proponents of polygamy vigorously. Richardson's friend, Dr. Patrick Delany, for example, wrote a treatise, *Reflections upon Polygamy*, whose somewhat hysterical tone suggests a deep alarm. He feared that although 'Polygamy is indeed at present abolished . . . how long it may continue so, under the present increase of infidelity and licentiousness, is not easy to pronounce'.[1] His book, which Richardson printed in 1737, probably supplied the material for the discussion of polygamy in the second part of *Pamela*, where Mr. B. appropriately makes use of the arguments of the licentious Deists, although his bride eventually makes him renounce 'that foolish topic'.[2] Lovelace, however, continues in Mr. B.'s evil ways and proposes an ingenious and characteristic variant—an Act of Parliament for annual marriages: such a practice, he argues, would stop polygamy being 'panted after'; it would end the prevalence of 'the spleen or vapours'; and it would ensure that there would no longer remain a single '*old maid* in Great Britain and all its territories'.[3]

There is, then, a considerable variety of evidence to support the view that the transition to an individualist social and economic order brought with it a crisis in marriage which bore particularly hard upon the feminine part of the population. Their future depended much more completely than before on their being able to marry and on the kind of marriage they made, while at the same time it was more and more difficult for them to find a husband.

The acuteness of this problem surely goes far to explain the enormous contemporary success of *Pamela*. Servant girls, as we have seen, constituted a fairly important part of the reading public, and they found it particularly difficult to marry: no wonder, then, that Lady Mary Wortley Montagu thought that Pamela's matrimonial triumph had made her 'the joy of the chambermaids of all nations'.[4] More generally, it is likely that Richardson's heroine symbolised the aspirations of all the women in the reading public who were subject to the difficulties recounted above. Not only so. Somewhat similar difficulties have since become standard in modern society as a result of the combined effects of economic individualism and the conjugal family; and this would seem to explain why the great majority

[1] 2nd ed., 1739, p. viii.   [2] Everyman Edition, II, 296-339.
[3] *Clarissa*, III, 180-184.   [4] *Letters and Works*, II, 200.

of novels written since *Pamela* have continued its basic pattern, and concentrated their main interest upon a courtship leading to marriage.

Pamela, it is true, departs from the usual pattern in one important respect: even if we exclude Richardson's ill-advised continuation, the narrative does not end with the marriage, but continues for some two hundred pages while every detail of the marriage ceremony and the resulting new conjugal pattern is worked out according to Richardson's exemplary specifications. This particular emphasis is odd to us, and suggests a lack of formal proportion in the novel. Actually, it is probably a good pointer to Richardson's real intentions: in 1740 the middle-class concept of marriage was not yet completely established, and Richardson must have felt that his aim of producing a new model of conduct for the relations between men and women involved paying attention to many matters which we take for granted but on which there was not yet complete public agreement when he wrote.

One historical parallel to Richardson's earnest redefinition of marriage is to be found in the sphere of law. In 1753 the Marriage Bill, which laid the legal basis of modern practice, and which, in the words of a Victorian historian, did much to improve 'the conjugal relations of the people of England, high and low',[1] was introduced by Hardwick, the Lord Chancellor. Its main purpose was to end the confusion about what constituted a legal marriage, and to effect this it laid down in unequivocal terms that a valid marriage, except under certain specified and very exceptional circumstances, could only be performed by a minister of the Church of England in the parish church after public reading of banns on three consecutive Sundays, and with an official licence.[2]

This practice was already common; but, as the law had stood, marriages of mutual consent by word of mouth were also legal; and—more important—so were secret marriages performed by an ordained minister. This had led to many clandestine marriages, especially those performed by disreputable clergymen within the liberties of the Fleet Prison, and to other abuses, such

[1] Charles Knight, *Popular History of England* (London, 1856–1862), VI, 194.
[2] See Philip C. Yorke, *Life and Correspondence of Philip Yorke, Earl of Hardwick* (Chicago, 1913), II, 58 ff., 72 ff., 134 ff., 418 ff., 469 ff.

as the false marriage ceremonies which are often portrayed in Restoration comedy, and which reappear in Mr. B.'s efforts to delude Pamela with a mock marriage.[1]

The Marriage Bill aroused very strong Tory opposition, on the grounds that the civil authority had no competence in the matter, and that since the clergy were now officiating merely as agents of the state, the Whigs were subverting the orthodox sacramental view of marriage.[2] In fact, although such was certainly no important part of the intention of the bill, which was really a compromise between the needs of the law and common religious practice, the measure did assist the displacement of Filmer's traditional and religious attitude towards the family: for it incorporated the essential feature of Locke's view of the family by making marriage a civil contract between individuals —a view, incidentally, which Locke shared with the Puritans,[3] whose eighteenth-century successors, the Dissenters, supported the bill even though it meant they had to be married in Anglican churches.[4]

At the time there was considerable criticism of the elaborateness and the publicity that was now attached to the marriage ceremony. This was the view of Goldsmith,[5] for example, and of Shebbeare in his novel, *The Marriage Act* (1754), which must surely be the first work of fiction arising out of a piece of legislation; while Horace Walpole complained that 'every Strephon and Chloe . . . would have as many impediments and formalities to undergo as a Treaty of Peace'.[6]

Essentially, however, the act was, in the words of Richardson's friend Sir Thomas Robinson, what 'every good man ha[d] long wished for'.[7] It expressed in legal terms the air of pondered contractual protocol which Richardson had already given marriage in *Pamela*, whose heroine insists on a public ceremony.[8] *Sir*

---

[1] See Alan D. McKillop, 'The Mock-Marriage Device in *Pamela*', *PQ*, XXVI (1947), 285-288.
[2] See M. M. Merrick, *Marriage a Divine Institution*, 1754, and references given in notes 57, 60, 62.
[3] Chilton Latham Powell, *English Domestic Relations, 1487–1653* (New York, 1917), pp. 44-51.
[4] See Cobbett, *Parliamentary History* (London, 1803), XV, 24-31.
[5] *Citizen of the World*, Letters 72, 114.
[6] *Letters*, ed. Toynbee, III, 160 (May 24, 1753).
[7] From a letter to Hardwick, June 6, 1753 (B.M. Add. MSS. 35592, ff. 65-66). For Robinson's relations with Richardson, see Austin Dobson, *Samuel Richardson* (London, 1902), p. 170. [8] Everyman Edition, I, 253.

Charles Grandison appeared in the same year as the Marriage Bill was eventually passed into law; and its hero intrepidly supports the view that 'chamber-marriages' are neither 'decent' nor 'godly' by proclaiming that he would take 'glory in receiving' his wife's hand 'before ten thousand witnesses',[1] and he does in fact face a somewhat smaller congregation at his church wedding. Indeed Richardson's insistence in his novels on a properly ceremonial attitude to marriage was such that Lady Mary Wortley Montagu ironically suggested that their author must be 'some parish curate, whose chief profit depends on weddings and christenings'.[2]

IV

Pamela's success, it has been suggested, was largely due to its appeal to the interests of women readers: and before proceeding any further it is perhaps necessary to consider briefly the grounds for believing, not only that women constituted a sufficiently large proportion of the novel reading public to make this success possible, but also that Richardson himself was in a position to express their distinctive literary interests.

We have already seen that many women, especially those in the middle ranks of life who lived in towns, had much more leisure than previously, and that they used a good deal of it in literary and other cultural pursuits. This is reflected in the increasing tendency of booksellers and writers to address special appeals to the feminine audience. John Dunton founded the first periodical avowedly addressed to women, the *Ladies' Mercury*, in 1693: and there were many other similar efforts, such as *The Female Tatler* in 1709 and Eliza Haywood's *Female Spectator* in 1744. Addison, too, had set himself out to please the ladies, and Steele had compiled *The Ladies' Library* in 1714, to give them something more edifying than the frivolous material to which they were so often alleged to restrict themselves.

That most women read only romances and novels, as was endlessly asserted, is not likely. Many were certainly devoted to religious literature. But, at least as far as secular reading is concerned, it is likely that their lower educational standards made classical and learned literature out of the question for the great majority, and that they therefore tended to devote much of

[1] VI, 307-308, 354-365.   [2] *Letters and Works*, II, 289.

their leisure to whatever lighter reading was available. The fact that 'the novel-reading girl' became an established comic type early in the century,[1] with Biddy Tipkins in Steele's *The Tender Husband* (1705), certainly suggests that fiction was the main reading of younger girls; but it is more likely that she was an extreme case, and that most women read both fiction and more serious matter. This mixture of tastes is suggested at one social level by Shamela's library which included various religious works such as *The Whole Duty of Man*, as well as scabrous novels like *Venus in the Cloister; or the Nun in Her Smock*.[2] At a higher social level we have the representative feminine types Matilda and Flavia in William Law's *A Serious Call to a Devout and Holy Life* (1729), whose shelves are well stocked both with piety and wit; and many of the women in Richardson's own circle combined these tastes. It is very likely, therefore, that one of the reasons for the success of *Pamela* was the way that it enabled readers to enjoy the attractions both of fiction and of devotional literature at the same time and in the same work.

It would be very difficult to determine whether Richardson had any conscious intention of appealing to these two elements in feminine literary taste. His correspondence about his own writings certainly shows a great and indeed almost obsessive interest in the public's reaction to them; and one of his replies to Cheyne's objection to the 'fondling and gallantry' in *Pamela* seems to cover the present point at issue: 'if I were to be too spiritual, I doubt I should catch none but the grandmothers; for the granddaughters would put my Girl indeed in better company, such as that of the graver writers, and there they would leave her'.[3] On the other hand, there is no need to assume that the profound interest in women's problems which Richardson manifests in his novels is an attempt to please feminine taste, for everything we know about his own personality and way of life shows that he shared these tastes to a very remarkable degree. .

He was always happiest in feminine society, believing, as he once confided to Miss Highmore after the tedium of three meetings with his friend 'the good Dr. Heberden', that 'there is nothing either improving or delightful out of the company of intelligent women'.[4] He was very proud both of the fact that

---

[1] See Reynolds, *Learned Lady*, pp. 400-419.   [2] Letter 12.
[3] *Cit.* McKillop, *Richardson*, p. 62.   [4] *Ibid.* p. 189.

'the tendency' of his works 'was to exalt the sex', and of the abundant homage with which he had been repaid; 'no man', he wrote, 'has been so honoured by the fine spirits of the sex as I have been'.[1] Indeed, there is much in his letters to suggest that he had a deep personal identification with the opposite sex which went far beyond social preference or cultural rapport. Such, certainly, is the implication of the fact that he was afraid of mice, or at least confessed to the future Mrs. Chapone, that he had 'ever had a kind of natural aversion to that species of animal'.[2]

One reflection of Richardson's closeness to the feminine point of view is to be found in the wealth of minutely described domestic detail in *Pamela*. Many contemporary readers apparently objected to the 'heap of trivial circumstances' in the novel; a gentleman in a coffee-house ironically 'wondered the Author had not told us the exact number of pins *Pamela* had about her when she set out for Lincolnshire, and how many rows of those pins she bought for a penny';[3] while Fielding parodied Richardson's explicitness about the least detail in matters of dress by making Shamela pack 'one Clog and almost another' when she leaves Squire Booby.[4] But if the men mocked, there can be little doubt that many feminine readers enjoyed these details for their own sake; Madame Du Deffand, for example, particularly praised 'tous les détails domestiques'[5] and preferred Richardson's novels to the French romances on their account.

The taste for domestic detail on the part of Richardson's feminine audience probably made an appreciable contribution to the narrative's air of everyday reality; romance-heroines, for instance, had made journeys often enough, but none before Pamela's had been so real as to confront them with the varied perplexities of assembling a suitable travelling wardrobe. In another respect, however, Richardson's closeness to the feminine point of view involved him in a very significant departure from the ordinary course of human life. Pamela's marriage to one so much above her economically and socially is an unprecedented victory for her sex; and although Mr. B. accepts his fate with a good grace the outcome cannot be regarded as bringing him equally great satisfaction; the direction of the plot, in fact, out-

[1] *Correspondence*, IV, 233; V, 265.
[2] *Cit.* C. L. Thomson, *Samuel Richardson* (London, 1900), p. 93.
[3] *Cit.* McKillop, *Richardson*, p. 67.
[4] Letter 12.   [5] *Cit.* McKillop, p. 277.

rageously flatters the imagination of the readers of one sex and severely disciplines that of the other.

Here, too, *Pamela* initiated a fairly constant feature in the tradition of the novel. The marriage of the protagonists usually leads to a rise in the social and economic status of the bride, not the bridegroom. Hypergamy, though not a convention of modern society, is a fairly constant convention of the novel; and its ultimate cause is surely the preponderance of women in the novel-reading public, a preponderance which this crucial detail of its matrimonial mystique directly reflects.

V

Richardson's *Pamela*, then, made a particular appeal to the feminine part of his audience; and we can now return to our main theme, and see how their marriage problems were such as to provide rich literary resources. We have already seen that numerous forces in the social history of Richardson's time were tending to heighten interest in Pamela's struggle to secure a mate: these forces were also closely related to very significant changes in the accepted attitude towards the moral and psychological roles of the sexes, changes which provide the fundamental basis for Richardson's presentation of his heroine's character and mode of action. It is because of these changes that in *Pamela* the courtship, if that is not too risible a euphemism for Mr. B.'s tactics, involves a struggle, not only between two individuals, but between two opposed conceptions of sex and marriage held by two different social classes, and between two conceptions of the masculine and feminine roles which make their interplay in courtship even more complex and problematic than it had previously been.

To determine what exactly these conceptions were is not easy. It is one of the general difficulties in applying social history to the interpretation of literature that, uncertain as our knowledge of any particular social change may be, our knowledge of its subjective aspects, the way it affected the thoughts and feelings of the individuals concerned, is even more insecure and hypothetical. Yet the problem cannot altogether be avoided; however important the external facts about the complexities of the social situation of women may have been, they presented themselves to Richardson in the form of the largely unconscious presuppositions of the people around him; and it was presumably these social and psychological orientations which dictated the way that his readers understood the thoughts and actions of the characters in *Pamela*. It is necessary, therefore, to attempt to discover what were the dominant considerations which formed the attitudes towards sex and marriage which are portrayed there.

One of these attitudes we have already noted—the tremendous fascination of marriage and every detail connected with it for the heroine; but this emphasis is complemented by another—an equally striking horror of any sexual advance or reference until the conjugal knot is tied. Both these tendencies are typical of Puritanism.

The assimilation of the values of romantic love to marriage, it was argued above, occurred particularly early in England, and was closely connected with the Puritan movement. Not, of course, that Puritanism approved of romantic love, but that its individualist and anti-ecclesiastical type of religion caused it to attribute supreme spiritual importance to the relation of man and wife, as is suggested by the title of Defoe's *Religious Courtship: Being Historical Discourses on the Necessity of Marrying Religious Husbands and Wives Only* (1722). This emphasis on the need for spiritual harmony between man and wife was often transferred to the intrinsic qualities of the relationship itself: the Hallers have described how Milton, for example, proceeded from 'magnifying the religious significance of marriage' to magnifying 'the emotional, romantic, and idealistic aspects of the marriage relation'.[1]

The two attitudes, of course, may well be combined; and it must be added that—whether they are combined or held separately—they are in no sense exclusively Puritan, and are found among many other Protestant sects. The idealisation of marriage is, however, distinctively Protestant, since in Roman Catholicism the highest religious values are connected with celibacy; and given the characteristic strength of Puritanism in applying its theory to every detail of social organisation and individual psychology, it is likely that it was the strongest single force in developing the new emphasis on the spiritual values of the marriage relationship, an emphasis which may be regarded

[1] William and Malleville Haller, 'The Puritan Art of Love', *HLQ*, V (1942), 265.

as the modern counterpart of the originally religious basis of courtly love.

Puritanism was certainly particularly vigorous in enforcing the complementary attitude—the sinfulness of all sexual activities outside marriage. Wherever it achieved political power, in Geneva, in Scotland, in New England, in England during the Commonwealth period, it made rigorous inquiry into the sexual behaviour of individuals, arraigned offenders, forced them to confess their sins publicly, and punished them severely. The climax of this movement is probably the Act passed in England in 1650 which made adultery punishable by death.[1]

In this, as in many other matters, Puritanism was merely placing a particularly heavy emphasis on ideas which are not themselves peculiar to it, and which reach back to the Pauline and Augustinian elements in the Christian tradition. Man's physical nature and its desires were viewed as radically evil, the *damnosa hereditas* of the Fall: consequently virtue itself tended to become a matter of suppressing the natural instincts. This—in Puritanism as in St. Paul—was at first regarded merely as a negative step: to overcome the flesh might give the law of the spirit a better chance to operate. Later, however, as secularisation increased, there arose a widespread tendency to ethical rigorism for its own sake, a tendency which is Puritan only in the sense that Victorian morality was Puritan: resistance to the desires of the body became the major aim of secular morality; and chastity, instead of being only one virtue among many, tended to become the supreme one, and applied to men as well as to women.

It is interesting to notice that this particular ethical tendency is peculiarly suited to an individualist society. Aristotle's ethics are largely social; potential moral eminence varies according to the individual's capacity for outstanding qualities of citizenship. Such a code, however, accords ill with a civilisation whose members are primarily oriented towards achieving their own individual purposes in the economic, social and religious spheres; and it is particularly unsuitable for the feminine sex, who had little more opportunity in eighteenth-century England than in fourth-century Athens to realise the virtues of the

---

[1] G. May, *The Social Control of Sex Expression* (London, 1930), p. 152. See also L. L. Schücking, *Die Familie im Puritanismus* (Leipzig and Berlin, 1929), pp. 39-44, 137-153.

citizen, the warrior or the philosopher. On the other hand, what are often called the Puritan virtues, with their emphasis on sexual continence, are wholly suited to an individualist social order, and offer women as large possibilities of achievement as men.

It is, at all events, very evident that the eighteenth century witnessed a tremendous narrowing of the ethical scale, a redefinition of virtue in primarily sexual terms. Dr. Johnson, for example, held that 'man's chief merit consisted in resisting the impulses of nature';[1] and these impulses, significantly, were increasingly identified with 'the passion of love'.[2] Such, certainly, was Richardson's view. Sir Charles Grandison's mentor, Dr. Bartlett, 'said that the life of a good man was a continual warfare with his passions',[3] and Richardson's novels suggest that these passions are very largely sexual ones. The same tendency can be seen at work on the ethical vocabulary itself: words such as virtue, propriety, decency, modesty, delicacy, purity, came to have the almost exclusively sexual connotation which they have since very largely retained.

One aspect of this moral transformation which is particularly important for *Pamela* is the eighteenth-century attack on the double standard. Many women writers protested against the injustice it did their sex: Mrs. Manley, for example, attacked it in *The New Atalantis* (1709);[4] and in 1748 another erring matron, Laetitia Pilkington, asked, 'Is it not monstrous that our seducers should be our accusers?'[5] Most of the masculine reformers of the age also campaigned against the still fashionable assumption that sexual purity was not so important for men as for women. In 1713 the *Guardian* 'ventured to recommend to its readers Chastity as the noblest male virtue';[6] and in the mid-century Richardson, to the incredulous laughter of Colly Cibber, and the even more scandalous consternation of some of the ladies, made the principle quite explicit by insisting that his ideal man, Sir Charles Grandison, was a virgin until marriage.[7]

---

[1] 'Recollections' of Miss Reynolds, *Johnsonian Miscellanies*, ed. Hill, II, 285.
[2] See, for example, Mrs. Manley, *Power of Love* . . ., 1720, p. 353; Anon, *Reasons against Coition*, 1732, p. 7; Ned Ward, *The London Spy* (1698–1709; London, 1927 ed.), p. 92.
[3] III, 251.　　　　　　　　　　　　　　　[4] II, 190–191.
[5] *Memoirs* (1748; London, 1928 ed.), p. 103.　　[6] No. 45.
[7] See the anonymous pamphlet, possibly by Francis Plumer, *A Candid Examination of the History of Sir Charles Grandison*, 1754, p. 48.

In the matter of the double standard, as in many other aspects of the eighteenth-century concern with the reform of sexual morality, there were marked differences of attitude between classes, and it was, of course, the middle class which displayed the greatest zeal.

For many reasons. In the history of mankind strictness in sexual relations tends to coincide with the increasing importance of private property—the bride must be chaste so that her husband can be sure that it is his son who will inherit. This consideration must have been particularly important to those whose values were primarily those of trade and commerce; and its effect was reinforced by at least two other features of middle-class life. There is, first of all, the opposition between economic and sexual goals which was well explained by William Law when he remarked of his typical man of business, Negotius: 'If you ask me what it is that has secured Negotius from all scandalous vices, it is the same thing that has kept him from all strictness of devotion, it is his great business'.[1] Secondly, the merchant or tradesman is likely to feel resentment and mistrust against those whose way of life is not mainly directed towards economic ends, and who therefore have both the leisure and the leisure attributes which enable them to pursue the wives and daughters of the citizenry successfully, as the gallants of the court and the polite end of the town so notoriously did.

For these and many other reasons,' which must certainly include a long history of political and religious conflict, sexual prowess and sexual licence both tended to be linked with the aristocracy and the gentry in middle-class belief. Defoe, for example, placed the responsibility for the immorality of the times squarely on the upper classes: ''Twas the Kings and the Gentry which first . . . degenerated from that strict observation of moral virtues, and from thence carried vice on to that degree it now appears in. . . . We the poor Commons . . . have really been debauched into vice by their examples.'[2]

The quotation is from *The Poor Man's Plea* (1698), one of Defoe's main contributions to the various moral crusades begun in the reign of William and Mary by the new Societies for the Reformation of Manners. The most significant literary aspect of the work of these societies was that whose most notable expression is Jeremy Collier's *Short View of the Profaneness and Immorality*

[1] *Serious Call, Works* (Brockenhurst, 1892–1893), IV, 121-122.   [2] P. 6.

of the English Stage, also published in 1698.[1] It was natural that dislike of upper-class licence should extend to the literature which expressed it, and one result of this attitude was of particular importance to the development of the middle-class sexual code. Many writers felt that the public should be warned not only against the flagrant immorality of the kind that Collier attacked, but against the equally dangerous romantic concepts that underlay the sentiments of Restoration drama in general, and that were used with sophisticated duplicity by the courtly enemies of feminine virtue. Steele, for instance, pointed out that 'Notions of Gallantry' had latterly been 'turned topsie-turvey, and the knight errantry of this profligate age is destroying as many women as they can',[2] while in his *Critical Essay Concerning Marriage* (1724) Thomas Salmon emphasised the dangers occasioned by the ambiguities in the use of such words as 'honour and gallantry' in common speech.[3] Defoe, of course, persistently puts before us the realities of sexual intrigue, stripped of their conventional verbal decorations, and he mocks romantic professions of love wherever they occur. This trend was continued by Richardson, who included in his *Familiar Letters on Important Occasions* letters 'ridiculing a romantic Rhapsody in Courtship',[4] and who warned in *Pamela* that 'Platonic Love is Platonic Nonsense'.[5]

If virtuous daughters were to be forced to see the sordid aims that were concealed behind what Eliza Haywood's Alderman Saving called 'the romantic idle notions of the other end of the town',[6] even the word 'love' was dangerous and its meaning had to be clarified. Here Richardson made a characteristic contribution, in the Postscript to *Clarissa*: 'What is too generally called *love* ought (perhaps as generally) to be called by another name', he wrote, and bitingly suggested as substitute '*Cupidity* or a *Paphian stimulus* . . . however grating they may be to delicate ears'.

The need to outlaw the 'Paphian stimulus' involved a redefinition of the relations between men and women which excluded the sexual passion, and which stressed making a sensible marriage choice with rational friendship as its eventual

[1] See J. W. Krutch, *Comedy and Conscience after the Restoration* (New York, 1924), p. 169.
[2] *The Lover*, No. 2 (1714).
[3] *Critical Essay Concerning Marriage*, p. 40.
[4] Letters 89, 96, 97, 98.
[5] II, 338.
[6] *Betsy Thoughtless*, 1751, I, 50.

aim. Swift, for example, in his *Letter to a Very Young Lady on Her Marriage* (1727) warned against expecting 'any mixture of that ridiculous passion which has no being but in playbooks and romances', and instead advocated a 'match of prudence and common good liking'.[1] This view was widely held in Richardson's circle. His friend Dr. Delany, for example, wrote to his future wife in 1743 that 'perfect friendship is nowhere to be found but in marriage',[2] while Richardson himself, believing that 'friendship . . . is the perfection of love',[3] defined marriage as 'the highest state of friendship that mortals can know'. The climax of this trend must surely be the scene in *Sir Charles Grandison* where Richardson celebrates the triumph of spiritual ties over those of the flesh, and even of marriage, by making Sir Charles and the two rivals for his affections swear allegiance to a triangle of eternal friendship, and solemnly dedicate a temple in honour of their compact.[4]

Sir Charles, unfortunately, was something of an exception as far as the male sex was concerned, and as a result the campaign against sexuality was forced to a peculiar compromise. As far as Mr. B. and his like were concerned, the best that could be hoped for was a social disciplining of the unregenerate Adam within by making marriage the only permitted means of sexual expression: Pamela and her sex, however, with the exception of a few wholly abandoned females, were reserved for higher things; the new ideology granted them a total immunity from sexual feelings, and if they married it was not because they had any need of *medicina libidinis*, but because the pieties of marriage and the family were safe only in their hands.

This particular biological discrimination is really something of a historical novelty. It is, for example, in complete contradiction both to the patriarchal outlook and to the classic tradition of the portrayal of love in our literature, from Chaucer's *Troilus and Criseyde* to Shakespeare's *Romeo and Juliet*. Even more striking, it is directly opposed to the earlier attitudes of Puritanism itself, where such figures as Calvin, John Knox and Milton were notoriously prone to lay more emphasis on the concupiscence of women than of men.

A different point of view, however, was already widely

[1] *Prose Works* (London, 1907), XI, 119.
[2] Mrs. Delany, *Autobiography and Correspondence*, ed. Woolsey (Boston, 1879), I, 246.
[3] *Correspondence*, III, 188.   [4] *Grandison*, I, 283; VII, 315.

established in the early eighteenth century. Defoe's novels, for example, tend to support his stated view in *The Review* (1706) that 'in our general Pursuit of the Sex, the Devil generally acts the Man, not the Woman'.[1] Exactly why the serpent's invidious connection with Eve should have been forgotten is not clear; one can only surmise that, by a devious process not unknown to the psychologist, the very difficulties in the situation of women at this time brought about a new concept of the feminine rol꞉ which masked their actual dependence on sexual attractivenɛ s to the male much more completely than before, and streng h-ened their tactical position in courtship by making their acc .pt-ance of a suitor a matter, not of joint personal satisfaction, but of *noblesse oblige*.

The question of the origins of this new sexual ideology is obviously very problematic: but there is at least very little doubt that the appearance of *Pamela* marks a very notable epiphany in the history of our culture: the emergence of a new, fully developed and immensely influential stereotype of the feminine role. The nature and later sway of this ideal of womanhood is the subject of an excellent study, *Pamela's Daughters* (1937), by R. P. Utter and G. B. Needham. Briefly, they show how the model heroine must be very young, very inexperienced, and so delicate in physical and mental constitution that she faints at any sexual advance; essentially passive, she is devoid of any feelings towards her admirer until the marriage knot is tied—such is Pamela and such are most of the heroines of fiction until the end of the Victorian period.

The nature of this new stereotype, incidentally, reflects many of the social and economic trends described earlier. Even Pamela's tendency to faint, for example, may be regarded as an expression of the changing economic basis of marriage: for, since middle-class wives tended to be increasingly regarded as leisure exhibits engaging in no heavier economic tasks than the more delicate and supervisory operations of housewifery, a conspicuously weak constitution was both an assertion of a delicately nurtured past and a presumptive claim to a similar future. It is true that Pamela's humble birth hardly entitles her to this trait; but in fact her full possession of it only shows that her total being has been so deeply shaped by ideas above her station that even her body exhibits—to invoke the assistance of

[1] *Review*, III (1706), No. 132.

a neologism for which there is in any case a regrettable need—a not uncommon form of what can only be called sociosomatic snobbery.

The conception of the feminine role represented in *Pamela* is an essential feature of our civilisation over the past two hundred years. Margaret Mead writes in *Sex and Temperament* that this civilisation has largely 'relied for the creation of rich and contrasted values upon many artificial distinctions, the most striking of which is sex'.[1] I have no wish to suggest that this particular distinction had previously escaped notice, nor even that it is wholly artificial; but it is surely true that the conception of sex we find in Richardson embodies a more complete and comprehensive separation between the male and female roles than had previously existed.

The difference between the two roles is emphasised in almost every aspect of speech and manners. Richardson's friend, Dr. Johnson, was of 'opinion that the delicacy of the sex shou'd always be inviolably preserved, in eating, in exercise, in dress, in everything';[2] while Richardson himself—who in *Pamela* was responsible for the first use of the word 'indelicacy'[3]—was an avowed reformer in this sphere: 'I would fain reduce delicacy to a standard', he wrote to Miss Highmore, but quickly corrected himself: 'Reduce did I say? Should not *exalt* be the word?'[4] Some further indication of his attitude is provided early in *Pamela* when Mr. B. gives the heroine some of her dead mistress's clothes: she is acutely embarrassed, and when he says, 'Don't blush, Pamela, dost think I don't know pretty maids should wear shoes and stockings', she reports that 'I was so confounded at these words, you might have beat me down with a feather'. Later, when her parents hear of Mr. B.'s 'free expressions about the stockings' they at once fear the worst.[5]

This linguistic sensitivity seems to be a rather new phenomenon. To some extent, no doubt, the language of women and of mixed company has always tended to be somewhat different from that of men, but these differences had not been so obvious before. In the late seventeenth century, however, Jeremy Collier had made much of the fact that 'the Poets make *women*

---

[1] London, 1935, p. 322.   [2] *Thraliana*, I, 172.
[3] *Pamela's Daughters*, p. 44.   [4] *Cit.* McKillop, p. 197.   [5] I, 8-9.

speak smuttily',[1] and in his *The She-Gallants* (1695) George Granville had even ironically indicated that a movement to reform this verbal indecency was afoot: he spoke of 'a dictionary that's preparing . . . to suit our language to the fair sex, and to castrate the immodest syllables in such words as begin and end obscenely'.[2]

Only a generation later the taboo on biological references seems to have been fully established: Mandeville noted that 'among well-bred people it is counted highly criminal to mention before company anything in plain words that is relating to this Mystery of Succession';[3] while among the shocking attributes that Edward Young had bestowed upon the unfeminine Thalestris in his satire 'On Women' (1728) was that 'What nature dares to *give* she dares to *name*'.[4] The movement proceeded apace, until by the end of the century even the *Tatler* and *Spectator* were found unsuited to women readers: Coleridge, at least, thought that they contained words 'which might, in our day, offend the delicacy of female ears and shock feminine susceptibility',[5] and his distress was echoed by Jane Austen in *Northanger Abbey*.[6]

Richardson played an important part in the adjustment of language to the new feminine code. His rewriting of L'Estrange's version of Aesop reveals him as one of our earliest bowdlerisers,[7] and his novels show a considerable concern for the proprieties of the feminine linguistic code. When Pamela becomes pregnant, for instance, she is shocked to find that Lady Davers 'in her quality way'[8] takes public note of the fact: but then Lady Davers, of course, is one of those 'termagant, hermaphrodite minds' attacked in the 'Introduction to the Second Edition';[9] and she is also a symbol of the notorious impurity of 'the quality'.

What may be called the decarnalisation of the public feminine role provides a further explanation of the fact that in *Pamela* as in most novels the courtship leads to a rise in the social status

---

[1] *Short View*, 3rd ed., 1698, p. 8.

[2] *Cit.* John Harrington Smith, *The Gay Couple in Restoration Comedy* (Cambridge, Mass., 1948), p. 165, n.15.

[3] *Fable of the Bees*, ed. Kaye, I, 143.   [4] *Love of Fame*, V, l. 424.

[5] *Lectures and Notes on Shakespeare* (London, 1885), p. 37.

[6] Oxford, 1948, p. 35.

[7] See Katherine Hornbeak, 'Richardson's Aesop', *Smith College Studies in Modern Languages*, XIX (1938), 38.

[8] As is pointed out in *Pamela's Daughters*, p. 15.   [9] 1741, I, XXIV.

not of the hero but of the heroine. Male readers would presumably prefer to see the hero win the hand of some noble lady; but a moment's reflection shows that such a gratification could not be afforded without forcing upon the heroine a grave breach of feminine decorum.

This point is raised in a discussion between Lady Davers and Mr. B. He argues that his mesalliance is in no sense as shocking as it would be if the roles were reversed, since 'a woman, tho' ever so nobly born, debases herself by a mean marriage'.[1] This was the accepted view; so humane a man as Dr. Johnson, for instance, regarded it as a 'perversion' for a woman to marry beneath her.[2] The reason for this is clear. Mr. B. can properly follow his fancy and marry beneath his station because it is undeniable and irremediable fact that men are subject to the sexual passion; but for a woman to do so would amount to an admission that she had lost her immunity from sexual feeling, an immunity which is one of the peculiar constants in the heroines of English fiction from *Pamela* until recently, and whose sudden collapse was such a startling feature of the twentieth-century novel.

VI

During Richardson's lifetime, then, many important and complex changes in the ways that the sexes oriented themselves to their roles were already far advanced. These changes are of considerable intrinsic interest, since they herald the establishment of what is substantially the concept of courtship, marriage and the feminine role that has obtained most widely in the last two centuries. The reason for our interest in them here, however, is of a more directly literary nature: it derives from the fact that these social and psychological changes go far to explain two of the major qualities posed by *Pamela*: its formal unity, and its peculiar combination of moral purity and impurity.

Dr. Johnson, with the *novella* in mind, defined a 'novel' as a 'small tale, generally of love'. When *Pamela* appeared it was called a 'dilated novel',[3] because its subject was essentially the single amorous episode which previous short novels had usually

[1] I, 389.   [2] Boswell, *Life*, ed. Hill-Powell, II, 328-329.
[3] *Cit.* George Sherburn, 'The Restoration and Eighteenth Century', *A Literary History of England*, ed. Baugh (New York, 1948), p. 803.

been concerned with, but its treatment was on a scale much closer to that of a romance.

The direct connection between this change of scale and the tremendous importance which Richardson allotted to sexual morality is made clear by the contrast with Defoe. In Defoe's novels sexual encounters, marital or otherwise, are treated as minor episodes within the larger context of the pursuit of economic security. Moll Flanders is 'tricked once by that cheat called love',[1] but it is a beginning, not an end; while Colonel Jacque comments on his faithful wife Moggy's 'slip in her younger days' that 'it was of small consequence to me one way or another'.[2]

In the world of *Pamela* such off-handedness is inconceivable, for there, in the words of Henry Brooke,

> The woman no redemption knows
> The wounds of honour never close.[3]

Mr. B., of course, regards Pamela's acceptance of such a view as evidence that her 'head is turned by romances and such idle stuff', but he is wrong. The ideal chastity of the romance heroines had been very completely incorporated into the general moral outlook; it was in much more humdrum literary sources that Pamela had 'read that many a man has been ashamed of his wicked attempts, when he has been repulsed', and chanced 'a night or two before' upon the crucial slogan which she announces in appropriate circumstances—'May I never survive, one moment, that fatal one in which I shall forfeit my innocence!' It was also, presumably, from some conduct book, although this time no literary indebtedness is acknowledged, that Pamela learned that 'Millions of gold will not purchase one happy moment of reflection on a past mis-spent life'.[4]

Defoe's heroines, of course, would not have thought twice, even for rewards much less than Mr. B.'s five hundred guineas: the novel is born because Pamela makes her epic resistance to a 'fate worse than death', that significantly euphemistic hyperbole which loomed so large in the later history of fiction.

There is, of course, nothing inherently new in making a fictional heroine regard her chastity as a supreme value; what

[1] I, 57. [2] Ed. Aitken (London, 1902), II, 90.
[3] *Collection of Pieces*, 1778, II, 45. [4] I, 78, 31, 20, 169.

was new was that Richardson attributed such motives to a servant-girl: for whereas romance had usually exalted feminine
chastity, the other forms of fiction which dealt with characters
of humbler social origins had tended to take an opposite view
of feminine psychology. It is this historical and literary perspective which makes clear the importance of *Pamela*: Richardson's novel represents the first complete confluence of two previously opposed traditions in fiction; it combines 'high' and
'low' motives, and, even more important, it portrays the conflict between the two.

Richardson thus initiated the novel's radical departure from
the *Stiltrennung* in the crucial area of sexual relations. Not only
so: he also broke down the separation of 'high' and 'low' life'—
the class aspect of the *Stiltrennung*, and for the same reason. The
movement for moral reform, we have seen, tended to be mainly
supported by the middle class, who fortified their outlook as a
group with the assumption that their social superiors were their
moral inferiors. This, of course, is the situation in *Pamela*—the
rakish squire versus the humble but virtuous maid—and it
lends the story a much larger significance than the purely individual matters at issue between the protagonists.

This use of the conflict between social classes is typical of the
novel in general; its literary mode is radically particular, but it
achieves a universality of meaning by making its individual
actions and characters represent larger social issues. Defoe's
plots are not such as to allow the relationships between his
characters to go very far in developing this type of significance,
whereas the much greater simplicity of the action of *Pamela*
makes it far easier for the struggles of Pamela and Mr. B. to
mirror larger contemporary conflicts between two classes and
their way of life.

The enactment of the triumph of the middle-class code in
sexual ethics brings with it, not only Mr. B.'s offer of marriage,
but his complete re-education in the proper attitudes to sex and
marriage. These, of course, are mainly a matter of subjective
personal values, and their adjustment involves a progressive
revelation throughout the novel of the inner lives of the protagonists which continues until the hero's conversion is so complete that he becomes a 'Puritan'[1] as far as Lady Davers is
concerned.

[1] I, 391.

The relationship between Pamela and Mr. B. is therefore able to develop a much richer psychological and moral content than that between the traditional lovers in romance. The barriers between them that have to be broken down are not external and contrived but internal and real; and for this reason, combined with the fact that these barriers are based on the differences in their respective class outlooks, the dialogue between the lovers is not, as it is in romance, a conventional exercise in rhetoric, but an exploration of the forces that have made them what they are.

There is one final and very important contribution to the structure of *Pamela* which is directly related both to the middle-class Puritan sexual code, and to the major difference between that code and the tradition of courtly love.

Courtly love separated the sexual roles in a similar way—the carnal male adored the godlike purity of the female, and the contradiction between the two roles was absolute. In theory, at least; for if the lady yielded to her lover's suit it meant a total breakdown of the convention. Puritanism, however, by providing marriage with a large spiritual and social meaning, provided a possible bridge between the spirit and the flesh, between the convention and social reality. The bridge was not an easy one, because, as Richardson had explained in his popular contribution to the *Rambler* in 1751, the feminine role in courtship made it immoral as well as impolitic for a girl to allow herself to feel love for a suitor until he had actually asked for her hand in marriage.[1] The very difficulty, however, and the sudden reversal of the lady's attitude which was implied, supplied Richardson with a vital plot resource, since it made it possible for Richardson to withhold from us any idea of Pamela's real feelings towards Mr. B. until the crisis in the action.

When Pamela leaves him to return to her parents it appears certain that all is over between them; actually a counter-movement at once begins. On the one hand, she is surprised to discover 'something so strange . . . so *unexpected*' in her feelings that she is forced to wonder whether she is not in fact sorry to be leaving;[2] on the other hand, Mr. B.'s deepest feelings, as revealed in his parting letter, show that he is not merely the

[1] No. 97. It was the most popular of the *Ramblers*, according to Walter Graham (*English Literary Periodicals*, New York, 1930, p. 120).   [2] I, 222.

stereotype of the licentious squire but a man whose intentions may become honest, and who may quite possibly be a fit mate for Pamela. These sudden revelations of the disparity between the conventional and the actual attitudes of the lovers thus enabled Richardson to work out their relationship in a plot of the type which Aristotle considered to be the best, a complex action in which the peripety and the recognition coincide. The dramatic resolution of the plot of *Pamela*, in fact, was made possible by the actual moral and social attitudes of the time, which had produced an unprecedented disparity between the conventional roles of the sexes and the actual tenor of the oracles of the heart.

This conflict between public and private attitudes is one with which the novel in general has been much concerned, and which it is indeed peculiarly fitted to portray. There is, however, considerable doubt as to how far Richardson was aware of the duplicities involved in the feminine role, or as to how we should interpret the narrative which embodies them.

As is well known, *Pamela* has always been subject to very contradictory interpretations. Soon after its first publication one anonymous pamphleteer reported that there were, 'particularly among the ladies, two different parties, *Pamelists* and *Antipamelists*', who disagreed as to 'whether the young virgin was an example for ladies to follow . . . or . . . a hypocritical crafty girl . . . who understands the art of bringing a man to her lure'.[1] The most famous work in the controversy, of course, is *Shamela*, where, as his title implies, Fielding interpreted Richardson's heroine as a hypocrite whose masterly deployment of the resources of the feminine role enabled her to entrap a rich booby into marriage, although her purity did not in fact go beyond the conventional public pretence suggested by Mrs. Lucretia Jarvis when she speaks of the need to avoid 'what we women call rude, when done in the presence of others'.[2]

Fielding's pamphlet certainly draws attention to an important ambiguity in *Pamela*, but when later critics suggest that we must choose between Fielding's interpretation or Richardson's they are surely overlooking the possibility that the ambiguity need not spring from conscious duplicity on Pamela's part, since it is implicit in the feminine code by which she acts. It seems evident,

[1] *The Tablet, or Picture of Real Life*, 1762, p. 14.   [2] Letter VII.

for example, that the code's tremendous emphasis on the differentiation of the sexes in behaviour and dress is open to a very similar criticism to that which Fielding made of *Pamela*. 'Decency', as Bernard Shaw has reminded us, 'is indecency's conspiracy of silence', and the concern of the eighteenth-century moralists with feminine purity suggests imaginations only too ready to colour everything with impure sexual significances.

Sarah Fielding speaks in *Ophelia* (1760) of how Mrs. Darkins thought a 'girl ought not to set eyes on a baby that was not of the feminine gender';[1] the corrupt assumptions of this attitude are made clear when we remember that it is the lecherous Lady Wishfort in Congreve's *Way of the World* who prided herself on not allowing her infant daughter to play with little boys.[2] Similarly, we can interpret Addison's campaign against naked bosoms in the *Guardian*[3] by recalling that Tartuffe's unhealthy prurience is revealed by his throwing a handkerchief over Dorine's breasts,[4] and Bridget Allworthy's by her scandalised outcry against the revelatory Sunday finery of the farmers' daughters.[5] Richardson's own mind was certainly obsessed with sex in a similar way, as we can see in some of his own pronouncements on sexual modesty. In the *Familiar Letters*, for example, writing in the guise of an uncle, he chides his niece's 'manly air' in these terms: 'I have been particularly offended . . . at your *new riding-habit*; which is made so extravagantly in the mode, that one cannot easily distinguish your sex by it. For you look neither like a *modest girl* in it, nor an *agreeable boy*.'[6]

The ambivalent implications of a conspicuous concern for feminine modesty suggest themselves with equal force in the case of Richardson's heroine. It is certainly tempting to explain her continual concern with decency of dress, for example, by reference to the views of Dr. Gregory, an influential exponent of the new feminine code: in his *Father's Legacy to His Daughters* (1774) he concluded his warnings against 'denudation' with the Machiavellian parenthesis—'The finest bosom in nature is not so fine as what imagination forms'.[7] Be that as it may, there is at least no doubt that Mr. B. finds Pamela's virtuous

---

[1] II, 42. [2] Act V, sc. v. [3] No. 116 (1713).
[4] *Tartuffe*, Act III, sc. ii. [5] *Tom Jones*, Bk. I, ch. 8.
[6] Letter 90. [7] 1822 ed., p. 47.

resistance infinitely more provocative than any compliance could have been, and thus provides an involuntary tribute to the efficacy of the new feminine role in encompassing its ultimate aim.

That, however, does not justify us in assuming, as the Fielding interpretation suggests, that Pamela is only modest because she wants to entrap Mr. B. It is surely better to regard her as a real person whose actions are the result of the complexities of her situation and of the effects, both conscious and unconscious, of the feminine code. Steele pointed out that prude and coquette are alike in that they have 'the distinction of sex in all their thoughts, words and actions':[1] the code that commanded the allegiance of Pamela and her author is itself open to either interpretation. Similarly, although Pamela's acceptance of Mr. B. as a husband suggests that she regards his early advances as less heinous than she could publicly admit at the time, the inconsistency can be fully explained as the result of the falsity of the public code, rather than of her own character. Certainly if we condemn Pamela for such departures from absolute openness and sincerity in courtship, we must not forget how widely the charge could be brought against others in similar circumstances, both in her age and in ours.

Richardson's own attitude is difficult to determine. Like his heroine, he is alternately fascinated and repelled by Mr. B.'s licentious attempts, and his moral protestations are not wholly convincing. As an artist, however, Richardson seems to have been more aware of both points of view with respect to Pamela's sexual ethics than has been generally recognised, although he implicitly disavows the opposite position by making the odious Mrs. Jewkes its most vocal representative. When Pamela, for example, remarks that 'to rob a person of her virtue is worse than cutting her throat' she answers with an incomprehension which, though lamentable, is not without illustrious precedent: 'Why now, how strangely you talk! Are not the two sexes made for one another? Is it not natural for a gentleman to love a pretty woman? And suppose he can obtain his desires, is that so bad as cutting her throat?' The remark would not be out of place in *Shamela*; nor would Mrs. Jewkes's contemptuous retort when Pamela begs her not to let the master in lest she be undone—'Mighty piece of undone!'[2]

[1] *Cit. Pamela's Daughters*, p. 64.   [2] *Pamela*, I, 95-96, 174.

As a novelist, then, Richardson is capable of considerable objectivity; but it is clear that as a conscious moralist he is completely on the side of Pamela, and it is here that the most serious objections to his novel arise. His sub-title, 'Virtue Rewarded', draws attention to the immitigable vulgarity of the book's moral texture; it is surely evident that Pamela is in any case chaste only in a very technical sense which is of scant interest to the morally perceptive, and that Fielding hit upon the major moral defect of the story when he made Shamela remark: 'I thought once of making a little fortune by my person. I now intend to make a great one by my vartue.'[1] As to Mr. B.'s vaunted reformation it is difficult to see that it amounts to any more than a promise, in Mandeville's words, 'never to be a deer-stealer, upon condition that he shall have venison of his own'.[2]

Mandeville, of course, was the self-appointed *agent provocateur* of the bourgeois unconscious, determined to draw attention to all the perplexities in public morality which Addison and Richardson were determined to ignore; and his cynical analogy brings us back to the very considerable extent to which the problems raised by Richardson's treatment of marriage are typical of modern Western culture as a whole. If we continue our comparison of *Pamela* with Chaucer's *Troilus and Criseyde* or Shakespeare's *Romeo and Juliet* it is surely apparent that although Richardson is much purer in his language and his overt attitudes, his work nevertheless concentrates much more exclusively on the sexual relationship itself. This combination has had a very wide currency in fiction since then and has even spread to the cinema. In the Hollywood film, as in the type of popular fiction which Richardson initiated, we have an unprecedentedly drastic and detailed Puritan censorship in conjunction with a form of art which is historically unique in its concentration on arousing sexual interests: while in it marriage figures as the moral *deus ex machina* which, as James Fordyce said of marriage in comedy, 'is converted into a sponge, to wipe out in a single stroke the stain of guilt'.[3]

The cause of this duality—in Richardson's time as in ours—is presumably that the tabooed object is always an indication of the deepest interest of the society that forbids. All the forces that combined to intensify the prohibitions against sexual activity

[1] *Shamela*, Letter 10.   [2] *Fable of the Bees*, I, 161.
[3] *Sermons to Young Women*, 1766, I, 156.

outside marriage, tended in practice to increase the importance of sex in the total picture of human life. That they did so in Richardson was suggested by one of his contemporary critics, the anonymous 'Lover of Virtue' who produced some *Critical Remarks on Sir Charles Grandison, Clarissa and Pamela* (1754). He coupled the fact that 'Love, eternal Love, is the subject, the burthen of all your writings' with Richardson's tremendous accentuation of what he called the 'political chastity' about which 'you and your heroines make such a rout and a pother', a chastity which in his opinion compared very unfavourably with that of the women of ancient Greece. Even so, the writer was at a loss to understand why so many 'public-spirited pen-men' thought it necessary to employ 'all their art and eloquence to keep people in remembrance, that they were composed of different sexes' when 'provident nature' unassisted could be trusted to 'prevent the world from coming to an end'.[1] The explanation, of course, was that the repression of the instincts of 'provident nature', combined with the increasing concealment of what our culture, with eloquent indirection, calls 'the facts of life', produced needs in the public which had to be gratified. One of the main functions of the novel since Richardson, it may be suggested, has been to serve a fictional initiation rite into the most fundamental mystery of its society.

Only by some such hypothesis can we explain the later course of the novel, or the remarkable paradox that Richardson, a leader in the crusade for sexual reform, and an avowed enemy of love both in its romantic and fleshly aspects, should have signalised his entry into the history of literature by a work which gave a more detailed account of a single amorous intrigue than had ever been produced before. It would seem that the opposite qualities in Richardson's outlook, his Puritanism and his prurience, are the result of the same forces, and this no doubt explains why their effects are so intricately connected. The complexities of the forces juxtaposed are largely responsible for the unique literary qualities which *Pamela* brought into fiction: they make possible a detailed presentation of a personal relationship enriched by a series of developing contrasts between the ideal and the real, the apparent and the actual, the spiritual and the physical, the conscious and the unconscious. But if the latent ambiguities of the sexual code helped Richardson

[1] Pp. 38, 35, 27-30, 39.

to produce the first true novel, they at the same time conspired to create something that was new and prophetic in quite another sense: a work that could be praised from the pulpit and yet attacked as pornography, a work that gratified the reading public with the combined attractions of a sermon and a strip-tease.

CHAPTER VI

Private Experience and the Novel

AARON HILL was perhaps the most ebullient member of the vociferous Richardson *claque*, but when he announced that 'a force that can tear the heartstrings' had appeared 'to gild the horror of our literary midnight'[1] he was only slightly exaggerating the emotional enthusiasm with which *Pamela* and *Clarissa* were received by most of his contemporaries both in England and abroad.[2] We have already seen that one reason for this enthusiasm was the way that Richardson's subject-matter endeared him to feminine readers; but the men, on the whole, seem to have been almost equally excited, and so we must seek for further explanations.

One fairly common view has been that Richardson's novels gratified the sentimental tendencies of his age. 'Sentimentalism' in its eighteenth-century sense denoted an un-Hobbesian belief in the innate benevolence of man, a credo which had the literary corollary that the depiction of such benevolence engaged in philanthropic action or generous tears was a laudable aim. There are undoubtedly features in Richardson's work which are 'sentimental' in this as well as in the current sense, but the term is nevertheless somewhat misleading when applied either to his own outlook or to the characteristic literary quality of his novels. For, as we have seen, Richardson's moral theory was opposed to the cult of love and emotional release in general, while in his practice as a novelist he presented a much wider range of feelings than those to which the sentimentalists proper usually restricted themselves. What is distinctive about Richardson's novels is not the kind or even the amount of emotion, but rather the authenticity of its presentation: many writers of the period talked about 'sympathetic tears'; even more deplorably Richardson talked about 'pellucid fugitives',[3] but he made them flow as no one else and as never before.

How Richardson made them flow, how he involved his

---

[1] Letter to Richardson, March 8, 1749 (Forster MSS. XII, ii, f. 110).
[2] See McKillop, *Richardson*, pp. 43-106.   [3] *Clarissa*, III, 29.

readers so deeply in the sentiments of his characters, is well described by Francis Jeffrey in the *Edinburgh Review* (1804):

> Other writers avoid all details that are not necessary or impressive. . . . The consequence is, that we are only acquainted with their characters in their dress of ceremony, and that, as we never see them except in those critical circumstances, and those moments of strong emotion, which are but of rare occurrence in real life, we are never deceived into any belief of their reality, and contemplate the whole as an exaggerated and dazzling illusion. With such authors we make a visit by appointment, and see and hear only what we know has been prepared for our reception. With Richardson, we slip, invisible, into the domestic privacy of his characters, and hear and see every thing that is said and done among them, whether it be interesting or otherwise, and whether it gratify our curiosity or disappoint it. We sympathise with the former, therefore, only as we sympathise with the monarchs and statesmen of history, of whose condition as individuals we have but a very imperfect conception. We feel for the latter, as for our private friends and acquaintance, with whose whole situation we are familiar. . . . In this art Richardson is undoubtedly without an equal, and, if we except De Foe, without a competitor, we believe, in the whole history of literature.[1]

One of the constituents of the narrative method described by Jeffrey was noted in the first chapter—the more minutely discriminated time-scale, and the much less selective attitude to what should be told the reader, which are characteristic of Richardson's formal realism. But this unselective amplitude of presentation does not alone explain how Richardson enables us to 'slip into the domestic privacy of the characters': we must take account of the direction as well as of the scale of his narrative. This direction, of course, is towards the delineation of the domestic life and the private experience of the characters who belong to it: the two go together—we get inside their minds as well as inside their houses.

It is primarily this re-orientation of the narrative perspective which gives Richardson his place in the tradition of the novel. It distinguishes him from Defoe, for example: since although both writers were, as Mrs. Barbauld wrote, 'accurate describers, minute and circumstantial . . . the minuteness of Defoe was more employed about things, and that of Richardson about

---

[1] *Contributions to the Edinburgh Review* (London, 1844), I, 321-322.

persons and sentiments'.[1] In combination with his fullness of presentation it also distinguishes him from the rival French claimants to the paternity of the modern novel. When George Saintsbury, for example, concludes that *Pamela* is indeed the first novel, he does so because the only answer he can give to the question 'Where are we to find a probable human being, worked out to the same degree, before?' is—'Nowhere'.[2] There are many equally probable and perhaps more interesting characters in literature before Pamela, but there are none whose daily thoughts and feelings we know so intimately.

What forces influenced Richardson in giving fiction this subjective and inward direction? One of them is suggested by the formal basis of his narrative—the letter. The familiar letter, of course, can be an opportunity for a much fuller and more unreserved expression of the writer's own private feelings than oral converse usually affords, and the cult of such correspondence was one which had largely arisen during Richardson's own lifetime, and which he himself both followed and fostered.

In itself it involved a very significant departure from the classical literary perspective; as Madame de Staël wrote, 'the ancients would never have thought of giving their fiction such a form' because the epistolary method 'always presupposes more sentiment than action'.[3] Richardson's narrative mode, therefore, may also be regarded as a reflection of a much larger change in outlook—the transition from the objective, social and public orientation of the classical world to the subjective, individualist and private orientation of the life and literature of the last two hundred years.

The contrast is a fairly familiar one. It is implied in Hegel's comparison between ancient and modern tragedy, or in Goethe's and Matthew Arnold's yearning for the impersonality and objectivity of Greek and Roman art, as opposed to the feverish subjectivity of their own romantic literature; and its most important aspect from our point of view is expressed by Walter Pater in *Marius the Epicurean*, when he comments on how the ancients were 'jealous for the most part of affording us a glimpse of that interior self, which in many cases would have actually doubled the interest of their objective informations'.[4]

---

[1] 'Life', prefixed to *Correspondence of Samuel Richardson*, I, xx.
[2] *The English Novel* (London, 1913), pp. 86-87.
[3] *De l'Allemagne*, in *Œuvres complètes*, XI, 86-87.   [4] London, 1939, p. 313.

Some of the most important causes of the very different modern emphasis have already been mentioned. Christianity in general, for example, was essentially an inward, individualist and self-conscious kind of religion, and its effects were strongest in Puritanism, with its stress on the inner light; while the indispensable Madame de Staël drew attention to the influence of the changed philosophical outlook of the seventeenth century on the novel's subjective and analytic approach to character: 'ce n'est même que depuis deux siècles que la philosophie s'est assez introduite en nous-mêmes pour que l'analyse de ce qu'on éprouve tienne une si grande place dans les livres'.[1] The secularisation of thought which accompanied the new philosophy tended in the same direction: it produced an essentially man-centred world, and one in which the individual was responsible for his own scale of moral and social values.

Finally, the rise of individualism is of great importance. By weakening communal and traditional relationships, it fostered not only the kind of private and egocentric mental life we find in Defoe's heroes, but also the later stress on the importance of personal relationships which is so characteristic both of modern society and of the novel—such relationships may be seen as offering the individual a more conscious and selective pattern of social life to replace the more diffuse, and as it were involuntary, social cohesions which individualism had undermined. Individualism also contributed to Richardson's emphasis on private experience in at least two other respects: it provided an audience deeply enough interested in all the processes that occur in the individual consciousness to find *Pamela* absorbing; and its economic and social development eventually led to the development of the urban way of life, a fundamental formative influence on modern society which seems to be connected in many ways with the private and subjective tendency both of Richardson personally and of the novel form in general.

I

Eighteenth-century London had an importance in the national life of the time that was unequalled elsewhere. Throughout the period it was over ten times as large as any

[1] *De l'Allemagne*, p. 87.

other town in England,[1] and, perhaps even more important, it was there that such social changes as the rise of economic individualism, the increase in the division of labour, and the development of the conjugal family, were most advanced; while, as we have seen, it also contained a very large proportion of the reading public—from 1700 to 1760 over half of the booksellers of England were established there.[2]

The continual increase of the size of London was noted by many observers. They were especially struck by the proliferation of buildings beyond the ancient limits of the twin cities of London and Westminster, which became particularly evident after the Great Fire of 1666.[3] Fashion moved westward and northward, while to the east settlements arose which were almost exclusively inhabited by the labouring poor. This increasing segregation of classes was commented on by many writers. Addison's remarks in the *Spectator* are particularly significant: 'When I consider this great city in its several quarters and divisions, I look upon it as an aggregate of several nations, distinguished from each other by their respective customs, manners and interests. . . . In short, the inhabitants of St. James's, notwithstanding they live under the same laws, and speak the same language, are a distinct people from those of Cheapside, who are likewise removed from those of the Temple on the one side, and those of Smithfield on the other.'[4]

This process—the growth of London and its accompanying social and occupational differentiation—has been seen as 'perhaps the most important single feature of the social history of the late Stuart period'.[5] It is at least the plainest of many indications that something approaching the modern urban pattern was gradually imposing itself on the more cohesive community that Shakespeare knew: and we should therefore expect to find that some of the distinctive psychological features of modern urbanisation began to manifest themselves at the same time.[6]

[1] See O. H. K. Spate, 'The Growth of London, A.D. 1660–1800', *Historical Geography of England*, ed. Darby (Cambridge, 1936), pp. 529-547.

[2] Plant, *English Book Trade*, p. 86.

[3] See, for example, T. F. Reddaway, *The Rebuilding of London after the Great Fire* (London, 1951), pp. 300-308.

[4] No. 403 (1712); see also Fielding, *Covent Garden Journal*, No. 37 (1752).

[5] Max Beloff, *Public Order and Public Disturbances, 1660–1714* (London, 1938), p. 28.

[6] I base the ensuing generalisations mainly upon the area of agreement indicated in Louis Wirth's sociological analysis in 'Urbanism as a Way of Life', *American*

The growth of the population of London in the last decades of the seventeenth century from about 450,000 in 1660 to 675,000 in 1700,[1] combined with the increasing residential segregation of its inhabitants, and the extension of the metropolitan area, was certainly on a large enough scale to make the contrast between the rural and urban ways of life much deeper and more complete than it had been previously. Instead of the countryman's unchanging landscape, dominated by the regular alternation of the seasons, and the established hierarchy of social and moral order symbolised by the manor-house, the parish church and the village green, the citizen of eighteenth-century London had a horizon that was in many ways like that of modern urban man. The streets and places of resort in the various quarters of the town presented an infinite variety of ways of life, ways of life that anyone could observe, and yet for the most part utterly alien to any one individual's personal experience.

This combination of physical proximity and vast social distance is a typical feature of urbanisation, and one of its results is to give a particular emphasis to external and material values in the city-dweller's attitude to life: the most conspicuous values —those which are common to the visual experience of everyone —are economic; in eighteenth-century London, for example, it was the coaches, fine houses and expensive clothes which pervade the outlook of Moll Flanders. There was no real metropolitan equivalent to the expression of the community values available to all represented by the parish church in the country. In many of the new centres of population there was no church at all, and, consequently, according to Swift, 'five parts in six of the people of London [were] absolutely hindered from hearing divine service';[2] and in any case the atmosphere of what was fast becoming 'a mart of infidelity'[3] tended to discourage church-going—Bishop Secker said that 'people of fashion' often attended 'Divine worship in the country . . . to avoid scandal',

Journal of Sociology, XLIV (1938), 1-24, and Lewis Mumford's imaginative and historical treatment in *The Culture of Cities* (1938). I should perhaps make clear that no comparative evaluation of the urban as opposed to the rural way of life is intended here: the stability of the latter, for example, may well be a euphemism for what Marx and Engels once so impoliticly characterised as 'the idiocy of rural life'.

[1] Spate, 'Growth of London', p. 538.
[2] 'A Project for the Advancement of Religion and the Reformation of Manners', 1709, *Prose Works*, ed. Davis (Oxford, 1939), II, 61.
[3] Bishop Sherlock's phrase (1750), *cit.* Carpenter, *Sherlock*, p. 284.

but that they 'seldom or never [did so] in the town'.[1] This decline of religious values in the town made way for the supremacy of material values, a supremacy that was symbolised in the way that London was rebuilt after the Great Fire: under the new plan it was the Royal Exchange and not St. Paul's which became the architectural focus of the City.[2]

An environment so large and various that only a little of it can be experienced by any one individual, and a system of values that is mainly economic—these have combined to provide the novel in general with two of its most characteristic themes: the individual seeking his fortune in the big city and perhaps only achieving tragic failure, so often described by the French and American Realists; and, frequently in association with this, the milieu studies of such writers as Balzac, Zola and Dreiser, where we are taken behind the scenes, and shown what actually happens in the places we know only by passing them in the street or reading about them in the newspapers. Both these subjects also feature prominently in eighteenth-century literature, where the novel supplemented the work of journalists and pamphleteers[3] and revealed all the secrets of the town: both Defoe and Richardson appeal to this interest, and it is even more marked in such works as Fielding's *Amelia* and Smollett's *Humphrey Clinker*. At the same time London figured in much of the drama and fiction of the time as the symbol of wealth, luxury, excitement and perhaps a rich husband: for Steele's novel-reading girl Biddy Tipkins, and for Eliza Haywood's Betsy Thoughtless it is the milieu where everything happens, where people really live: triumph in the big city has become the Holy Grail in the individual's secular pilgrimage.

Few participated in the glories and miseries of London life more intensely than Defoe. London born and bred, he ran the gamut of court and jail, and finally, like the Complete Tradesman he wanted to be and in a sense was, finished life with coach and country-house. He was intensely interested in all London's problems, as is evident in such studies as *Augusta Triumphans*

---

[1] *Cit.* W.E. Lecky, *History of England in the Eighteenth Century* (New York, 1878), II, 580.   [2] Reddaway, *Rebuilding of London*, p. 294.
[3] For example, John Gay, *Trivia*, 1716; Richard Burridge, *A New Review of London*, 1722; James Ralph, *The Taste of the Town: or A Guide to all Public Diversions*, 1731; and see also Paul B. Anderson, 'Thomas Gordon and John Mottley, *A Trip through London*, 1728', *PQ*, XIX (1940), 244-260.

(1728), an interesting essay in urban reform, as well as in many of his other works; and he planned to profit directly from London's growth by establishing his ill-fated manufacture of bricks and tiles at Tilbury.

Defoe's novels embody many of the positive aspects of urbanisation. His heroes and heroines make their way through the competitive and immoral metropolitan jungle in the pursuit of fortune, and as we accompany them we are given a very complete picture of many of the London milieus, from the Customs House to Newgate Prison, from the poor tenements of Ratcliff to the fashionable parks and houses of the West End. Yet although the picture has its selfish and sordid aspects, it has one very significant difference from that presented by the modern city. Defoe's London is still a community, a community composed by now of an almost infinite variety of parts, but at least of parts which still recognise their kinship; it is large, but somehow remains local, and Defoe and his characters are a part of it, understanding and understood.

There are probably many reasons for Defoe's buoyant and secure tone. He had some memory of the days before the Great Fire, and the London he had grown up in was still an entity, much of it enclosed by the City Wall. But the major reason is surely that although Defoe had since seen enormous changes, he himself had participated in them actively and enthusiastically; he lived in the hurly-burly where the foundations of the new way of life were being laid: and he was at one with it.

Richardson's picture of London is totally different. His works express, not the life of the whole community, but a deep personal distrust and even fear of the urban environment. Especially in *Clarissa*: its heroine, like Pamela, is not one of the 'townwomen' whose 'confident' mien Richardson so disliked, but a pure country girl; and her fall is caused by the fact that, as she later tells Belford, 'I knew nothing of the town and its ways'. It is this which prevents Clarissa from realising that Mrs. Sinclair is 'a very vile creature'; and although she notices that the tea which is being used to drug her 'has an odd taste' she is easily put off with the explanation that it contains 'London milk'. When she attempts to escape from her enemies she is equally at a disadvantage, never knowing what duplicities are hidden in the behaviour of the people she meets, or what horrors are being perpetrated behind the walls of its houses. Eventually she must die, because the pure heart cannot survive the immoral brutality of the 'great wicked town';[1] but not until she has dragged herself through all her Stations of the Cross, from St. Albans to the brothel off fashionable Dover Street, from the shady resorts of Hampstead to the sponging-house in High Holborn, to find peace only when she returns to her native countryside for burial.

It is interesting to note that one at least of Richardson's contemporaries, the anonymous author of the 1754 *Critical Remarks on Sir Charles Grandison, Clarissa and Pamela*, saw the agents of Clarissa's downfall as typical products of urbanisation. He wrote that 'such characters as Lovelace and his associates, or mother Sinclair and her nymphs' could only subsist 'in a city like London, the overgrown metropolis of a powerful empire, and an extensive commerce', and added: 'all these corruptions are the necessary and unavoidable consequence of such a constitution of things'.[2]

There can be little doubt that some of the differences between the attitudes of Defoe and Richardson to urban life are due to the considerable changes that occurred in the middle decades of the century. This period witnessed many innovations such as the replacement of signs by house numbers, the demolition of the city wall, the creation of central authorities for paving and lighting the streets, water and sewerage, the reform of the police system by Fielding; they are not particularly important in themselves, but they show that conditions demanded quite different methods from those which had formerly sufficed:[3] changes of scale had reached a point which made changes of social organisation imperative. Nevertheless, the great contrast between Defoe and Richardson as Londoners cannot be explained only, or even mainly, as the result of the effects of increasing urbanisation: the two men were, after all, only a generation apart—Defoe was born in 1660, Richardson in 1689. The major reason for their very different portrayal of urban life is undoubtedly that they were poles apart in physical and psychological constitution.

[1] *Clarissa*, I, 353, III, 505, 368, I, 422; see also III, 68, 428.   [2] P. 54.
[3] See Ambrose Heal, 'The Numbering of Houses in London Streets', *N. & Q.*, CLXXXIII (1942), 100-101; Sir Walter Besant, *London in the Eighteenth Century* (London, 1925), 84-85, 88-101, 125-132; George, *London Life*, pp. 99-103.

Even here, however, their differences have a certain representative quality. Defoe had all the vigour of the textile tradesmen pictured by Deloney over a century earlier; like them he was in part a countryman, knowledgeable about crops and cattle, as much at home riding up and down the country as in shop or the counting-house; even in London the 'Change, the coffee-house and the streets supply him with the equivalent of the watching countryside of saga: and wherever he goes he is at home. But if Defoe harks back to the days of the heroic independence of the citizenry, Richardson offers us a glimpse of the middle-class tradesman to come, bounded by the horizons of the office in the city and the gentility of the suburban home.

London itself certainly provides no way of life in which he can participate. On the one hand, he is deeply aware of the social differences between the tradesmen of the City and the people of quality who inhabit Westminster, and this awareness is not qualified by Defoe's confident preference for his own class. 'There is a bar between us', Richardson wrote to Mrs. Delany in 1753 concerning a mutual acquaintance, 'Temple-Bar. Ladies who live near Hill Street, and Berkeley and Grosvenor Squares, love not to pass this bar. They speak of it, as if it were a day's journey.' On the other hand, Richardson participated very little in the life of his own environment. He was 'not able to bear a crowd', and stopped going to church on that account; while even in his own printing-shop he preferred to supervise his own workmen by looking through 'a spy window'.[1] As for the pleasures of the town, they were the road to damnation of such abandoned females as Sally Martin in *Clarissa*, and made him long for 'the last age, when there were no Vauxhalls, Ranelaghs, Marybones, and such-like places of diversion, to dress out for and gad after'.[2] Even the life of the streets was rapidly becoming something which only the poor shared. Certainly not Richardson if we can judge from the description he gave Lady Bradshaigh of how he walked abroad:

One hand generally in his bosom, the other a cane in it, which he leans upon under the skirts of his coat usually, that it may imperceptibly serve him as a support, when attacked by sudden tremors or startings, and dizziness, which too frequently attack him. . . . Looking directly foreright, as passers by would imagine, but

[1] *Correspondence*, IV, 79-80, I, clxxix, III, 225.   [2] *Clarissa*, IV, 538.

observing all that stirs on either hand of him without moving his short neck; hardly ever turning back . . . a regular even pace, stealing away ground, rather than seeming to rid it.[1]

There is something about Richardson's gait and posture which is distinctively urban; indeed even his ailments have this quality, being, as his friend Dr. George Cheyne told him, the ills typical of 'those obliged to follow a sedentary occupation'. Cheyne suggested that Richardson, whose nerves did not allow him to ride horseback, should at least get a 'chamber-horse', a 'liver-shaking device', as B. W. Downs has described it,[2] much used at this time. But exercise could not allay the fever of his nerves, and here Cheyne diagnosed the 'English Malady' or 'nervous hyp', which was no more, he confessed, than 'a short expression for any kind of nervous disorder',[3] and which may be regarded as the eighteenth-century version of anxiety neurosis, the typical derangement of the urban Psyche.

Richardson, then, is an example of many of the less salutary effects of urbanisation, and here the contrast with his great contemporary Fielding is as great as that with Defoe. It also had equally marked literary consequences, as was pointed out by Richardson's acquaintance Mrs. Donnellan, who linked his poor health with his characteristic sensibility as a writer, in an attempt to console Richardson for his perpetual ill-health:

> . . . the misfortune is, those who are fit to write delicately, must think so; those who can form a distress must be able to feel it; and as the mind and the body are so united as to influence one another, the delicacy is communicated, and one too often finds softness and tenderness of mind in a body equally remarkable for those qualities. Tom Jones could get drunk, and do all sorts of bad things in the height of his joy for his uncle's recovery. I dare say Fielding is a robust, strong man.[4]

Fielding had indeed much of the countryman's robustness, and the disparity between the two novelists and their works may therefore stand as a representative example of a fundamental parting of the ways in the history of English civilisation, a partng in which it is the urban Richardson who reflects the way hat was to triumph. D. H. Lawrence was keenly aware of the

[1] *Correspondence*, IV, 290-291.   [2] *Richardson* (London, 1928), p. 27.
[3] *Letters of Cheyne to Richardson*, pp. 34, 59, 61, 109, 108.
[4] *Correspondence*, IV, 30.

moral and literary effects of this revolution, and he recapitulated many of them in *Apropos of Lady Chatterley's Lover*, his defence of a novel whose treatment of sex may be said to bring the trend initiated by *Pamela* full circle. Briefly he suggests that economic changes and Protestantism combined to destroy man's sense of harmony with the natural life and with his fellows, and as a result created 'the feeling of individualism and personality, which is existence in isolation'. This harmony had existed 'in the old England' until the middle of the eighteenth century: 'we feel it', Lawrence wrote, 'in Defoe or Fielding. And then, in the mean Jane Austen, it is gone. Already this old maid typifies "personality" instead of character, the sharp knowing in apartness.'[1]

Lawrence, of course, was a refugee from 'personality' and personal relationships, from a world of 'nothing but people'.[2] By being so, he was, perhaps, a refugee from the novel. For the world of the novel is essentially the world of the modern city; both present a picture of life in which the individual is immersed in private and personal relationships because a larger communion with nature or society is no longer available; and it is surely Richardson, rather than his successor Jane Austen, who is the first novelist in whom all the tendencies which make for a 'sharp knowing in apartness' are apparent.

The connection between urbanisation and the novel's concentration on personal relationships is stated in E. M. Forster's *Howard's End*. Its heroine, Margaret Schlegel, comes to feel that 'London was but a foretaste of this nomadic civilisation which is altering human nature so profoundly, and throws upon personal relations a stress greater than they have ever borne before'.[3] The ultimate reason for the connection would seem to be one of the most universal and characteristic features of the city-dweller's experience: the fact that he belongs to many social groups—work, worship, home, leisure—but no single person knows him in all his roles, and nor does he know anyone else in all theirs. The daily round, in fact, does not provide any permanent and dependable network of social ties, and since there is at the same time no other over-riding sense of community or common standards there arises a great need for a kind of

---

[1] London, 1930, pp. 57-58.
[2] *Letters of D. H. Lawrence*, ed. Huxley (London, 1932), p. 614.   [3] Ch. 31.

emotional security and understanding which only the shared intimacies of personal relationships can supply.

In Defoe there is little suggestion of this need; the personal contacts of Moll Flanders are transient and shallow, but she seems to revel in the multiplicity of her roles and the only kind of security she seeks is economic. By the middle of the century, however, there are signs that a different attitude was coming into being. London, for example, is the milieu where, as the sub-title of her novel *David Simple* (1744) announces, Sarah Fielding's hero travels cheerlessly 'Through London and Westminster in Search of a Real Friend', lonely and anonymous in an anarchic environment where personal contacts are mercenary, fleeting and faithless.

Richardson's recoil from this environment would seem to have been very similar. Fortunately, however, there was a way out: urbanisation provided its own antidote, the suburb, which offered an escape from the thronged streets, and whose very different mode of life symbolised the difference between the multifarious but casual relationships depicted in Defoe's novels and the fewer but more intense and introverted ones which Richardson portrayed.

Defoe had spent his last years at Stoke Newington, but the pattern of living in the suburbs even before retirement was still relatively new, as was pointed out in the introduction of the 1839 edition of the *Complete English Tradesman*, which comments disdainfully that from Defoe's 'insisting so much on the wives of tradesmen acquainting themselves with their husbands' business, and his scarcely making any allusion to out-of-town houses for the families of tradesmen . . . we readily see that a simple state of things then existed in London, such as is now perhaps found only in fourth-rate towns'.[1] Very soon, however, the movement of the prosperous into the suburb became very marked, and indeed caused a decline of the population within the city limits.[2] This was one urban trend in which Richardson could unreservedly participate; on week-ends and holidays he was happy to leave his place of business in Salisbury Court off the Strand to luxuriate in the peace of his handsome retreats first at 'agreeable suburbane North End', and after 1754 at Parson's Green. Both were in Fulham which, in 1748, according to Kalm, was a 'pretty town' with all the houses of brick, set

[1] Edinburgh, p. 3.   [2] George, *London Life*, p 329.

in a countryside that 'is everywhere nothing but a pleasaunce'.[1] Here Richardson established his little court, where, according to Miss Talbot, 'his very poultry [were] made happy by fifty little neat contrivances'.[2]

The suburb is perhaps the most significant aspect of the segregation of classes in the new urban pattern. Both the very rich and the very poor are excluded, and so the middle-class pattern can develop unmolested, safe both from the glittering immorality of the fashionable end of town and from the equally affronting misery and shiftlessness of the poor—the word 'Mob' is a significant late seventeenth-century coinage which reflects a growing distaste and at times even fear of the urban masses.

The contrast between the old urban way of life and the new social pattern which replaced it is perhaps best suggested by the different implications of the words 'urbane' and 'suburban': the one is a Renaissance idea, the other typically Victorian. 'Urbanity' denotes the qualities of politeness and understanding which are the product of the wider social experience which city life makes possible; with it goes the spirit of comedy which, in Italian, French or English comedy of the sixteenth and seventeenth centuries, centres on the gay life of the streets and the squares, where the walls of houses afford a purely nominal privacy. 'Suburban', on the other hand, denotes the sheltered complacence and provinciality of the sheltered middle-class home: as Mumford has said, the suburb is a 'collective attempt to live a private life';[3] it offers a peculiar combination of the solace of society with the safety of personal privacy; it is dedicated to an essentially feminine ideal of quiet domesticity and selective personal relationships which could only be portrayed in the novel, and which found its first full literary expression in the works of Richardson.

The privacy of the suburb is essentially feminine because it reflects the increasing tendency already discussed to regard the modesty of womanhood as highly vulnerable and therefore in need of a defensive seclusion; and the seclusion of the suburb was increased by two other developments of the period—the greater privacy afforded by Georgian housing, and the new pattern of personal relationships made possible by familiar

[1] *Account*, p. 36.   [2] *Cit.* McKillop, *Richardson*, p. 202.
[3] *Culture of Cities* (London, 1945), p. 215.

letter-writing, a pattern which, of course, involves a private and personal relationship rather than a social one, and which could be carried on without leaving the safety of the home.

In the mediaeval period nearly all the life of the household went on in the common hall. Then gradually the private bedroom and separate dining quarters for masters and servants became current; by the eighteenth century the final refinements of domestic privacy had fully established themselves. There was much more emphasis than before on separate sleeping quarters for every member of the family, and even for the household servants; a separate fireplace in all the main rooms, so that everyone could be alone whenever they wished, became one of the details which the up-to-date housewife noted with approbation; and locks on doors—still a great rarity in the sixteenth century—became one of the modernisations on which the genteel insisted, as Pamela does when she and Mr. B. are preparing a house for her parents.[1] Pamela, of course, has good reason to pay attention to this matter: during her ordeals being able to lock the door of her various sleeping places was a matter of life or a fate worse than death.

Another characteristic feature of the Georgian house is the closet, or small private apartment usually adjoining the bedroom. Typically, it stores not china and preserves but books, a writing desk and a standish; it is an early version of the room of one's own which Virginia Woolf saw as the prime requisite of woman's emancipation; and it was much more characteristically the locus of woman's liberty and even licence than its French equivalent, the boudoir, for it was used, not to conceal gallants but to lock them out while Pamela writes her 'saucy journal' and Clarissa keeps Anna Howe abreast of the news.

Richardson was something of a propagandist for this new forcing-house of the feminine sensibility; in a letter to Miss Westcomb, for example, he contrasts the 'goose-like gabble' of social conversation with the delights of epistolary intercourse for the lady who makes 'her closet her paradise'.[2] His heroines do not and cannot share the life of the street, the highways and the places of public resort with Defoe's Moll Flanders and even Fielding's Miss Western, whom Richardson described with characteristically outraged horror as 'inn-frequenting Sophia';[3]

---

[1] *Pamela*, Pt. II, p. 2. [2] *Correspondence*, III, 252-253.
[3] Letter to Miss G[rainger], Jan. 22, 1750, in *N. & Q.*, 4th ser., III (1869), 276.

they inhabit substantial houses that are quiet and secluded but where each room has its feverish and complicated inner life. Their drama unrolls in a flow of letters from one lonely closet to another, letters written by an occupant who pauses only to listen with wild surmise to footsteps in some other part of the house, and who communicates the intolerable sense of strain which arises when an opening door threatens some new violation of a cherished privacy.

In their devotion to familiar letter-writing Richardson's heroines reflect a cult which is one of the most distinctive features of eighteenth-century literary history. The basis of the cult was the great increase in the leisure and literacy of middle-class women; and it was materially assisted by a very great improvement of postal facilities. A penny post was established in London in 1680, and by the twenties of the next century it gave a service whose cheapness, speed and efficiency were, according to Defoe at least, unrivalled throughout Europe; while the ensuing decades also witnessed a great improvement in the postal system of the rest of the country.[1]

With the increase in the writing of letters went a significant change in their nature. In the sixteenth century and earlier most regular correspondences were of a public nature, concerned with commercial, political or diplomatic affairs. Letters were of course written about other matters, about literature, family concerns and indeed love: but they seem to have been fairly rare and confined to a relatively restricted social circle. There is certainly little indication of the existence of the 'scribbling treaties', as Lady Mary Wortley Montagu called them,[2] that were so common in the eighteenth century—correspondences in which people of very varying social classes habitually exchanged news and opinions about their ordinary lives. A fairly recent parallel to the kind of change that seems to have occurred is afforded by the telephone: long reserved for important transactions, usually of a business nature, its use, as facilities improved and cheapened, was gradually extended, especially under feminine influence perhaps, to the purposes of ordinary sociability and even intimate converse.

At all events, by 1740 it was apparently not wholly implausible that a servant-girl such as Pamela should keep regularly in

---

[1] Howard Robinson, *The British Post Office: A History* (Princeton, 1948), pp. 70-103.   [2] *Letters and Works*, I, 24.

touch with her parents; and it was, of course, the wide diffusion of the letter-writing habit which provided Richardson with the initial impetus to write her adventures, since it led two of his bookselling associates to suggest that he prepare a volume of 'Familiar Letters' 'in a common style, on such subjects as might be of use to those Country Readers, who were unable to indite for themselves'.[1]

Pamela's epistolary expertness, however, suggests a somewhat higher-class position than the one which she is supposed to have —she patently needs no help in inditing! She is, in fact, a heroine after the pattern of those innumerable eighteenth-century gentlewomen who took Richardson's own advice as to the employment of their leisure: 'The pen is almost as pretty an implement in a woman's fingers, as a needle'.[2]

We are now in a position to see more clearly the main links between urbanisation and Richardson's emphasis on private experience. The same causes which brought about Richardson's rejection of city life and his preference for the suburb, made him find his supreme satisfaction in familiar letter-writing, the form of personal intercourse most suited to the way of life which the suburb represents. Only in such a relationship could Richardson circumvent the deep inhibitions which made him silent and ill at ease in company, and caused him to prefer to communicate with his workmen in the printing-house, and even with his own family, by means of 'little notes'.[3] All these inhibitions could be forgotten when he was engaged in real or fictitious correspondences: it was a necessity of his being so deep that his friends said that 'whenever Mr. Richardson thought himself sick, it was because he had not a pen in his hand'.[4]

The pen alone offered him the possibility of satisfying his two deepest psychological needs, needs which were otherwise mutually exclusive: withdrawal from society, and emotional release. 'The pen', he wrote, 'is jealous of company. It expects, as I may say, to engross the writer's whole self; every body allows the writer to withdraw.' At the same time the pen offered an escape from solitude into an ideal kind of personal relationship. As he wrote to Miss Westcomb, 'Correspondence is, indeed, the cement of friendship; it is friendship avowed under hand and

---

[1] *Correspondence*, I, liii.   [2] *Ibid.*, VI, 120.   [3] *Ibid.*, I, clxxxi.
[4] *Cit.* Thomson, *Richardson*, p. 110.

seal: friendship upon bond, as I may say. More pure, and yet more ardent, and less broken in upon, than personal conversation can ever be amongst the most pure, because of the deliberation it allows, from the preparation to, and action of writing.'[1] So insistent, indeed, was Richardson's conviction that epistolary converse gave him the emotional satisfaction which ordinary life denied, that he supported his belief with a revelatory, though erroneous, etymology: 'familiar letter writing', Lovelace explains in *Clarissa*, 'was writing from the heart . . . as the very word "*Cor-respondence*" implied', and adds 'Not the heart only; the *soul* was in it'.[2]

II

The literary advantages and disadvantages of the epistolary form in fiction have been much discussed.[3] The disadvantages are particularly obvious—the implausibility of such incessant recourse to the pen, and the repetition and prolixity which the method imposes, often make us sympathise with Lovelace's imprecation, 'Rot the goose and the goose quill!'[4] The major advantage, of course, is that letters are the most direct material evidence for the inner life of their writers that exist. Even more than the memoir they are, to repeat Flaubert's phrase, 'le réel écrit', and their reality is one which reveals the subjective and private orientations of the writer both towards the recipient and the people discussed, as well as the writer's own inner being. As Dr. Johnson wrote to Mrs. Thrale: 'A man's letters . . . are only the mirror of his breast, whatever passes within him is shown undisguised in its natural process. Nothing is inverted, nothing distorted, you see systems in their elements, you discover actions in their motives'.[5]

The main problem in portraying the inner life is essentially one of the time-scale. The daily experience of the individual is composed of a ceaseless flow of thought, feeling and sensation; but most literary forms—biography and even autobiography for instance—tend to be of too gross a temporal mesh to retain

---

[1] *Correspondence*, III, 247, 245.   [2] *Clarissa*, II, 431.
[3] See G. F. Singer, *The Epistolary Novel* (Philadelphia, 1933), especially pp. 40-59; F. G. Black, *The Epistolary Novel in the Late Eighteenth Century* (Eugene, Oregon, 1940); and for the European background Charles E. Kany, *The Beginnings of the Epistolary Novel in France, Italy and Spain* (Berkeley, 1937).
[4] *Clarissa*, IV, 375.   [5] Oct. 27, 1777.

its actuality; and so, for the most part, is memory. Yet it is this minute-by-minute content of consciousness which constitutes what the individual's personality really is, and dictates his relationship to others: it is only by contact with this consciousness that a reader can participate fully in the life of a fictional character.

The nearest record of this consciousness in ordinary life is the private letter, and Richardson was fully aware of the advantages to be derived from his 'writing to the minute' technique, as he called it. He was most explicit about this advantage in the Preface to *Clarissa*: 'All the letters are written while the hearts of the writers must be supposed to be wholly engaged in their subjects . . . so that they abound, not only with critical situations, but with what may be called *instantaneous* descriptions and reflections'. This present-tense recording of the action, Richardson felt, also gave him a great advantage over the autobiographical memoir which Defoe and Marivaux had used as the basis of their narrative technique. For, as a contemporary critic pointed out in a letter which Richardson reproduced in the Postscript to *Clarissa*, 'The minute particulars of events, the sentiments and conversation of the parties' were in his method 'exhibited with all the warmth and spirit that the passion supposed to be predominant at the very time could produce'; on the other hand, 'Romances in general, and Marivaux's amongst others, are wholly improbable, because they suppose the history to be written after the series of events is closed by the catastrophe; a circumstance which implies a strength of memory beyond all example and probability'.[1]

The argument of improbability is not a very convincing one; the epistolary method is by no means exempt from it in other ways, and both methods must be accepted for what they are, literary conventions. But it is true that the use of the epistolary method impels the writer towards producing something that may pass for the spontaneous transcription of the subjective reactions of the protagonists to the events as they occur and thus to break even more completely than Defoe did with the more patently selective and summarising tendency of classical writing. For, if events are remembered long after the event, the

---

[1] The Everyman and many other editions do not reprint the prefatory matter of the novels, nor the important Postscript of *Clarissa*. Quotations here are from the Shakespeare Head Edition (Oxford, 1930).

memory performs a somewhat similar function, retaining only what led to significant action and forgetting whatever was transitory and abortive.

Richardson's attempt to achieve what in the 'Preface by the Editor' to *Pamela* he called 'an immediate impression of every circumstance' obviously led to much that was trifling and ridiculous. This aspect of his narrative was nicely parodied by Shenstone: 'So I sat down and wrote thus far: scrattle, scrattle, goes the pen—why, how now? says I—what's the matter with the pen? So I thought I would make an end of the letter, because my pen went scrattle, scrattle . . .'[1] Pamela's repetitions and her habit of conversing with herself over trivialities are fair enough game; but even in Shenstone's parody, especially when read in its entirety, it is evident that this very garrulity itself brings us extremely close to Pamela's inner consciousness; it is necessary that the train of thought should often be ephemeral and transparent in this way, so that we can feel sure that nothing is being withheld. The very lack of selectiveness, indeed, impels us to a more active involvement in the events and feelings described: we have to pick significant items of character and behaviour out of a wealth of circumambient detail, much as in real life we attempt to gather meaning from the casual flux of circumstance. This is the kind of participation which the novel typically induces: it makes us feel that we are in contact not with literature but with the raw materials of life itself as they are momentarily reflected in the minds of the protagonists.

Previous traditions of letter-writing would not have encouraged this narrative direction. John Lyly's *Euphues* (1579), for example, is also an exemplary tale told in letters: but, in keeping both with the literary and the epistolary traditions of his time, Lyly's emphasis was on producing new models of eloquence; the characters and their actions are of very secondary importance. But by the time of *Pamela* the majority of the literate public cared little for the traditions of courtly rhetoric, and used letters only for the purpose of sharing their daily thoughts and acts with a friend; the cult of familiar letter-writing, in fact, provided Richardson with a microphone already attuned to the tones of private experience.

The fact that Richardson was using an essentially feminine, and from a literary point of view, amateur, tradition of letter-

---

[1] *Letters*, ed. Mallam, p. 24.

writing, also helped him to break with the traditional decorums of prose and use a style that was wholly suited to embody the kind of mental process with which his narrative was concerned. In this, as in many other things, he was a good deal more conscious and even sophisticated about his literary purpose than he sometimes allowed; there is at least a strong suggestion in *Clarissa* that he regarded his own literary style as infinitely superior to those of the classically educated for his particular purposes: Anna Howe tells us that '*mere* scholars' too often 'spangle over their productions with *metaphors*; they rumble into *bombast*: the *sublime* with them, lying in *words* and not in *sentiment*'; while others 'sinking into the *classical* pits, there poke and scramble about, never seeking to show genius of their own'.[1]

On the other hand, the familiar letters both of Richardson and his less educated feminine correspondents were simpler and less conscious: everything was subordinated to the aim of expressing the ideas passing in the mind at the moment of writing. This can be seen in Richardson's real letters as well as his fictional ones: in this passage to Lady Bradshaigh, for example:

> Another there was whom his soul loved; but with a reverence—Hush! Pen, lie thee down!—
> A timely Check; where, else, might I have ended? This lady—how hard to forbear the affecting subject! But I *will* forbear. This man presumed not—Again going on! not a word more this night.[2]

There is a complete break here with the mode of Augustan prose, but it is an essential condition for Richardson's success in transcribing the inner drama of impulse and inhibition.

In the novels Richardson's use of language is concentrated on producing what his characters might plausibly write in the circumstances. One expression of this is Richardson's use of popular words and phrases. In *Pamela*, for example, we get such colloquialisms as 'fat-face', 'no better than he should be', and 'you might have beat me down with a feather'[3]—neither elegant nor pungent enough to have been used in comedy or satire, yet redolent of the moral and social milieu of the book. But Richardson's most characteristic linguistic innovation was in vocabulary, and here, too, his aim was to create a literary vehicle for the more exact transcription of psychological processes. One anonymous pamphleteer, for instance, complained about

---

[1] *Clarissa*, IV, 495.   [2] *Correspondence*, I, clx.   [3] I, 356, 6, 8.

Richardson's 'many new-coined words and phrases, Grandison's *meditatingly*, Uncle Selby's *scrupulosities*, and a vast variety
of others' which, he feared, might 'by the laborious industry of
some future compiler' be 'transferred into a Dictionary'.[1] As
it happens, these particular words had been used before
although Richardson may well have coined them independently.
In any case, they both indicate Richardson's characteristic literary direction: 'meditatingly' shows the need for the accurate
transcription of the feeling-tones of the characters; while
'scrupulosities' is a useful piece of shorthand to denote all the
restraints great and small which dominate the inner world of
his characters.

Lord Chesterfield, interestingly enough, seems to have been
aware of the connection between Richardson's breach with
linguistic decorum and the fact that his eye was on a new literary
object. He connected Richardson's uneducated 'small talk'
with his 'great knowledge and skill both in painting and in
interesting the heart', and conceded that Richardson had 'even
coined some expressions for those little secret movements that
are admirable'.[2] He did not, unfortunately, specify what words
he had in mind, but three of Richardson's actual coinages may
be cited which offer some support for his view: 'Childbed
matronises the giddiest spirits'[3] is evidence of the need to pin
down a whole complex psychological development in a single
word; *Clarissa* offers us the first recorded usage of the word
'personalities' meaning 'individual traits', long before its
modern usage in the singular was established; while *Grandison*
provides us with 'femalities' which is indeed 'a peculiar but
expressive word of Mr. Selby's'.[4]

The letter form, then, offered Richardson a short-cut, as it
were, to the heart, and encouraged him to express what he
found there with the greatest possible precision, even at the cost
of shocking the literary traditionalists. As a result, his readers
found in his novels the same complete engrossment of their inner
feelings, and the same welcome withdrawal into an imaginary

[1] *Critical Remarks on Sir Charles Grandison, Clarissa and Pamela* . . . By a Lover
of Virtue, 1754, p. 4. Shenstone parodied Richardson's neologisms in the passage
cited above, which contains the first use of 'scrattle' recorded in the *O.E.D.*
[2] Letter to David Mallet, 1753; *cit.* McKillop, *Richardson*, p. 220.
[3] *Familiar Letters on Important Occasions*, 1741, Letter 141; the first reference given
in the *O.E.D.*, also by Richardson, is from *Grandison*.   [4] *Grandison*, VI, 126.

world vibrant with more intimately satisfying personal relationships than ordinary life provided, that they had afforded Richardson in the writing: both author and readers, in fact, were continuing the tendencies and interests which had originally led to the development of the formal basis of the narrative mode of *Pamela*—the development of the cult of familiar letter-writing.

III

On the stage, or through oral narration, the intimate and private effect of the letter form would be lost: print is the only medium for this type of literary effect. It is also the only possible mode of communication for modern urban culture. Aristotle thought that the proper size of the city should be limited by the need for the citizens to conduct their affairs in one meeting-place;[1] beyond this size the culture ceases to be oral, and writing becomes the main means of intercommunication; and with the later invention of printing there comes into being that typical feature of modern urbanisation which Lewis Mumford has called 'the pseudo-environment of paper' whereby 'what is visible and real . . . is only what has been transferred to paper'.[2]

The literary importance of the new medium is difficult to analyse. But it is at least clear that all the major literary forms were originally oral, and that this continued to affect their aims and conventions long after the advent of print. In the Elizabethan period, for instance, not only poetry but even prose were still composed primarily with a view to performance by the human voice. That literature was eventually to be printed was a minor matter, compared to pleasing patrons whose taste was formed on the old oral models. It was not until the rise of journalism that a new form of writing arose which was wholly dependent on printed performance, and the novel is perhaps the only literary genre which is essentially connected with the medium of print: it is therefore very appropriate that our first novelist should have been a printer himself.

Richardson's reliance on his trade for some of his characteristic literary effects has been noted by F. H. Wilcox: 'the very typographical form of Richardson's writings', he points out, 'bears witness to his passion for fidelity to the actual fact. No English writer has understood so well the literary possibilities

[1] *Politics*, Bk. VII, ch. 4, sects. ii-xiv.   [2] *Culture of Cities*, pp. 355-357.

of punctuation marks . . . for inflections and rhythms of actual conversation.'[1] Richardson's freedom with italics, large letters, and the dash to indicate an incomplete sentence, certainly help to convey the impression of a literal transcript of reality, although they must surely have been regarded by many of his contemporaries as merely the result of an imperfect command of the normal resources of literary style. Their view, indeed, perhaps finds some justification in two very obtrusive typographical devices in *Clarissa*: the heroine's disjointed outbursts in her delirium are expressed in a jumble of poetical fragments printed at varying angles on the page in imitation of her original demented doodlings on 'Paper X'; and Lovelace's final cry 'LET THIS EXPIATE' is rendered in extra large capitals.[2]

Richardson, however, exploited the resources of his medium in other and much more important ways. Print, as a mode of literary communication, has two characteristics which derive from its total impersonality: they may be called the authority and the illusion of print, and they give the novelist a tremendous flexibility of narrative approach, since they enable him to modulate effortlessly from the public to the private voice, from the realities of the Stock Exchange to those of the daydream.

The authority of print—the impression that all that is printed is necessarily true—was established very early. If Autolycus's ballads were in print, Mopsa was 'sure they are true'.[3] The innkeeper in *Don Quixote* has the same conviction about romances.[4] Print, to the reader, is no fallible specimen of humanity—no actor, bard or speaker who must prove himself worthy of credence: it is a material reality which can be seen by all the world and will outlive everyone in it. Nothing printed has any of the individuality, the margin of error, the assertion of personal idiosyncrasy, which even the best manuscript retains; it is more like an impersonal fiat which—partly because the State and the Church print their messages, and so hallow the medium—has received the stamp of universal social approbation. We do not, instinctively at least and until experience has made us wise, question what has appeared in print.

Defoe, obviously, made great use of this authority of print: his stories tend towards the purely impersonal, historic narration

[1] 'Prévost's Translations of Richardson's Novels', *Univ. California Pubs. in Modern Philology*, XII (1927), p. 389.   [2] *Clarissa*, III, 209; IV, 530.
[3] *The Winter's Tale*, Act IV, sc. iv.   [4] Part I, ch. 32.

of events which is the method of journalism and reportage. It is of the essence of the newspaper that it pretends to be impersonal, to prevent the reader from asking 'Who made this up?'

The impersonal authority of print is complemented by its capacity for securing a complete penetration of the reader's subjective life. The mechanically produced and therefore identical letters set with absolute uniformity on the page are, of course, much more impersonal than any manuscript, but at the same time they can be read much more automatically: ceasing to be conscious of the printed page before our eyes we surrender ourselves entirely to the world of illusion which the printed novel describes. This effect is heightened by the fact that we are usually alone when we read, and that the book, for the time being, becomes a kind of extension of our personal life —a private possession that we keep with us in our pocket or under the pillow, and that tells of an intimate world of which no one speaks out loud in ordinary life, a world which had previously found utterance only in the diary, the confession or the familiar letter, forms of expression exclusively addressed to one person, whether the writer himself, the priest or the close friend.

The private nature of the novel's mode of performance was a necessity both for the author and for the reader of *Pamela* or *Clarissa*. It is probable that, for psychological reasons, Richardson, as he himself said, could only have become an author with 'the umbrage of the editor's character to screen [himself] behind';[1] while as for the reader, it is a matter of common observation that the reactions of a group tend to be quite different from the reactions which the same individuals would make when alone. Richardson was quite aware of this. When the Rev. Dr. Lewen urges that Clarissa bring Lovelace to public trial for the rape she answers, quite realistically: 'Little advantage *in a court* . . . would some of those pleas in my favour have been, which *out of court*, and to a *private* and *serious* audience, would have carried the greatest weight against him'. A bare summary of the events might suggest that Clarissa courted her fate; only a full knowledge of her sentiments and aspirations, and the certainty that Lovelace understood them well enough to realise the enormity of his offence, enable us to understand the real nature of the story. This is further exemplified in the brilliantly executed scene at the ball given by Colonel Ambrose

[1] *Correspondence*, I, lxxvi.

where Lovelace secures acceptance from a social group of which many members are friends of Clarissa's and know of his behaviour towards her: even Anna Howe is unable in public to make the effective protest that her feelings demand.[1]

But the supreme reason for Richardson's dependence on the novel's mode of performance is, of course, his concern with that most private aspect of experience, the sexual life. The stage, in Western Europe at least, has never been able to go very far in the description of sexual behaviour, whereas in his novels Richardson was able to present much that in any other form would have been quite unacceptable to an audience whose public demeanour, at least, was very severely controlled by the intensified taboos of a Puritan morality.

Clarissa is an extreme example of this. Richardson's impersonal and anonymous role allowed him to project his own secret fantasies into a mysterious next room: and the privacy and anonymity of print placed the reader behind a keyhole where he, too, could peep in unobserved and witness rape being prepared, attempted and eventually carried out. Neither the reader nor the author were violating any decorum: they were in exactly the same situation as Mandeville's virtuous young woman who exemplified the curious duality of public and private attitudes to sex. Her modesty in public was easily ruffled, but 'let them talk as much bawdy as they please in the room next to the same virtuous young woman, where she is sure that she is undiscovered, and she will hear, if not hearken to it, without blushing at all'.[2] Ironically enough, Richardson himself seems to have used a similar argument to defend himself against those who had censured the 'warm' scenes in *Clarissa* as exceeding 'the bounds of decency'. He either wrote himself, or inspired Mr. Urban to write, in the *Gentleman's Magazine* that 'a nice person of the sex may not . . . be able to bear those scenes in action, and on the stage, in presence of a thousand witnesses, which she may not think objectible in her closet'.[3]

The printing-press, then, provided a literary medium much less sensitive to the censorship of public attitudes than the stage, and one intrinsically better suited to the communication of private feelings and fantasies. One result of this was very apparent

---

[1] *Clarissa*, IV, 184, 19-26. [2] 'Remark C', *Fable of the Bees*, I, 66.
[3] *Cit.* Dobson, *Richardson*, pp. 100-101.

in the later development of the novel. After Richardson, many authors, publishers and circulating-library operators began to engage in the mass production of fiction which merely provided opportunities for daydreaming. Such, at least, was the opinion of Coleridge, in a memorable passage of *Biographia Literaria*:

> As to the devotees of the circulating libraries, I dare not compliment their *pass-time* or rather *kill-time* with the name of *reading*. Call it rather a sort of beggarly day-dreaming, during which the mind of the dreamer furnishes for itself nothing but laziness and a little mawkish sensibility. While the whole *materiel* and imagery of the dose is supplied *ab extra* by a sort of *camera obscura* manufactured at the printing office, which, *pro tempore* fixes, reflects, and transmits the moving phantasms of one man's delirium, so as to people the barrenness of a hundred other brains afflicted with the same trance or suspension of all common sense and all definite purpose. . . .[1]

It would be unjust to Richardson, however, to suggest that the main advantage which he derived from the private circuit which print offered between himself and his readers was to present them with the content of his own daydreams, much less make possible the description of actions which could not be presented publicly owing to censorship. For although much has been said about Richardson's 'keyhole view of life', which he undoubtedly used on occasion for unwholesome ends, it is also the essential basis of his remarkable opening up of the new domain of private experience for literary exploration. We must, after all, remember that the term itself is merely the pejorative form of the metaphor by which another great and dedicated student of the inner life, Henry James, expressed his belief in the necessity for the author's objectivity and detachment: for him the role of the novelist in the house of fiction is, if not that of the peeper through keyholes, at least that of 'the watcher at the window'.[2]

IV

Many social and technical changes, then, combined to assist Richardson in giving a fuller and more convincing presentation of the inner lives of his characters and of the complexities of

[1] Ed. Shawcross, I, 34, n.
[2] See Prefaces, *Portrait of a Lady*, *Wings of the Dove* (*Art of the Novel*, ed. Blackmur (London, 1934), pp. 46, 306).

their personal relationships than literature had previously seen. This in turn brought about a much deeper and unqualified identification between the reader and these characters. For obvious reasons: we identify ourselves not with actions and situations but with the actors in them, and there had never before been such opportunities for unreserved participation in the inner lives of fictional characters as were offered by Richardson's presentation of the flow of consciousness of Pamela and Clarissa in their letters.

The contemporary reception of Richardson's novels shows this very clearly. Aaron Hill, for example, in a letter which Richardson reproduced in the prefatory matter to *Pamela*, described how he was transformed into all the characters in turn as he read: 'Now and then, I am *Colbrand* the Swiss; but, as *broad* as *I stride*, in that Character, I can never escape *Mrs. Jewkes*: who often keeps me awake in the Night';[1] while Edward Young considered *Clarissa* 'his last amour'.[2] The testimony of Diderot shows that in France also Richardson's characters were felt to be completely real persons. In his *Éloge de Richardson* (1761) he relates how, when reading *Clarissa*, he would cry out involuntarily to the heroine: 'Don't believe him! He's deceiving you! If you go you'll be ruined!' As his reading drew to a close he 'felt the same sensations that people feel when they are about to part with close friends with whom they have lived for many years', and when he had finished he 'suddenly felt that he had been left alone'. The experience, indeed, had been so exhausting that when his friends saw him afterwards they wondered if he had been ill, and asked if he'd lost a friend, or a parent.[3]

To some extent, of course, identification is a necessity of all literature, as it is of life. Man is a 'role-taking animal'; he becomes a human being and develops his personality as the result of innumerable outgoings of himself into the thoughts and feelings of others;[4] and all literature obviously depends upon this human capacity for projection into other people and their situations. Aristotle's theory of catharsis, for instance, presumes that the audience identifies itself to some extent with the tragic

[1] *Pamela*, 2nd ed., 1741, I, xxx.   [2] Richardson, *Correspondence*, II, 18.
[3] *Œuvres*, ed. Billy (Paris, 1946), pp. 1091, 1090, 1093.
[4] On this see G. H. Mead, *Mind, Self, and Society* (Chicago, 1934), especially pp. xvi-xxi, 134-138, 173, 257.

hero: how could you be purged but by taking the same dose of salts?

Greek Tragedy, however, like the other literary forms which preceded the novel, contained many elements which limited the extent to which identification could take place. The circumstance of public theatrical performance, the nobility of the hero and the exceptional horror of his fate, all reminded members of the audience that what they were seeing was not life but art, and an art that was depicting people and situations very different from those offered by their own daily experience.

The novel, on the other hand, was inherently devoid of the elements which restricted identification, and this more absolute power over the reader's consciousness does much to account for the peculiar triumphs and degradations of the novel form in general. On the one hand it is capable of the unrivalled subtlety in the exploration of personality and personal relationships which is found in the work of the greatest novelists; 'the vast importance of the novel' for D. H. Lawrence is that it can 'inform and lead into new places the flow of our sympathetic consciousness . . . lead our sympathy away in recoil from things gone dead . . . reveal the most secret places of life'.[1] On the other hand, it is the same power over the consciousness which, far from extending psychological and moral awareness, makes possible the novel's role as a popular purveyor of vicarious sexual experience and adolescent wish-fulfilment.

Richardson has a unique place in the tradition of the novel because he initiates both these directions. Every discovery is rich in irony, because it is susceptible to such varied uses, but there is a particularly complete irony in the divergent uses to which Richardson put his literary discovery in his first work: for *Pamela* is both a very remarkable psychological study and an exploitation, as Cheyne wrote to Richardson, of what St. Paul 'like a polite man as well as a deep Christian' had forbidden when he wrote 'It is a shame for you to speak of those things that are done by you in secret'.[2]

Cheyne was hinting at Fielding's most extreme accusation in *Shamela*—the view that *Pamela*'s popularity was due to the fact that it provided vicarious sexual stimulation. It is interesting to note that this charge is made in an introductory letter by Thomas Tickletext which is a close parody of Aaron Hill's

[1] *Lady Chatterley's Lover*, ch. 9.   [2] *Letters to Richardson*, pp. 68-69.

eulogy of Richardson's power to bring about a complete identification with his characters. Tickletext writes: '. . . if I lay the book down *it comes after me*. When it has dwelt all day long upon the ear, it takes possession all night of the Fancy. It has witchcraft in every page of it.—Oh! I feel an emotion even while I am relating this: Methinks I see Pamela at this instant, with all the Pride of Ornament cast off.'

Fielding's mockery was not undeserved; some of the scenes in *Pamela* are more suggestive than anything in Boccaccio's *Decameron*, for example, although it is at first sight difficult to see why this should be so, given Richardson's virtuous intentions. One reason is certainly the greater secrecy surrounding sex in Richardson and his society. In Boccaccio the protagonists of both sexes freely avow their sexual feelings; and their deeds are related orally to a mixed audience without anyone being very seriously shocked, or even excited. Things were very different in the world of Richardson, and the secrecy surrounding the sexual life meant that every move made by Mr. B. engaged the shocked attention of Richardson's readers much more thoroughly than Boccaccio's treatment of the sexual act itself.

Another reason is probably to be found in the superficial decency of Richardson's descriptions—what Lawrence tellingly described as Richardson's union of 'calico purity and underclothing excitements'.[1] The moralists who approved of *Pamela* might well have heeded Dennis's argument that 'it is a very great error in some persons at present, to be so shy of bawdy, and so fond of love. For obscenity cannot be very dangerous, because it is rude and shocking; but love is a passion, which is so agreeable to the movements of corrupted nature, that by seeing it livelily touched and often represented, an amorous disposition insensible insinuates itself into the chastest breast.'[2] There is, indeed, some reason to believe that Richardson himself was not unaware of this antinomy; he remarked contemptuously of Sterne that 'one extenuating circumstance attends his works, that they are too gross to be inflaming'.[3] He might have said the same of Boccaccio, and we might reply that nothing could be less gross and yet more 'inflaming' than some of the passages in *Pamela*.

[1] 'Introduction to These Paintings', *Phoenix*, ed. MacDonald (London, 1936), p. 552.   [2] 'A Large Account of Taste in Poetry', *Critical Works*, I, 284.
[3] *Correspondence*, V, 146.

The main reason, however, why Richardson's erotic scenes are so much more suggestive than Boccaccio's is merely that the feelings of the actors involved are so much more real. We cannot know Boccaccio's characters in the *Decameron*, since they are only necessary devices for the presentation of an amusing situation; we do know Richardson's characters, and his exhaustive treatment of their reactions to each incident makes us imagine that we are participating in every fascinating advance and retreat as it is reflected in Pamela's excited sensibility.

The major objection, however, to *Pamela* and to the novelette tradition it inaugurates, is perhaps not so much that it is salacious but that it gives a new power to age-old deceptions of romance.

The story of *Pamela*, of course, is a modern variant of the age-old Cinderella theme. As the original occupations of both the heroines suggest, both stories are essentially compensations for the monotonous drudgery and limited perspectives of ordinary domestic life. By projecting themselves into the position of the heroine the readers of *Pamela* were able to change the impersonality and boredom of the actual world into a gratifying pattern whose every element was converted into something that gave excitement and admiration and love. Such are the attractions of romance, and Richardson's novel bears everywhere the marks of its romance origin—from Pamela's name, which is that of Sidney's princess in the *Arcadia*, to her assertion of the pastoral heroine's freedom from economic and social realities when she proposes to seek refuge in nature and 'live, like a bird in winter, upon hips and haws'.[1] But it is romance with a difference: the fairy godmother, the prince and the pumpkin are replaced by morality, a substantial squire and a real coach-and-six.

This is no doubt the reason why Richardson, who so rarely gave his approval to any fiction except his own, was able to forget how close he was to providing exactly the same satisfactions as the romances he derided. His attention was so largely focussed on developing a more elaborate representational technique than fiction had ever seen before that it was easy to overlook the content to which it was being applied—to forget that his narrative skill was actually being used to re-create the pseudo-realism of the daydream, to give an air of authenticity

[1] *Pamela*, I, 68.

to a triumph against all obstacles and contrary to every expectation, a triumph which was in the last analysis as improbable as any in romance.

This combination of romance and formal realism applied both to external actions and inward feelings is the formula which explains the power of the popular novel: it satisfies the romantic aspirations of its readers in a literary guide which gives so full a background and so complete an account of the minute-by-minute details of thought and sentiment that what is fundamentally an unreal flattery of the reader's dreams appears to be the literal truth. For this reason, the popular novel is obviously liable to severe moral censure where the fairy story or the romance is not: it pretends to be something else, and, mainly owing to the new power which accrued to formal realism as a result of the subjective direction which Richardson gave it, it confuses the differences between reality and dream more insidiously than any previous fiction.

The confusion itself, of course, was not new, at least since *Don Quixote*. But if we compare *Don Quixote* with *Madame Bovary*, its classic equivalent as regards the effects of the novel, the result of the novel form's apparent realism of action and background combined with its focus on the emotional life of the characters become apparent. Don Quixote is, after all, mad, and the distortions produced by romance issue in actions whose ridiculous unreality is evident to everyone, and even, eventually, to himself; whereas Emma Bovary's conception of reality and her own role in it, though equally distorted, is not seen to be so by her or by anyone else because its distortions exist primarily in the subjective sphere, and the attempt to carry them out does not involve any such obvious collisions with reality as those of Cervantes's hero: she is mistaken, not about sheep and windmills but about herself and her personal relationships.

In this Emma Bovary pays involuntary tribute to the way in which the novel's access to the inner life gives it a more pervasive and enduring sway than the romance, and one which is much more difficult either to escape or to assess. As far as this sway is concerned, indeed, the question of literary quality is not of first importance. For good and ill the novel's power over private experience has made it a major formative influence on the expectations and aspirations of the modern consciousness; as Madame de Staël truly wrote: . . . 'les romans, même les plus purs, font du mal; il nous ont trop appris ce qu'il y a de plus secret dans les sentiments. On ne peut plus rien éprouver sans se souvenir presque de l'avoir lu, et tous les voiles du cœur ont été déchirés. Les anciens n'auraient jamais fait ainsi de leur âme un sujet de fiction.'[1]

The development of the novel's concentration on private experience and personal relationships is associated with a series of paradoxes. It is paradoxical that the most powerful vicarious identification of readers with the feelings of fictional characters that literature had seen should have been produced by exploiting the qualities of print, the most impersonal, objective and public of the media of communication. It is further paradoxical that the process of urbanisation should, in the suburb, have led to a way of life that was more secluded and less social than ever before, and, at the same time, helped to bring about a literary form which was less concerned with the public and more with the private side of life than any previous one. And finally, it is also paradoxical that these two tendencies should have combined to assist the most apparently realistic of literary genres to become capable of a more thorough subversion of psychological and social reality than any previous one.

But the novel is capable of great illumination too, and so it is natural that our feelings about the genre itself and its social context should be mixed. Perhaps the most representative and inclusive presentation of the problem in all its dubieties is to be found in the supreme culmination of the formal trend that Richardson initiated—James Joyce's *Ulysses*. No book has gone beyond it in the literal transcription of all the states of consciousness, and no book in doing so has depended more completely on the medium of print. Further, its hero, as Lewis Mumford has pointed out, is a very complete symbol of the urban consciousness, regurgitating 'the contents of the newspaper and the advertisement, living in a hell of unfulfilled desires, vague wishes, enfeebling anxieties, morbid compulsions and dreary vacuities'.[2] Leopold Bloom is representative, too, in his devotion as a reader to the vicarious sexual prowesses offered in such novelettes as *Sweets of Sin*, and his relation, such as it is, with his wife, is coloured by their mutual addiction to such delights, and to the clichés they derive from them. Again

[1] *De l'Allemagne*, p. 84.   [2] *Culture of Cities*, p. 271.

typically urban, Bloom does not belong to any one social group, but participates superficially in a great many of them; none, however, provide him with the affectionate understanding and the stable personal relationships for which he yearns, and his loneliness leads him to imagine that he has found in Stephen Dedalus the magic helper of folklore and daydream, the 'real friend' that David Simple sought.

There is nothing heroic about Bloom, nothing outstanding in any way; it is difficult at first sight to see why anyone should want to write about him; and there is, indeed, only one possible reason, which is also the reason by which the novel in general lives: despite all that can be said against Bloom his inner life is, if we can judge, infinitely more various, more interesting and certainly more conscious of itself and its personal relationships than that of his Homeric prototype. In this, too, Leopold Bloom is the climax of the tendencies we have been concerned with here: and Richardson, who is surely his spiritual kin, must be explained and, perhaps, justified by the same reasons.

CHAPTER VII

Richardson as Novelist: 'Clarissa'

EARLY in 1741 Richardson explained to Aaron Hill that he had written *Pamela* in the hope that it 'might possibly introduce a new species of writing'.[1] This claim antedates that of Fielding, made the following year in the preface to *Joseph Andrews*, and indicates that, unlike Défoe, Richardson was a conscious literary innovator.

There was certainly no accidental quality about *Clarissa*, whose plot was already in his mind in 1741, and whose actual composition occupied him fairly continuously from 1744 to 1749 when the last volumes were published: nor can there be any doubt that in *Clarissa*, even more completely than in *Pamela*, Richardson resolved the main formal problems which still confronted the novel by creating a literary structure in which narrative mode, plot, characters and moral theme were organised into a unified whole. For, although *Clarissa* contains something like a million words and is almost certainly the longest novel in the language, Richardson was justified in asserting that 'long as the work is, there is not one digression, not one episode, not one reflection, but what arises naturally from the subject, and makes for it, and [carries] it on'.[2]

I

Richardson's use of the letter form in *Clarissa* was much better adapted to the presentation of personal relationships than was the case in his first novel. In *Pamela* there was only one main correspondence—that of the heroine and her parents; as a result there was no direct presentation of Mr. B.'s point of view, and our picture of Pamela herself was completely one-sided. This posed a very similar critical problem to that in *Moll Flanders*: it was difficult to know how far the heroine's own interpretation of her character and actions was to be accepted. The parallel,

[1] *Correspondence*, I, lxxiii-lxxiv; on its date see McKillop, *Richardson*, p. 26, n.
[2] McKillop, *Richardson*, p. 127.

indeed, can be continued, for the fact that Richardson had essentially only one narrative source, Pamela herself, meant not only that he occasionally had to intervene himself as editor and explain such matters as how Pamela got from Bedfordshire to Lincolnshire, but, more important, that the epistolary convention itself gradually broke down, the letters turned into 'Pamela's Journal', and the later parts of the novel therefore produced a kind of narrative effect not unlike that of the autobiographical memoir in Defoe.

In *Clarissa*, however, the epistolary method carries the whole burden of the story which is, therefore, as Richardson says in his Postscript, a 'dramatic narrative' rather than a 'history'. Its main and obvious difference from drama, indeed, is a significant one: the characters express themselves not by speaking but by writing letters, a distinction which is entirely in keeping with the inward and subjective nature of the dramatic conflict involved. This conflict is also such as to justify the way Richardson organised his narrative 'in a double yet separate correspondence, between two young ladies of virtue . . . and two gentlemen of free lives'[1]—the basic formal division is both an expression of the dichotomisation of the sexual roles which is at the heart of Richardson's subject, and an essential condition of the candid self-revelation by the characters which would have been inhibited by a mixed correspondence.

The use of two parallel series of letters, then, has great advantages, but it also presents considerable difficulties; not only because many of the actions have to be recounted separately and therefore repetitively, but because there is a danger of dispersing the reader's attention between two different sets of letters and replies. Richardson, however, handles the narrative sequence in such a way as to minimise these disadvantages. At times the attitudes of the protagonists to the same events are so different that we have no sense of repetition, while at others he intervenes editorially to explain that some letters have been suppressed or shortened—the distinction, incidentally, between such intervention, which is limited to clarifying the handling of the original documents, and that which occurs in *Pamela*, where the author becomes the narrator, is an important one.

Richardson's main method of resolving the narrative problem,

---

[1] Preface, *Clarissa*. On this subject see A. D. McKillop, 'Epistolary Technique in Richardson's Novels', *Rice Institute Pamphlet*, XXXVIII (1951), 36-54.

however, is to give us large groups of letters from one side or the other and to organise these major compositional units in such a way that there is a significant relationship between the action and the mode of its telling. At the outset, for example, the letters between Clarissa and Anna Howe occupy most of the first two volumes. It is only when their characters and background have been fully established, and Clarissa has taken the fateful step and placed herself in Lovelace's power, that the main male correspondence begins and at once reveals the full danger of Clarissa's situation. The climax of the story brings another very effective piece of counterpoint: the rape is announced briefly by Lovelace, but the reader has to undergo several hundred pages of anguished expectation before hearing a word of Clarissa's account of the affair, and the events that preceded it. By then her death is already in sight and it precipitates another significant reordering of the epistolary pattern: the rigid canalisation of correspondences is broken down by a flood of letters surrounding Clarissa with admiring and anxious attention, while Lovelace becomes a more and more isolated figure, to have his eventual death reported by a French travelling valet.

Richardson prevents the fundamental simplicity of his handling of the main epistolary structure from becoming obvious or boring by a great variety of auxiliary devices. There is, first of all, the contrast between the totally different worlds of the male and female correspondences; and within them there are further contrasts of character and temperament: Clarissa's anxious restraint is juxtaposed to Anna's pert volubility, and Lovelace's Byronic alternations of mood are set off against the increasingly sober tenor of Belford's letters. From time to time further contrasts of tone are provided by the introduction of new correspondents, such as Clarissa's heavy Uncle Anthony, Lovelace's illiterate servant Joseph Leman, the ridiculous pedant Brand or by the inclusion of incidents of a contrasted kind, varying from the full-dress description of the moral and physical squalor of Mrs. Sinclair's death to the social comedy of some of the disguise scenes in which Lovelace participates.

For—contrary to general opinion—Richardson had considerable humorous gifts. Much has been made of his unintentional humour, and *Clarissa* is certainly not free from it—witness the letter where Clarissa informs her Cantabrigian brother that she is 'truly sorry to have cause to say that I have heard it often remarked, that your uncontrolled passions are not a credit to your liberal education'.[1] But there is also a great deal of effective conscious humour in the novel; Fielding found 'much of the true comic force' in the widow Bevis,[2] and some very lively and sardonic irony is obtained, especially in the central portions of the book, from the interplay of characters and of their very different standards and assumptions. One brief example must suffice. After the dinner in Mrs. Sinclair's parlour before Clarissa realises the true nature of the establishment, Lovelace dryly reports Clarissa's approving comment on the dissolute Sally Martin's quite imaginary prospective alliance with a woollen draper: 'What Miss Martin particularly said of marriage, and of her humble servant, was very solid'.[3] The comment enforces the pathos of Clarissa's charitable ignorance, and yet leads us on to savour the total irony of the scene, an irony which depends upon the fact that it is Lovelace who is writing mockingly to Belford about Clarissa's penchant for the 'very solid'.

Richardson also shows great skill in varying the tempo of the narrative: after a very prolonged preparation, for example, the rape is reported so swiftly that it comes as a surprise whose full impact reverberates through the atmosphere of slowly developing leaden horror that ensues. Such calculated alternations combine with the tenor of the action itself to produce a curious and wholly characteristic literary effect. Richardson's very slowness communicates a sense of continual tension held lightly in check: the poised, almost processional, tempo of the narrative with its sudden lapses into brutality or hysteria is itself the perfect formal enactment of the universe which *Clarissa* portrays, a universe where the calm surface of repressive convention and ingrown hypocrisy is momentarily—but only momentarily—threatened by the irruption of the secret violences which it provokes but conceals.

Richardson was as careful and skilful in his characterisation as in his epistolary technique. He claimed in the Postscript that 'the characters are various and natural; well distinguished and

---

[1] I, 138.

[2] This letter to Richardson was discovered by E. L. McAdam, Jr., and was published by him in 'A New Letter from Fielding', *Yale Review*, XXXVIII (1948), 304.   [3] II, 221.

uniformly supported and maintained'; and his assertion is very largely justified. All characters of any importance are given a complete description, which includes an account, not only of their physical and psychological nature, but of their past life and of the ramifications of their family and personal relationships; while in the 'Conclusion Supposed to be Written by Mr. Belford' Richardson anticipates a later convention of the novel by acknowledging his responsibility for all his *dramatis personae* and rounding off his narrative with a brief account of their later careers.

Many modern readers, it is true, have found Clarissa too good and Lovelace too bad to be very convincing, but this was not the view of Richardson's contemporaries, who infuriated him, as he recounts in the Postscript, by their tendency, on the one hand, to condemn the heroine as 'too cold in her love, too haughty, and even sometimes provoking', and on the other to succumb to the hero's rakish charms. 'Oh that I could not say, that I have met with more admirers of Lovelace than of Clarissa', Richardson lamented to Miss Grainger;[1] and this despite the fact that he had already added footnotes to his original text so as to emphasise Lovelace's cruelty and duplicity. This very different attitude to Richardson's protagonists lasted until well into the nineteenth century: Balzac, for example, thought it appropriate in 1837 to illustrate the point that there are always two sides to a question by asking, with what was certainly meant to be a rhetorical flourish—'Who can decide between a Clarissa and a Lovelace?'[2]

On the other hand, there is no doubt that it was a major part of Richardson's intention to establish Clarissa as a model of feminine virtue—he stated very explicitly in the Preface that she was 'proposed as an exemplar to her sex'—and that this interposes considerable barriers between us and the heroine. When we are told that Clarissa knew some Latin, was distinguished for the correctness of her orthography, was even 'a perfect mistress of the four rules of arithmetic', we find it a strain to muster the proper awe. Clarissa's systematic apportionment of time seems ridiculous, with its fantastic book-keeping carried on by such entries as 'debtor to the article of benevolent visits, so many hours' if perchance she has skimped on

---

[1] *Cit.* McKillop, *Richardson*, p. 205.
[2] *Les Illusions perdues* (Paris, 1855), p. 306.

philanthropy by running over the three hours allotted daily to epistolary amusements; we are gratified rather than otherwise when Clarissa bewails the fact that her fall has deprived her of the pleasure of visiting the 'cots of my poorer neighbours, to leave lessons for the boys and cautions for the elder girls'; and we pine for more substantial concessions to human frailty than are indicated by Anna Howe's admission that her friend did not excel 'in the executive part' of painting.[1]

None of these things would have seemed so ridiculous to Richardson's contemporaries. Theirs was an age of very deep class distinctions; an age when the position of women was still such as to make any effective intellectual achievement on their part a legitimate cause of admiration; an age when the ceremonies of benevolence were commonly performed with a blandly patronising pomp. Even Clarissa's care in the management of her time, though extreme by any standard, would probably have found wide approval as a laudable schematisation of an established Puritan tendency.

The ideals of Richardson's time and class, then, combined with the somewhat limited literary perspective prevalent in his day according to which the didactic function of art was best served by making characters paradigms of vice or virtue, go far towards explaining much that we find incredible or uncongenial in Clarissa's personality. But in any case such a defence is only necessary for a small part of the book—the beginning and especially the end when she is overwhelmed in the obituary pieties of her friends; during most of the narrative our attention is deflected from her perfections towards the tragic consequences of her error of judgement in leaving the parental roof in the company of Lovelace. Nor is this all: with a psychological penetration which shows how, if the need arises, Richardson the novelist can silence Richardson the writer of conduct books, it is made clear that this error of judgement was itself the result of Clarissa's very excellencies: 'So desirous', she taunts herself, 'to be considered an *example*! A vanity which my partial admirers put into my head! And so secure in my own virtue.' Indeed, with a supreme objectivity, Richardson connects his heroine's downfall with her attempt to realise the aims of the campaign of sexual reformation described above. Clarissa eventually comes to realise that she fell into Lovelace's power

[1] IV, 494, 496, 507; III, 521; IV, 509.

because of her spiritual pride, which led her to believe 'that I might be an humble means in the hands of Providence to reclaim a man who had, as I thought, good sense enough at bottom to be reclaimed'.[1]

In the case of Clarissa, then, Richardson's strong tendency towards making his characters exemplifications of some rather obvious moral lesson is to a large extent redeemed by his equally strong if not stronger tendency towards a very powerful imaginative projection into a much more complicated psychological and literary world. There is a similar qualification of his didactic tendency in his portrayal of Lovelace—Richardson refused, for example, to satisfy the narrow moralists who wanted him to add atheism to Lovelace's other sins, on the grounds that this would have made it impossible for Clarissa even to consider him as suitor.[2] But the main objections to Lovelace's character are of a somewhat different order: we object not so much to his exemplary viciousness as to its artificial, self-conscious and single-minded quality. Richardson undoubtedly had Lothario in Rowe's *Fair Penitent* (1703) in mind,[3] as well as several real persons of his acquaintance; he had 'always' been 'as attentive . . . to the profligate boastings, of the one sex as . . . to the disguises of the other':[4] and as a result produced a character who is not so much a real individual as a conflation of a variety of rakish traits that Richardson derived partly from personal observation and partly from his considerable reading in the drama.

Yet, although the artificial and composite elements in Lovelace's character cannot be denied, there is, as we shall see, much else that is convincingly human about him; and, as with Clarissa, an appreciation of the contemporary social context does much to relieve Richardson of the grosser charges against the credibility of his creation. For the eighteenth-century rake was very different from its twentieth-century counterpart. Lovelace belonged to an age before the public schools had enforced a code of manly reticence upon even the most hypertonic of aristocratic cads;[5] nor did cricket and golf provide alternative channels for the superfluous energies of the leisured male. Lady

---

[1] II, 378-379; III, 335.   [2] Postscript.
[3] See H. G. Ward, 'Richardson's Character of Lovelace', *MLR*, VII (1912), 494-498.   [4] *Correspondence*, V, 264.
[5] On this interpretation of the character see H. T. Hopkinson, 'Robert Lovelace, The Romantic Cad', *Horizon*, X (August 1944), 80-104.

Mary Wortley Montagu tells us that in 1724 one of Richardson's possible models for Lovelace, Philip, Duke of Wharton, was the moving spirit in a 'committee of gallantry', the Schemers, who met 'regularly three times a week to consult on gallant schemes for the advantage and advancement of that branch of happiness';[1] and there is much other evidence to suggest that a single-minded devotion to the chase was the exception rather than the rule among the gentry of the time, and that many of the younger set differed from Squire Western only in preferring a sport that had no closed season and where the quarry was human and feminine.

The moral theme of *Clarissa* is open to objections somewhat similar to those against its characterisation, but there can at least be no doubt that Richardson's purpose, as stated in the title, is carried out considerably more carefully than is the case in *Moll Flanders*. The title reads: *Clarissa: or, The History of a Young Lady: Comprehending the Most Important Concerns of Private Life, and Particularly Showing the Distresses that May Attend the Misconduct Both of Parents and Children, in Relation to Marriage.* What follows bears this description out: both parties are wrong—the parents in trying to force Solmes on their daughter, and their daughter in entertaining the private addresses of another suitor, and leaving home with him; and both parties are punished—Clarissa dies, and is shortly followed to the grave by her remorseful parents, while the fates bring to her sister and brother respectively the appropriate scourges of a faithless husband and a wife who brings, not the anticipated fortune but only 'a lawsuit for life'.

In the Postscript, however, Richardson also laid claim to a much larger moral purpose. Considering that 'when the Pulpit fails other expedients are necessary', he resolved to 'throw in his mite' to reform the infidel age and to '*steal in* . . . the great doctrines of Christianity under the guise of a fashionable amusement'. Whether this lofty ambition is achieved is open to serious question.

The crux of the matter is Clarissa's death. In the Postscript Richardson adversely criticises previous tragedy on the grounds that 'the tragic poets have . . . seldom made their heroes . . . in their deaths look forward to a future hope'. He, on the

[1] *Letters and Works*, I, 476-477.

contrary, prides himself that he is 'well justified by the *Christian system*, in deferring to extricate suffering virtue to the time when it will meet with the *completion* of its reward' and goes on to discuss the theory of poetic justice, with copious quotations, notably from Addison's essay on the subject in the *Spectator*.[1] This has led B. W. Downs to argue that Richardson was merely continuing the 'virtue rewarded' theme of *Pamela* with the single difference that he post-dated 'the reward', and paid it 'in different currency from that in common use at B—— Hall': that Richardson, in fact, merely 'substituted a transcendental for a sublunary audit'.[2]

Although a transcendental audit is aesthetically more satisfying in the circumstances than the very sublunary one which is found, not only in *Pamela*, but in many eighteenth-century works which attempt to combine the tragic mode with a happy ending, it must be admitted that Richardson has at best a shallow notion of religion: as a writer in the *Eclectic Review* (1805) said of him, with damning brevity: 'his views of Christianity are general and obscure'.[3] On the other hand, if all examples of Christian art—or theology for that matter—in which some form of transcendental reward played an important part were to be rejected, there would be very little left, especially from the eighteenth century; we cannot fairly condemn Richardson too strongly either for sharing the complacent piety of his age or for failing to overcome the very general tendency of the Christian view of the after-life to modify the usual effect of the death of the tragic hero.

In any case, the overpowering sense of waste and defeat actually conveyed by Clarissa's death, combined with the fortitude she displays in facing it, actually succeed in establishing a true tragic balance between the horror and the grandeur of Clarissa's death, a balance which reveals an imaginative quality of a much higher order than the jejune eschatology of Richardson's critical defence in the Postscript would suggest. Here again, however, the modern reader encounters what seems to be an insuperable obstacle—the tremendous scale on which every detail of Clarissa's death is described, up to her embalming and the execution of her will. The reality of this obstacle must be in part admitted: to devote nearly one-third of the novel to the heroine's death is surely excessive. On the other hand, Richardson's emphasis can

[1] No. 40.   [2] *Richardson*, p. 76.   [3] I (1805), 126.

be to some extent explained on both historical and literary grounds.

Puritanism had been opposed to all the joyous festivals of the church, but it had approved of protracted rituals and even of emotional abandon where death and burial were concerned. Consequently the scope and importance of funeral arrangements had increased until, by Richardson's day, they had attained an unprecedented elaboration.[1] Once again, therefore, it would seem that what appears to be a false note to us in *Clarissa* is also evidence of how Richardson, for good and ill, acted as a sounding board for the dominant notes of his age, and in this case, incidentally, for a note which has echoed from the Pyramids to the cemeteries of twentieth-century Los Angeles.

The later part of *Clarissa*, in fact, belongs to a long tradition of funeral literature. J. W. Draper has shown how one specifically Puritan contribution to poetry was the Funeral Elegy;[2] and death-bed reflections were often published separately as pamphlets for evangelical purposes. Eventually both these sub-literary genres developed into a larger literary trend which exploited all the thoughts and emotions concerned with death and burial; and it was the decade in which *Clarissa* was published that saw the triumph of this movement in such works as Blair's *The Grave* (1743), Edward Young's *Night Thoughts on Life, Death, and Immortality* (1742–1745) and Hervey's very popular *Meditations among the Tombs* (1746–1747), the last two of which Richardson printed.[3]

Theological works dealing with death were also among the best-sellers of the time—among them Drelincourt's *On Death*, to which Defoe's *The Apparition of Mrs. Veal* was commonly appended. It was undoubtedly part of Richardson's intentions to supply another work of this kind, a conduct book for death and burial. He wrote to Lady Bradshaigh hoping that she would place *Clarissa* on her shelf with Jeremy Taylor's *Rule and Exercises of Holy Living and Holy Dying*;[4] and would have been happy to know that Thomas Turner, grocer of East Hoathly, and a

---

[1] See H. D. Traill and J. S. Mann, *Social England* (London, 1904), V, 206; H. B. Wheatley, *Hogarth's London* (London, 1909), pp. 251-253; Goldsmith, *Citizen of the World*, Letter 12.

[2] *The Funeral Elegy and the Rise of English Romanticism* (New York, 1929), especially pp. 3, 82, 269.

[3] William Sale, Jr., *Samuel Richardson, Master Printer* (Ithaca, 1950), pp. 174-175, 218-221.   [4] *Correspondence*, IV, 237.

devotee of Drelincourt, Sherlock and other specialists in the literature of death, accorded him this status: 'My wife read to me that moving scene of the funeral of Miss Clarissa Harlowe', he wrote in 1754, and concluded, 'Oh, may the Supreme Being give me grace to lead my life in such a manner as my exit may be in some measure like that divine creature's'.[1]

The reason for this emphasis on death seems to have been the belief that the growing secularisation of thought could best be combated by showing how only faith in the future state could provide a secure shelter from the terrors of mortality; for the orthodox at least, death, not ridicule, was the test of truth. This was one of the main themes of Young's *Night Thoughts*; and Richardson himself was responsible for the insertion into Young's *Conjectures on Original Composition* of the story of how Addison had called a young unbeliever to his bedside so that he could 'see in what peace a Christian can die'.[2] To us Clarissa's preoccupation with her own coffin can only seem morbid affectation; but it must have seemed a convincing confirmation of her saintly fortitude to an age which made Newgate criminals about to be executed kneel round a coffin on their last Sunday alive while the 'condemned sermon' was preached.[3]

To his contemporaries, then, Richardson's funerary emphasis would have seemed justified for its own sake; and we, perhaps, can only try to regard it in the same light as we do a good deal of baroque memorial sculpture—forget the crushing banality of the symbolism and notice only the elaborate assurance of its presentation. At the same time we must recognise that there are strong literary reasons why Richardson should have placed such an emphasis on the death of his heroine. A very considerable length of time is required before we can forget the sordid scenes through which Clarissa has passed and remember only the final radiance, the 'sweet smile' that remains on her face when Colonel Morden opens the coffin. A very complete description is necessary before we can fully appreciate, in Belford's words, 'the infinite difference, on the same awful and affecting occasion, between a good and a bad conscience'. Clarissa meets

[1] *Diary*, ed. Turner (London, 1925), pp. 4-5. Turner's reaction was exactly the one which Richardson hoped to inspire (see *Correspondence*, IV, 228).

[2] Young, *Works*, 1773, V, 136; A. D. McKillop, 'Richardson, Young, and the *Conjectures*', *MP*, XXII (1925) 396-398.

[3] Besant, *London Life in the Eighteenth Century*, pp. 546-548; the scene is depicted in Ackermann's *Microcosm of London*, 1808.

her end with tragic serenity, asking Belford to tell Lovelace 'How happily I die:—and that such as my own, I wish to be his last hour'.[1] But Lovelace falls suddenly and unprepared, whereas by his unhurried emphasis Richardson has contrived to give Clarissa's death all the appearance of an act of the will—it is no hasty surrender to man's mortality but a beautifully staged collaboration with the powers above that have already marked her for their own.

II

In *Clarissa*, then, Richardson solved many of the formal problems of the novel, and brought the new form into relation with the highest moral and literary standards of his day. The epistolary method, it is true, lacks the pace and crispness of Defoe's narrative manner, but *Clarissa* is, what *Moll Flanders* is not, a work of serious and coherent literary art, and one which, by the almost unanimous consent of his contemporaries at home and abroad, was the greatest example of the genre ever written: Dr. Johnson called Richardson 'the greatest genius that had shed its lustre on this path of literature', and considered *Clarissa* 'the first book in the world for the knowledge it displays of the human heart',[2] while Rousseau wrote in the *Lettre à d'Alembert* (1758) that 'no one, in any language, has ever written a novel that equals or even approaches *Clarissa*'.[3]

That this is not the modern view does not prove that it is wrong; but it is undeniable that the moral and social preoccupations of the age obtrude themselves much more insistently in *Clarissa* than in the novels of Defoe or of Richardson's great contemporaries, and thus tend to render it much less immediately palatable to the modern reader (Defoe's moralising, we have seen, is usually viewed ironically today; while Fielding, Smollett and Sterne, being primarily comic or satirical writers, do not demand our acceptance of their positive standards in the same way). This, combined with the enormous length of *Clarissa*, and Richardson's occasional tendency to a harrowing moral and stylistic vulgarity in which Dreiser is perhaps his only peer among the great novelists, has denied the first masterpiece of the novel form the tribute which it so freely earned in its own day, and to which it is still largely entitled.

---

[1] IV, 398, 327, 347.   [2] *Johnsonian Miscellanies*, ed. Hill, II, 190, 251.
[3] *Cit.* McKillop, *Richardson*, p. 279.

It is entitled to it primarily because Richardson's very responsiveness to the dictates of his time and his class, which did much to render *Clarissa* unpalatable today, also helped to make it a more modern novel in a sense than any other written in the eighteenth century. Richardson's deep imaginative commitment to all the problems of the new sexual ideology and his personal devotion to the exploration of the private and subjective aspects of human experience produced a novel where the relationship between the protagonists embodies a universe of moral and social conflicts of a scale and a complexity beyond anything in previous fiction; after *Clarissa* one has to wait until Jane Austen or Stendhal for a comparable example of a work which develops so freely and so profoundly under the impetus of its own fictional imperatives.

Richardson was, as has often been noted, obsessed by class distinctions. Not consciously perhaps; he seems rather to have combined an acute sense of class differences with something of the moral democracy of the earlier Puritans which eventually led to the Victorian view as expressed by G. M. Young that 'the great dividing line . . . is . . . the respectable and the others'.[1] Some such duality is perhaps responsible for the very unsatisfactory treatment of the class issue in *Pamela*: virtuous indignation at upper-class licentiousness jars very unpleasantly with the heroine's abject regard for Mr. B.'s social status. In *Clarissa*, however, and perhaps because there is nothing like the same social distance between hero and heroine, Richardson achieves a much more powerful rendering not only of the social conflict itself, but of its moral implications.

Both Clarissa and Lovelace come from the wealthy landed gentry and have aristocratic connections. Those of the Harlowes, however, are only on the mother's side, and they are in no sense the equivalent of Lovelace's uncle, Lord M., or his titled half-sisters. The Harlowe 'darling view', as Clarissa bitterly explains, is that of '*raising a family* . . . a view too frequently . . . entertained by families which having great substance, cannot be satisfied without rank and title'. The chief repository of this ambition is James, the only son: if the family fortune, combined with those of his two childless uncles, can be concentrated on him, his enormous wealth and its accompanying

[1] *Last Essays* (London, 1950), p. 221.

political interest 'might entitle him to hope for a peerage'. Lovelace's courtship of Clarissa, however, threatens the realisation of this aim. Lovelace has even higher expectations, and James is afraid that his uncles may encourage the match by diverting some of their fortunes from him to Clarissa. For this reason, combined with a personal animosity towards Lovelace and perhaps an envious fear lest his sister outstrip him in the race for a coronet, James uses every possible means to make his family force Clarissa to marry Solmes. Solmes is very rich but he is meanly born, and in return for such a grand alliance will not expect any more dowry from Clarissa than her grandfather's estate, which is already hers and whose loss therefore cannot in any case be avoided.[1]

•At the outset, therefore, Clarissa is placed in a complicated conflict of class and family loyalties. Solmes is most unpleasantly typical of the rising middle class: mercenary with the squalid concentration of '*an upstart man* . . . not born to the immense riches he is possessed of', as Clarissa scornfully reports. He is totally devoid of social grace or intellectual cultivation, repulsive physically and a poor speller to boot. Lovelace, on the other hand, seems to possess the very qualities which Clarissa misses in her own environment: a generous landlord, a 'person of reading, judgement and taste',[2] and what is more, his suit is primarily motivated not by economic interest but by genuine personal admiration of Clarissa's beauty and accomplishments. As a potential lover he is immensely superior to the males of the Harlowe milieu—not only to Solmes but to her previous suitors and to Anna Howe's rather tame admirer Hickman; and there is therefore every reason why Lovelace should at first represent for Clarissa a very desirable escape from the constrictions of the Harlowe way of life, and the immediate threat of being forced to marry Solmes.

Events soon demonstrate, however, that Lovelace actually menaces her freedom and self-respect even more dangerously, and this for reasons also closely connected with his social affiliations. Primarily, of course, it is his aristocratic licentiousness, and his cynical distaste for matrimony, which are at issue, but they are accompanied by a quite conscious enmity to the moral and social attitudes of the middle class in general. Clarissa's sexual virtue is his great 'stimulative' as he says, and it must

[1] I, 53-54.   [2] I, 59, 166, 12.

be regarded as an expression of the moral superiority of her class: 'were it not for the *poor* and the *middling*', he comments, 'the world would probably, long ago have been destroyed by fire from Heaven'. He has already deceived and ruined a Miss Betterton, of a rich trading family that 'aimed at a new line of gentry'; and one of the factors which poisons his love of Clarissa is his resolve to win a much greater victory for his caste against the Harlowe family that has insulted him, and that he despises as a house 'sprung up from a dunghill, within every elderly person's remembrance'.[1]

Clarissa, therefore, is without allies, and this is fitting since she is the heroic representative of all that is free and positive in the new individualism, and especially of the spiritual independence which was associated with Puritanism: as such she has to combat all the forces that were opposed to the realisation of the new concept—the aristocracy, the patriarchal family system, and even the economic individualism whose development was so closely connected with that of Puritanism.

The authoritarian nature of the family is what precipitates Clarissa's tragedy. Her father goes beyond what was generally agreed to be his legitimate paternal rights: he demands not only that she give up Lovelace but that she marry Solmes. This she must refuse, and in an interesting letter to her Uncle John enumerates the absolute dependence of her sex upon their marriage choice, and concludes that 'a young creature ought not to be obliged to make all these sacrifices but for such a man as she can love'.[2]

The patriarchal authoritarianism of the Harlowe family is exacerbated by the unrestrained dominance of the dictates of economic individualism; and Clarissa is caught between the two. Much of the initial animosity that her brother and sister feel towards her is based on the fact that their grandfather has singled her out to inherit his estate. In doing so, of course, he has disregarded primogeniture, and the fact that his grandson James is the only relative who could possibly continue the family name; instead he has chosen Clarissa, a younger granddaughter, and this purely on grounds of personal preference, that is on grounds of an individual, not a family relationship. At the same time Clarissa's plight is increased by James's hatred of the traditional system of dowries: 'daughters', he likes to

[1] II, 491, 218, 147; I, 170.   [2] I, 153.

say, 'are chickens brought up for the tables of other men', and he cannot bear to think that to achieve this, 'the family stock must be impaired into the bargain'.[1]

The combination of family authority with the attitudes of economic individualism not only denies Clarissa any freedom of choice, but even leads her family to treat her with calculated cruelty, on the grounds that, as her Uncle Anthony puts it, she prefers 'a noted whoremonger . . . before a man that is merely a money-lover'.[2] Richardson here suggests how rigid middle-class morality, combined with a primary regard for material considerations, express themselves in a concealed and self-righteous sadism; and this was recognised by one member of his circle, Jane Collier. In her *Essay on the Art of Ingeniously Tormenting* (1753)—an early study of the minor persecutions of genteel family life—she comments on 'How much must an old Harlowe enjoy himself in loading a Clarissa with money, clothes, jewels, and etc., whilst he knows, that all she wants from him, is kind looks, and kind words'.[3]

A perfectly realised scene depicting this kind of persecution occurs when her sister Arabella tortures Clarissa by pretending not to understand why she is unwilling to talk about the trousseau which has been ordered for her wedding with Solmes. Clarissa, who has been confined to her room for disobedience, thus reports the visit of Arabella and her aunt:

> My sister left my aunt musing at the window, with her back towards us; and took that opportunity to insult me still more barbarously: for, stepping to my closet, she took up the patterns which my mother had sent me up, and bringing them to me, she spread them upon the chair by me; and, offering one, and then another, upon her sleeve and shoulder, thus she ran on, with great seeming tranquillity, but whisperingly, that my aunt might not hear her. *This*, Clary, is a pretty pattern enough: but *this* is quite *charming*! I would advise you to make your appearance in it. And *this*, were I you, should be my wedding night-gown, and *this* my second dressed suit! Won't you give orders love, to have your grandmother's jewels new set? Or will you think to show away in the new ones Mr. Solmes intends to present to you? He talks of laying out two or three thousand pounds in presents, child! Dear Heart, how gorgeously you will be arrayed! What! Silent my dear! . . .[4]

[1] I, 54.   [2] I, 160.   [3] P. 88.   [4] I, 235-236.

Clarissa escapes from such oppressions and the struggle is transferred to the purely individual place. Even here, however, she is under great disadvantages. The mere fact that she has left home to protect her own freedom and not out of love for him gives deep offence to Lovelace's pride; while the main issue that separates them, that of marriage, presents peculiar difficulties. As far as Lovelace is concerned, to consent to marriage is to yield Clarissa too easy a triumph: it means that 'a man is rather to be *her* prize, than she *his*'. Lovelace therefore tries by every stratagem to make her love 'come forward and show itself', to have the attraction of his maleness fully acknowledged; and it is only when this fails, and he fears that 'she presumes to think that she can be happy *without* me' that he uses force, hoping that then at least family pressure and public opinion will force her to remain with him.[1]

The way that Lovelace exploits every disadvantage of her situation means that Clarissa continues to be confronted with the issue which parental tyranny first raised—the power of all the forces which deny her sex their just equality with men. She is indeed, as Richardson implies during Belford's discussion of *The Fair Penitent*, engaged in the same cause as Rowe's heroine Calista, and asks with her:

> Wherefore are we
> Born with high souls, but to assert ourselves,
> Shake off this vile obedience they exact,
> And claim an equal empire o'er the world?[2]

Unlike Calista, however, and because she is pure and guiltless, Clarissa is eventually able to conquer her Lothario with spiritual weapons. At first Lovelace proclaimed himself 'a very Jew' in believing 'that women have no souls', but he is finally convinced of the reality of considerations which had not previously entered his mind: Clarissa's behaviour as she undergoes her terrible trials persuades him that 'justly did she tell me . . . that her soul was my soul's superior'.[3] Such is the wholly unexpected result of his experiment to vanquish her with the methods he has previously employed so successfully against other members of Clarissa's sex: for the first time he has been brought up against the fact that the individual is ultimately a spiritual entity and that Clarissa is a finer one than he.

---

[1] II, 426-427; III, 150.   [2] Act III, sc. i.   [3] II, 474; III, 407.

In a sense, therefore, Clarissa's triumph is one in which her sex is irrelevant and looks forward to the new and inward ethical sanction which an individualistic society requires, and of which Kant was to be the philosophical spokesman. His categorical imperative was based on the premise that 'persons, because their very nature points them out as ends in themselves ... must not be used merely as means'.[1] Lovelace uses Clarissa, as he uses everybody else, as a means to gratify his pride in his caste, his sex and his intellect; Clarissa at first fails in the eyes of the world because she does not use others as means, but eventually she proves that no individual and no institution can destroy the inner inviolability of the human personality. This realisation completely cows him: as he confesses, 'I never knew what fear of man was—nor fear of woman neither, till I became acquainted with Miss Clarissa Harlowe; nay, what is *most* surprising, till I came to have her in my power'.[2]

If Richardson had stopped here, *Clarissa* would have been a work analogous to such later portrayals in the Puritan tradition of the tragedy of feminine individualism as George Eliot's *Middlemarch* and Henry James's *Portrait of a Lady*. The three novels reveal the all but unendurable disparity between expectation and reality that faces sensitive women in modern society, and the difficulties that lie before anyone who is unwilling either to be used, or to use others, as a means. Richardson's fascinated absorption in the sexual issue, however, produced a treatment of the theme which is starker, less reticent, and, perhaps, even more revealing.

Clarissa is, among other things, the supreme embodiment of the new feminine stereotype, a very paragon of delicacy. This is a crucial factor in her relations with Lovelace, who carefully contrives not to propose marriage in such a way as would enable Clarissa to agree without compromising her delicacy, which she refuses to do: 'Would he have me catch at his first, his *very* first word?' she asks on one occasion, and on another, when Lovelace cruelly asks if she has any objections to delaying a few days until Lord M. can attend the wedding, she is forced by her sense of 'due decorum' to answer, 'No, no, You cannot

---

[1] *Fundamental Principles of the Metaphysic of Morals* (1785), in *Kant's Critique of Practical Reason and Other Works*, trans. Abbott (London, 1898), p. 46.
[2] III, 301.

think that I should imagine there can be reasons for such a hurry'. As a result, even Anna Howe thinks that Clarissa is 'over-nice, over-delicate', and she strongly urges that Clarissa 'condescend to clear up his doubts'. Richardson, however, points out in a footnote that 'it was not possible for a person of her true delicacy of mind to act otherwise than she did, to a man so cruelly and insolently artful': and in fact Lovelace understood this very well, as he explained to Belford: 'Never, I believe, was there so true, so delicate a modesty in the human mind as in that of this lady . . . this has been my security all along'.[1]

The reinforced taboo on women avowing their feelings in courtship is, therefore, primarily responsible for the way that the deadlock between Clarissa and Lovelace drags out so long, becoming uglier and more desperate in the process. Richardson, indeed, with remarkable objectivity, even makes Lovelace challenge the whole basis of the code. He wonders whether women should really be proud of having 'wilful and *studied* delays, *imputed to them*' over marriage: 'are they not', he suggests, 'indelicate in their affected delicacy; for do they not thereby tacitly confess that they expect to be the greatest gainers in wedlock; and that there is *self-denial* in the pride they take in delaying'.[2]

Lovelace is himself a representative of the masculine stereotype against which the feminine code is a defence. He believes, for example, that the hypocritical bashfulness of the '*passive sex*' justifies his own in using forceful methods. 'It is cruel to ask a modest woman for her consent', he writes, and finds a kind of support in the views of Anna Howe who believes that 'our sex are best dealt with by boisterous and unruly spirits'. Clarissa sees that a larger issue is at stake, and pleads that a 'modest woman' should 'distinguish and wish to consort with a modest man' such as the unexciting Hickman: but Lovelace knows better; women do not really desire such a lover—'a *male virgin*—I warrant!' For, as he rather wittily puts it, a virtuous woman can 'expect . . . the confidence *she* wants' if she marries a rake, whereas she cannot but consider the virtuous male 'and herself as two parallel lines; which, though they run side by side, can never meet'.[3]

[1] II, 28, 312, 156; I, 500; II, 156, 475.   [2] II, 457.
[3] III, 214; II, 147, 73, 126; III, 82.

Lovelace himself, like the rakes and heroes of Restoration drama, gives his allegiance to a debased form of romantic love, thus underlining his historical role as the representative of the Cavalier attitude to sex, in conflict with the Puritan one represented by Clarissa. Sexual passion is placed upon a different and higher plane than the institutional arrangement of marriage, and so, although the divine Clarissa Harlowe can almost make him think of 'foregoing the *life of honour* for the *life of shackles*', his darling hope is 'to prevail upon her to live with [him] what [he] call[s] the life of honour', in which he will promise 'never to marry any other woman', but in which their felicity will be uncontaminated by the rites of matrimony.[1]

That, at least, is his scheme: to win her on his own terms; with always the possibility that he can marry her afterwards, once his personality and his code have had their triumph. 'Will not the generality of the world acquit me, if I *do* marry?' he asks. 'And what is that injury which a *church rite* will not at any time repair? Is not the *catastrophe of every story that ends in wedlock accounted happy?*'[2]

As the world goes, Lovelace is perhaps as close to the average view as Clarissa, and his attitude finds some support in the story of *Pamela*. But Richardson was now in a much more serious mood, and, as he announced in the Preface, was now determined to challenge 'that dangerous but too-commonly-received notion, *that a reformed rake makes the best husband*'. So he introduced the rape when Clarissa is unconscious from opiates, which is perhaps the least convincing incident in the book, but which serves a number of important moral and literary purposes.

First, and most obviously for Richardson's didactic purpose, it puts Lovelace wholly beyond the pale of any conception of honour, and proclaims to all the barbarity which lies below the genteel veneer of rakery; this Lovelace himself comes to realise, and curses himself for having taken the advice of Mrs. Sinclair and her crew. Not, of course, out of moral compunction, but because it is an admission of complete defeat: in his own eyes, since, as he says, 'there is no triumph in *force*. No conquest over the will':[3] and in the eyes of the world, since, as John Dennis cynically remarked, 'A rape in tragedy is a panegyrick upon the sex . . . for . . . the woman . . . is supposed to remain innocent, and to be pleased without her consent; while the man, who is ac-

[1] I, 147; II, 496.   [2] III, 281.   [3] II, 398.

counted a damned villain, proclaims the power of female charms, which have the force to drive him to so horrid a violence'.[1]

Once Lovelace has found that, contrary to his expectation, it is not a case of '*once overcome . . . for ever overcome*', Clarissa is able to demonstrate the falsity of his view of the feminine code, and defy him in the famous words, 'That man who has been the villain to me that you have been shall never make me his wife'. Clarissa's sense of her own honour is much more important than her reputation in the eyes of the world; the code, in fact, is not a hypocritical sham; Lovelace's assumption that 'the for-better and for-worse legerdemain' would 'hocus pocus . . . all the wrongs I have done Miss Harlowe into acts of kindness and benevolence to Mrs. Lovelace' is completely disproved, and he succumbs to such 'irresistible proofs of the love of virtue for its own sake'.[2]

If this were all, the conflict in *Clarissa* would still, perhaps, be too simple for a work of such length. Actually, however, the situation is much more complex and problematic.

Freud showed how the artificiality of the modern sexual code 'must incline [the members of society] to concealment of the truth, to euphemism, to self-deception, and to the deception of others'.[3] In *Pamela* this self-deception produces irony: the reader contrasts the heroine's pretended motives with her transparent but largely unconscious purpose. In *Clarissa*, however, a similar unawareness of sexual feeling on the heroine's part, which by others may be interpreted as gross lack of self-knowledge, if not actual dishonesty, becomes an important part of the dramatic development, deepening and amplifying the overt meaning of the story.

Johnson observes of Clarissa that 'there is always something which she prefers to truth'.[4] But Anna Howe justly points out that as far as women's communication with men is concerned, this duplicity is imposed by the sexual code: for, as she says, if a woman writes 'her heart to a man practised in deceit, or even to a man of some character, what advantage does it give him over her!'[5] The real tragedy, however, is that the code also makes Clarissa withhold her sexual feelings from Anna Howe,

[1] *Critical Works*, II, 166.   [2] III, 318, 222, 412, 222.
[3] '"Civilised" Sexual Morality and Modern Nervousness', *Collected Papers* (London, 1924), II, 77.   [4] *Johnsonian Miscellanies*, I, 297.   [5] III, 8.

and even from her own consciousness, and it is this which creates the main psychological tension in the early volumes, for which Johnson particularly admired Richardson.[1] The correspondence of Clarissa, and, to a lesser extent, of Lovelace, is an absorbing study because we can never assume that any statement should be taken as the complete and literal truth. Perhaps one of the reasons for Johnson's admiration was that, although as we have seen he believed that a man's 'soul lies naked' in his letters, he also knew that 'There is . . . no transaction which offers stronger temptations to fallacy and sophistication than epistolary intercourse'.[2]

The counterpoint of these unconscious duplicities in the early volumes is built upon the fact that Anna believes that Clarissa is in love with Lovelace, and does not believe Clarissa's protestations that her elopement was entirely accidental and involuntary on her part. After the marriage has been long delayed, Anna Howe even thinks it necessary to write to Clarissa: 'What then have you to do but to fly this house, this infernal house! Oh that your heart would let you fly the *man*!' Lovelace, it is true, seizes the letter, and Clarissa escapes on her own initiative. Nevertheless, until half the book is done, there is a genuine ambiguity about the situation in everyone's mind; we are fully entitled to suspect Clarissa herself of not knowing her own feelings: and Lovelace is not altogether wrong in suspecting her of the 'female affectation of denying [her] love'.[3]

As the story develops, Clarissa herself gradually makes this discovery. Very early she has cause to wonder 'what turn my mind had taken to dictate so oddly to my pen' in the course of a letter about Lovelace; and her debates with Anna Howe about her real attitude to him eventually force her to question whether her original hope that she could reform Lovelace was not actually a mask for less creditable motives. 'What strange imperfect beings!' she reflects. 'But *self* here, which is at the bottom of all we do, and of all we wish, is the grand misleader.' 'Once you wrote', she confesses to Anna Howe, 'that men of his cast are the men that our sex do not *naturally* dislike: while I held that such were not (however *that* might be) the men we *ought* to like.' She cannot deny that she 'could have liked Mr. Lovelace above all men', and that there may be some justice in

[1] *Johnsonian Miscellanies*, I, 282.
[2] 'Pope', *Lives of the Poets*, ed. Hill, III, 207.   [3] III, 11; I, 515.

the tenor of Anna's raillery that she did not 'attend to the throbs' of her heart; her principle that we should 'like and dislike as reason bids us' was not so easy to practise as she imagined; and she convicts herself 'of a punishable fault' in having loved him, punishable because 'what must be that love that has not some degree of purity for its object?' But, as she realises, 'love and hatred' are not 'voluntary passions', and so, although without any full clarification of her feelings, she admits 'detection' by Anna of her passion for Lovelace: '*Detection*, must I call it?' she wonders, and adds defeatedly: 'What can I call it?'[1]

Throughout the novel Clarissa is learning more about herself, but at the same time she is also learning more about the much blacker deceptions of Lovelace. The minor reticences and confusions revealed in the feminine correspondence are insignificant compared to the much grosser discrepancies between Lovelace's pretended attitudes to Clarissa and the falsehoods and trickeries which his letters reveal. The masculine code allows him to practise, and even openly avow, his complete lack of truth and honour in his pursuit of the opposite sex. As Belford points out, '*our honour*, and *honour* in the *general acceptation* of the word are two things', and Lovelace's honour is such that he has 'never lied to man, and hardly ever said truth to woman'. As a result of these revelations we realise that the code which might seem to make Clarissa too prudent is not prudent enough when measured against the outrageous means which men allow themselves to gain their ends. But if Clarissa's code fosters the self-ignorance which helps to place her in Lovelace's power, it at least does not involve conscious deception; and so Lovelace is forced to see that since Clarissa cannot 'stoop to deceit and falsehood, no, not to save herself', Belford was right when he asserted that 'the trial is not a fair trial'.[2]

The sophistries both conscious and unconscious produced by the sexual code, then, helped Richardson to produce a pattern of psychological surprise and discovery very similar in nature to that in *Pamela*, although the counterpoint between feminine self-deception and masculine trickery is of a much more extended and powerful kind. But Richardson's explorations of the unconscious forms taken by the sexual impulse also took

[1] I, 47; II, 379, 438-439; I, 139; II, 439.
[2] II, 158; IV, 445; III, 407; II, 158.

him much further; and he added to the already complex series of dualities embodied in the relationship of Lovelace and Clarissa quite another range of meanings which may be regarded as the ultimate and no doubt pathological expression of the dichotomisation of the sexual roles in the realm of the unconscious.

The imagery in which the relation between the sexes is rendered indicates the basic tendency of Richardson's thought. Lovelace fancies himself as an eagle, flying only at the highest game; Belford calls him 'cruel as a panther'; while Anna sees him as a hyena. The metaphor of the hunt, indeed, informs the whole of Lovelace's conception of sex: he writes to Belford, for example: 'we begin when boys, with birds, and when grown up, go on with women; and both, perhaps, in turn, experience our sportive cruelty'. Then he gloats as he pictures 'the charming gradations' by which the bird yields to its captor as he hopes Clarissa will yield to him, and concludes, 'By my soul, Jack, there is more of the savage in human nature than we are commonly aware of'. But Jack is already aware of it, in Lovelace's case at least, and replies: 'Thou ever delightedst to sport with and torment the animal, whether bird or beast, that thou lovedst and hadst a power over'.

Sadism is, no doubt, the ultimate form which the eighteenth-century view of the masculine role involved: and it makes the female role one in which the woman is, and can only be, the prey: to use another of Lovelace's metaphors, man is a spider, and woman is the predestined fly.[1]

This conceptualisation of the sexual life has had an illustrious literary history since Richardson. Mario Praz has seen *Clarissa* as the beginning of what he calls 'the theme of the persecuted maiden', a theme which was taken up by de Sade, and played an important part in Romantic literature.[2] Later, in a somewhat milder form, this picture of the sexual relationship established itself in England. The Victorian imagination was haunted by the perpetual imminence of attacks on pure womanhood by cruel and licentious males, while, in a Rochester or a Heathcliff, the feminine and Puritan imaginations of Charlotte and Emily Brontë produced a stereotype of the male as a combination of terrifying animality and diabolic intellect which is equally pathological.

[1] II, 253; IV, 269; II, 245-249, 483, 23.
[2] *The Romantic Agony*, trans. Davidson (London, 1951), pp. 95-107.

The complement of the sadistic and sexual male is the maso-chistic and asexual female; and in *Clarissa* this conception is present both in the imagery connected with the heroine and in the underlying implication of the central action. As regards imagery, Clarissa, significantly, is symbolised not by the rose but the lily: Lovelace sees her on one occasion as 'a half-broken-stalked lily, top-heavy with the overcharging dews of morning', and Clarissa later arranges that her funeral urn be decorated with 'the head of a white lily snapped short off, and just falling from the stalk'.[1] In the realm of action, the rape itself, when Clarissa is unconscious from opiates, may be re-garded as the ultimate development of the idea of the feminine sexual role as one of passive suffering: it suggests that the ani-mality of the male can only achieve its purpose when the woman's spirit is absent.

Even so, Clarissa dies; sexual intercourse, apparently, means death for the woman. What Richardson intended here is not wholly clear, but it may be noted that he had already shown a remarkable awareness of the symbolism of the unconscious in *Pamela*. When the heroine is still terrified of Mr. B. she imagines him pursuing her in the shape of a bull with bloodshot eyes; later, when a happy resolution is in sight she dreams, appropri-ately enough, of Jacob's ladder.[2] It is significant, therefore, that just before her elopement, Clarissa should have a dream in which Lovelace stabs her to the heart; then, she reports, he 'tumbled me into a deep grave ready dug, among two or three half-dissolved carcasses; throwing in the dirt and earth upon me with his hands, and trampling it down with his feet'.[3] The dream is primarily a macabre expression of her actual fear of Lovelace; but it is also coloured by the idea that sexual inter-course is a kind of annihilation.

This connection haunts the later part of the story. Though afraid of Lovelace, she goes off with him; and later, when his intentions are becoming more evident, she several times offers him knives or scissors to kill her with. One of these occasions is thus reported by Lovelace: 'baring, with a still more frantic violence, part of her enchanting neck, Here, here, said the soul-harrowing beauty, let thy pointed mercy enter'. Unconsciously, no doubt, Clarissa courts sexual violation as well as death; and when the violation comes its equation with death is apparent to

[1] III, 193; IV, 257.   [2] *Pamela*, I, 135, 274.   [3] I, 433.

both parties. Lovelace announces, 'The affair is over. Clarissa lives'—as though the contrary might have been expected; while later Clarissa directs that if Lovelace insists 'upon viewing *her dead* whom he ONCE before saw in a manner dead, let his gay curiosity be gratified'.[1]

In a sense the coming death to which Clarissa here refers is a working out of her own initial masochistic fantasy: having equated sex and death, and having been violated by Lovelace, her self-respect requires that the expected consequence ensue: her decline is as the physician says, clearly not a bodily matter but 'a love case'.[2] Not much is said about the covert and implacable cause why her fate cannot be otherwise, but there is never any doubt about the fact itself: anything else would prove her deepest self to have been wrong.

This, of course, is not the only cause of her death, which has a very complex motivation. It is, for example, quite consistent with Richardson's beliefs that Clarissa should prefer death to the burden of her sexual desecration, even though it is, as Lovelace says, 'a mere *notional violation*'.[3] But there is also more than a hint that what Clarissa cannot face is not so much what Lovelace has done or what the world may think about it, but the idea that she herself is not wholly blameless.

This idea is most clearly expressed in one of the fragments which she writes in her delirium after the rape:

> A lady took a great fancy to a young lion, or a bear, I forget which—but of a bear, or a tiger, I believe it was. It was made her a present of when a whelp. She fed it with her own hand: she nursed up the wicked cub with great tenderness; and would play with it without fear or apprehension of danger . . . But mind what followed: at last, somehow, neglecting to satisfy its hungry maw, or having otherwise disobliged it on some occasion, it resumed its nature; and on a sudden fell upon her, and tore her in pieces, And who was most to blame, I pray? The brute, or the lady? The lady, surely! For what *she* did was *out* of nature, *out* of character, at least: what it did was *in* its own nature.[4]

Lovelace, being a man, had done only what was to be expected: but Clarissa had acted out of nature in toying with him. Looking back, she perhaps remembers that Anna Howe, mocking her own claim that 'she would not be in love with him

[1] III, 238, 196; IV, 416.   [2] II, 468.   [3] III, 242.   [4] III, 206.

233

for the world', had ironically congratulated her on 'being the first of our sex that ever I heard of who has been able to turn that lion, Love, at her own pleasure, into a lap-dog'. And this bitter reminder that she was wrong may have caused her to look within and glimpse the truth that even she was not above what Lovelace calls the 'disgraceful' weaknesses 'of sex and nature'.[1] With such a belief poisoning her mind, the need to be delivered from the body becomes imperative; she must act out in a very literal fashion the words of St. Paul in *Romans*: 'I delight in the law of God after the inward man. But I see another law in my members, warring against the law of my mind . . . O wretched man that I am! Who shall deliver me from the body of this death?'

In a historical perspective, it seems clear, Clarissa's tragedy reflects the combined effects of Puritanism's spiritual inwardness and its fear of the flesh, effects which tend to prevent the development of the sexual impulse beyond the autistic and masochistic stages. Freud and Horace are agreed that *Naturam expellas furca, tamen usque recurret*—a sentiment, incidentally, which was familiar to Richardson since Lovelace quotes it—and it is not surprising, therefore, that Clarissa's *Liebestod* should suggest that the erotic impulse has been channelled in varied and divergent directions. The perverse sensuous pleasure which she takes in every detail of the preparations for her coming death is primarily due to the feeling that she is at least about to meet the heavenly bridegroom: 'I am upon a *better preparation* than for an earthly husband', she proclaims. 'Never bride was so ready as I am. My wedding garments are bought . . . the easiest, the *happiest* suit, that ever bridal maiden wore.' But her pleasure in her own approaching demise also has a strong narcissistic quality. Belford reports that 'the principal device' she chose for her coffin 'is a crowned serpent, with its tail in its mouth, forming a ring, the emblem of eternity': emblem of eternity, doubtless, but also emblem of an endlessly self-consuming sexual desire.[2]

Opinions may well vary over the details of the meaning of the psychopathological aspects of *Clarissa*, but there can at least be no doubt that this was one of the directions which Richardson's imagination took, and that he there demonstrated a

[1] I, 49; III, 476; see also II, 420.   [2] II, 99; IV, 2, 303, 256-257.

remarkable insight into the by now notorious sophistries of the unconscious and subconscious mind. Further evidence of this is to be found in the scenes after the rape, and in Clarissa's incoherent letter to Lovelace: Fielding praised it as 'beyond anything I have ever read'.[1] Another great contemporary admirer, Diderot, specifically pointed to the exploration of the deeper recesses of the mind as Richardson's *forte*—a testimony which carries considerable authority in the light of his own treatment of the theme in *Le Neveu de Rameau*. It was Richardson, Diderot said, 'qui porte le flambeau au fond de la caverne; c'est lui qui apprend à discerner les motifs subtils et déshonnêtes qui se cachent et se dérobent sous d'autres motifs qui sont honnêtes et qui se hâtent de se montrer les premiers. Il souffle sur le phantôme sublime qui se présente à l'entrée de la caverne; et le More hideux qu'il masquait s'aperçoit.'[2] Such certainly is the nature of the voyage of discovery which we take in *Clarissa*; and the hideous Moor is surely the frightening reality of the unconscious life which lies hidden in the most virtuous heart.

Such an interpretation would imply that Richardson's imagination was not always in touch with his didactic purpose; but this, of course, is in itself not unlikely. The decorous exterior, the ponderous voice of the lay bishop, expresses an important part of Richardson's mind, but not all of it; and, his subjects being what they were, it is likely that only a very safe ethical surface, combined with the anonymity of print, and a certain tendency to self-righteous sophistry, were able to pacify his inner censor and thus leave his imagination free to express its profound interest in other areas of experience.

Some such process seems to have occurred in Richardson's portrayal of Lovelace as well as of Clarissa. There was probably a much deeper identification with his rake than he knew, an identification which left traces in such a remark as this of Lovelace: 'Were every rake, nay, were every man, to sit down, as I do, and write all that enters into his head or into his heart, and to accuse himself with equal freedom and truth, what an army of miscreants should I have to keep me in countenance!' Elsewhere, the prodigious fertility of Lovelace's sexual imagination surely suggests a willing co-operation on the part of his creator's far beyond the call of literary duty: Lovelace's plan, for instance, of wreaking his revenge on Anna Howe, not only by ravishing

[1] 'New Letter from Fielding', p. 305.   [2] *Œuvres*, ed. Billy, p. 1091.

235

her, but in having her mother abducted for the same fell purpose is a monstrously gratuitous fancy which is quite unnecessary so far as the realisation of Richardson's didactic intentions are concerned.[1]

The ultimate effect of Richardson's unconscious identification, however, would seem to be wholly justified from an aesthetic point of view. The danger in the original scheme of the novel was that Lovelace would be so brutal and callow that the relationship with Clarissa would be incapable of supporting a developing and reciprocal psychological pattern. Richardson, however, diminished the disparity between his protagonists by supplying their personalities with psychological undertones which do something to qualify the apparently diametrical opposition between them. He mitigated Clarissa's perfections by suggesting that her deeper self has its morbid aspects—a suggestion which actually increases the pathos of her story but which brings her closer in a sense to the world of Lovelace; and at the same time he led us to feel that, just as his heroine's virtue is not without its complications, so his villain's vices have their pitiable aspect.

Lovelace's name—in sound as in etymology—means 'loveless';[2] and his code—that of the rake—has, like Clarissa's, blinded him to his own deepest feelings. From the beginning one side of his character is continually struggling to express its love for Clarissa openly and honourably, and it often almost succeeds. Clarissa, indeed, is aware of this undercurrent in his nature: 'What *sensibilities*', she tells him, 'must thou have suppressed! What a dreadful, what a judicial hardness of heart must thine be; who canst be capable of such emotions as sometimes thou hast shown; and of such sentiments as sometimes have flown from thy lips; yet canst have so far overcome them all, as to be

---

[1] II, 492, 418-425.

[2] See Ernest Weekley, *Surnames* (London, 1936), p. 259. Names are often a guide to unconscious attitudes, and those of Richardson's protagonists tend to confirm the view that he secretly identified himself with his hero—Robert Lovelace is a pleasant enough name—and even unconsciously collaborated with Lovelace's purpose of abasing the heroine: 'Clarissa' is very close to 'Calista', Rowe's impure heroine; while Harlowe is very close to 'harlot'. This verbal association seems to be on the verge of consciousness in a letter of Arabella's to Clarissa: she tells her that James will treat her 'like a common creature, if he ever sees you', and then, referring to her doubts as to whether Lovelace will ever marry her, adds in a frenzy of contempt: '. . . this is the celebrated, the blazing Clarissa—Clarissa *what*? *Harlowe*, no doubt!—And Harlowe it will be, to the disgrace of us all.' (II, 170-171.)

able to act as thou hast acted, and that from settled purpose and premeditation.'[1]

This division in Lovelace between conscious villainy and stifled goodness provides yet another satisfying formal symmetry to the conduct of the narrative. For, just as Clarissa began by loving Lovelace unconsciously and then was forced to see that, in truth, he did not deserve it, so Lovelace begins with a feeling in which hate and love are mixed, but comes eventually to love her completely, although only after he himself has made it impossible for her to reciprocate. Clarissa could perhaps have married Lovelace, very much on her own terms, had she known her own feelings earlier, and not been at first so wholly unaware, and later so frightened, of her sexual component; so Lovelace need not have lost Clarissa, if he had known and been willing to recognise the gentler elements in his personality.

The ultimate reason why this was impossible is, indeed, the exact complement of that which causes Clarissa's virtual suicide: both their fates show the havoc brought about by two codes which doom their holders to a psychological attitude which makes human love impossible, since they set an impenetrable barrier between the flesh and the spirit. Clarissa dies rather than recognise the flesh; Lovelace makes it impossible for her to love him because he, too, makes an equally absolute, though opposite, division: if he wishes 'to prove her to be either angel or woman', Clarissa has no alternative but to make the choice she does, reject her physical womanhood, and prove, in Lovelace's words, that 'her frost is frost indeed'. At the same time for him also the only possibility of salvation lies in the rejection of his own illusion of himself which, like Clarissa's, is ultimately a projection of false sexual ideology. 'If I give up my contrivances', he writes in a moment of heart-searching, 'I shall be but a common man.' But, of course, he is, like Clarissa, so deeply attached to his own preconceptions of himself that he cannot change; the deadlock is complete, and, as he confesses, 'what to do with her, or without her, I know not'.[2]

For Lovelace also, therefore, death is the only way out. His end, it is true, is not a suicide, but it is like Clarissa's in the sense that he has in part provoked it, and that he has been forewarned in a dream, a dream where, thinking at last to embrace her, he sees the firmament open to receive her and then, left

[1] III, 152.   [2] II, 208; III, 190, 229.

alone, the floor sinks under him and he falls into a bottomless Inferno. His unconscious premonition is confirmed by the event, but not before he has made expiation, admitting to his slayer Colonel Morden that he has provoked his destiny, and imploring Clarissa's Blessed Spirit to look down with pity and forgiveness.[1]

So ends a relationship that, in this at least like those of the great lovers of myth and legend, endures beyond death. Clarissa and Lovelace are as completely, and as fatally, dependent on each other as Tristan and Isolde or Romeo and Juliet; but, in keeping with the novel's subjective mode of vision, the ultimate barriers that prevent the union of Richardson's star-crossed lovers are subjective and in part unconscious; the stars operate on the individual through varied psychological forces, forces which are eventually, no doubt, public and social, since the differences between the protagonists represent larger conflicts of attitude and ethic in their society, but which are nevertheless so completely internalised that the conflict expresses itself as a struggle between personalities and even between different parts of the same personality.

This is Richardson's triumph. Even the most apparently implausible, didactic or period aspects of the plot and the characters, even the rape and Clarissa's unconscionable time a-dying, are brought into a larger dramatic pattern of infinite formal and psychological complexity. It is this capacity for a continuous enrichment and complication of a simple situation which makes Richardson the great novelist he is; and it shows, too, that the novel had at last attained literary maturity, with formal resources capable not only of supporting the tremendous imaginative expansion which Richardson gave his theme, but also of leading him away from the flat didacticism of his critical preconceptions into so profound a penetration of his characters that their experience partakes of the terrifying ambiguity of human life itself.

[1] IV, 136, 529.

CHAPTER VIII

Fielding and the Epic Theory
of the Novel

SINCE it was *Pamela* that supplied the initial impetus for the writing of *Joseph Andrews*, Fielding cannot be considered as having made quite so direct a contribution as Richardson to the rise of the novel, and he is therefore given somewhat less extensive treatment here. His works in any case raise very different problems, since their distinguishing elements have their roots not so much in social change as in the neo-classical literary tradition. This in itself may be regarded as presenting something of a challenge to the basic argument of the present study: if the main features of *Tom Jones*, for example, were in fact the result of an independent and autonomous development within the Augustan world of letters, and if these features later became typical of the novel in general, it is evident that the crucial importance attributed above to the role of social change in bringing about the rise of the new form could hardly be sustained.

Fielding's celebrated formula of 'the comic epic in prose' undoubtedly lends some authority to the view that, far from being the unique literary expression of modern society, the novel is essentially a continuation of a very old and honoured narrative tradition. This view is certainly widely enough held, albeit in a rather general and unformulated way, to deserve consideration. It is evident that since the epic was the first example of a narrative form on a large scale and of a serious kind, it is reasonable that it should give its name to the general category which contains all such works: and in this sense of the term the novel may be said to be of the epic kind. One can perhaps go further, and, like Hegel, regard the novel as a manifestation of the spirit of epic under the impact of a modern and prosaic concept of reality.[1] Nevertheless, it is surely evident that the actual similarities are of such a theoretical and abstract nature that one cannot make much of them without neglecting most of the specific

[1] See *The Philosophy of Fine Art*, trans. Osmaston (London, 1920), IV, 171.

literary characteristics of the two forms: the epic is, after all, an oral and poetic genre dealing with the public and usually re-markable deeds of historical or legendary persons engaged in a collective rather than an individual enterprise; and none of these things can be said of the novel.

They certainly cannot be said of the novels of Defoe or Richardson; and as it so happens that their occasional remarks about the epic do something to illuminate the social and literary differences between the two genres, their views on the subject will be briefly considered before Fielding's conception of the epic analogy, and the nature of its contribution to his novels are investigated.

I

Apart from one rather conventional contrast between 'the immortal Virgil's . . . accurate judgement' and Homer's 'more fertile and copious invention and fancy',[1] Defoe's general attitude to epic was one of casual depreciation: 'It is easy to tell you the Consequences of Popular Confusions, Private Quarrels, and Party Feuds, without Reading *Virgil, Horace,* or *Homer*', he writes in *The Review* (1705),[2] and in a 1711 pamphlet, *The Felonious Treaty,* he tells us that the siege of Troy was all for 'the Rescue of a Whore'.[3] This view of Helen was not uncom-mon: but the terseness of Defoe's reduction of the whole matter to a simple moral judgement reminds us how the primacy of ethical considerations in the literary outlook of the middle class was likely to undermine much of the prestige of classical litera-ture. Defoe's condemnation of the 'long ago exploded . . . Latin bawdy authors Tibullus, Propertius and others',[4] and his lament that there was 'not a Moralist among the *Greeks* but *Plutarch*',[5] may serve as further confirmations of this tendency.

If Defoe did not approve of Homer as a moralist he was even more explicit in condemning him as a historian. Defoe's interest in literature was almost exclusively dictated by his voracious appetite for facts, and Homer's value as a repository of fact obviously had serious limitations, as did oral tradition in general. This theme occurs as early as the preface to *The Storm* in 1704,

---

[1] *The Life of Mr. Duncan Campbell* (Oxford, 1841), p. 86.
[2] No. 39 (1705).   [3] P. 17.
[4] *Mist's Journal,* April 5, 1719, *cit.* William Lee, *Daniel Defoe* (London, 1869), II, 31.   [5] *Essay upon Literature* (1726), p. 118.

and is very fully developed in Defoe's *Essay upon Literature*, published in 1726.

By literature Defoe means writing. His general thesis is that the art of writing was a divine gift given by Moses which enabled man to escape from 'that most corrupting, multiplying Usage of Tradition', that is, the primitive, 'oral History of Men and Things', which in fact always tended to turn history into 'Fable and Romance', 'Scoundrels' into 'Heroes', and 'Heroes' into 'Gods'. Homer was a very notable offender in this respect. His works are irreplaceable historical documents: we should know nothing of 'the Siege of Troy, were it unsung by Homer'; and yet, unfortunately, 'even now we scarce know whether it is a History, or that Ballad-Singer's Fable to get a Penny'.[1]

This last phrase echoes Defoe's most extended reference to Homer, which occurs in the course of a very amusing intervention in the controversy which arose over Pope's unacknowledged collaboration with Broome and Fenton on his translation of the *Odyssey*. Writing in *Applebee's Journal*, where indiscriminate impudence was at a premium, Defoe argues that it is ridiculous to single out Pope for attack, since all writers, from Homer down, have been plagiarists:

> . . . a Merry Fellow of my Acquaintance assures me, that our cousin *Homer* himself was guilty of the same *Plagiarism*. Cousin *Homer* you must note was an old blind Ballad Singer at *Athens*, and went about the country there, and at other Places in Greece, singing his Ballads from Door to Door; only with this difference, that the Ballads he sung were generally of his own making. . . . But, says my Friend, this *Homer*, in Process of Time, when he had gotten some Fame,—and perhaps more Money than Poets ought to be trusted with, grew Lazy and Knavish, and got one *Andronicus* a Spartan, and one Dr. S——l, a Philosopher of *Athens*, both pretty good Poets, but less eminent than himself, to make his songs for him; which, they being poor and starving, did for him for a small Matter. And so, the *Poet* never did much himself, only published and sold his Ballads still, in his own Name, as if they had been his own; and by that, got great Subscriptions, and a high Price for them.[2]

Defoe had close precedents for this picture of Homer—d'Aubignac and Perrault in France, and more recently Bentley

---

[1] Pp. 115, 17, 115, 117.
[2] July 31, 1725; Defoe's two letters on the topic are reprinted in Lee (III, 410-414).

and Henry Felton in England, had seen the Homeric poems as collections of the songs of a strolling bard;[1] but the account of Homer as a plagiary and a successful literary entrepreneur seems to have been invented to suit the argument of the moment. Defoe's strategy—to reduce all literary matters to their commercial equivalent—is perfectly calculated not only to undermine the prestige of epic and the classical premises of Augustan culture, but also to reduce the great ones of literature to the same low Grub Street level to which they had contemptuously relegated him.

Defoe had yet another important objection to Homer—the fact that he shared the pagan credulity of his age. One of his conclusions in *A System of Magic* (1727) is that 'the Greeks were the most superstitious of all the Devil-worshippers in the World, worse than the Persians and Chaldeans', and that their religious literature was vitiated by the 'infernal juggles' of the devil who continually 'chops in' with 'a horrid Rhapsody of complicated Idolatry'.[2] In another work, *The History and Reality of Apparitions* (1727), Defoe examines the statements of Homer and Virgil on apparitions, and concludes scornfully: 'What learned Nonsense, and what a great deal of it is here, to reconcile a thing, which, upon the Christian foundation, is made as easy as anything not immediately visible to the common eye can be made!'[3]

This note of hardly concealed impatience at the irrational and immoral idolatry of the ancients is a suitable one on which to leave Defoe. Homer could have been a most valuable source of historical evidence. But—partly because of his own inveterate ballad-mongering, and partly because of the obdurate superstitiousness of the Greek civilization—he sang 'the Wars of the Greeks . . . from a Reality, into a meer Fiction . . .'[4] If only Troy had had a really good journalist!

II

One would not expect from Richardson's cautious temperament the defiant assertion of personal opinion that came so naturally to Defoe; but, with two minor exceptions,[5] a

[1] See Donald M. Foerster, *Homer in English Criticism* (New Haven, 1947), pp. 17-23, 28.
[2] Oxford, 1840, pp. 226, 191, 193.   [3] Oxford, 1840, pp. 171-174.
[4] P. 22.   [5] See Postscript, *Clarissa*, and *Grandison*, I, 284.

similar hostility to the epic can be discerned in his novels and letters.

Richardson's main antipathy to the heroic genre was, as we should expect, based on the manners and morals which it exhibited. His most outspoken attack occurs in a letter to Lady Bradshaigh, who had apparently initiated a correspondence with him on the dire consequences of epic poetry:

> I admire you for what you say of the fierce, fighting Iliad. Scholars, judicious scholars, dared they to speak out, against a prejudice of thousands of years in its favour, I am persuaded would find it possible for Homer to nod, at least. I am afraid this poem, noble as it truly is, has done infinite mischief for a series of ages; since to it, and its copy the Eneid; is owing, in a great measure, the savage spirit that has actuated, from the earliest ages to this time, the fighting fellows, that, worse than lions or tigers, have ravaged the earth, and made it a field of blood.[1]

The ideas in the attack are not original. Pope had written that 'the most shocking' thing in Homer was 'that spirit of cruelty which appears too manifestly in the *Iliad*'.[2] And it is obvious that since, in epic, warfare is 'an essential rather than an accessory',[3] its moral world stands for values which are alien and unwelcome to the members of a peace-loving society. Richardson, however, goes a good deal further, and his talk of the 'infinite mischief' done by the *Aeneid* is substantially new, and anticipates Blake's more general accusation that '. . . it is the Classics . . . that Desolate Europe with Wars'.[4]

The dangerous sanction which the prestige of epic afforded vicious models of individual behaviour was an abiding preoccupation with Richardson. In *Grandison* Lady Charlotte repeats his views as given to Lady Bradshaigh almost verbatim, but finishes by broadening the charge:

> . . . men and women are cheats to one another. But we may, in a great measure, thank the poetical tribe for the fascination. I hate them all. Are they not inflamers of the worst passions? With regard to *epics*, would Alexander, madman as he was, have been

[1] *Correspondence*, IV, 287; the letter is undated but was probably written in 1749.
[2] Note, *Iliad*, IV, 75, cited by Foerster, *Homer*, p. 16.
[3] H. M. and N. K. Chadwick, *The Growth of Literature* (Cambridge, 1936), II, 488.
[4] In 'On Homer's Poetry' (*c.* 1820); *Poetry and Prose*, ed. Keynes (London, 1946), p. 583.

so *much* a madman, had it not been for Homer? Of what violences, murders, depredations, have not the epic poets been the occasion, by propagating false honours, false glory, and false religion?[1]

The epic's false code of honour, like that of heroic tragedy, was masculine, bellicose, aristocratic and pagan: it was therefore wholly unacceptable to Richardson, whose novels are largely devoted to attacking this ideology, and replacing it by a radically different one in which honour is internal, spiritual, and available without distinction of class or sex to all who had the will to act morally.

Richardson's fullest demonstration of the new type of heroism was *Sir Charles Grandison*, the result, he stated in his Preface, of the insistence of his friends that he 'produce into public view the character and actions of a man of TRUE HONOUR': and it makes much of the crucial social issue on which the new and the old codes of honour differ—the question of duelling. Although Grandison is an admirable swordsman, he is so determined an opponent of this barbarism that he even refuses a challenge. In the 'Concluding Note' Richardson defended this course of action very strongly. He reiterated Harriet Byron's opposition to the old code—'Murderous, vile word *honour*! . . . the very opposite to duty, goodness, piety, religion . . .';[2] pointed out that the 'notion of honour is evidently an absurd and mischievous one'; and insisted that challenges to a duel are nothing less than 'polite *invitations to murder*' which every man of Christian principles should refuse, since 'true bravery is to adhere to all duties under disadvantages'.

There is much else in *Grandison*, as well as in *Pamela* and *Clarissa*, to support the view that Richardson's novels are the climax of a long-standing movement in Christian and middle-class apologetics against the glamour of the pagan and warrior virtues. Steele had wondered 'why the Heathen struts, and the Christian sneaks in our imagination?'[3] Defoe had suggested as a solution that the real test of courage was 'to dare to be good'.[4] Richardson gave models of this daring: but the conflict between the active and extroverted ideals of the Homeric world and his own way of life is perhaps even more clearly shown in his

---

[1] VI, 315.   [2] *Grandison*, I, 304; see also *Clarissa*, IV, 461-463.
[3] *The Christian Hero*, ed. Blanchard (London, 1932), p. 15.
[4] *Applebee's Journal*, August 29, 1724, cited from Lee, III, 299-300.

sedentary and suburban reflection to Miss Highmore that 'In such a world as this, and with a feeling heart, content is heroism!'[1]

Richardson's distaste for the heroic virtues would alone, perhaps, have been enough to lead him to reject the epic as a literary model; but, of course, the rejection was very likely on many other grounds.

In the early half of the eighteenth century there was an increasing awareness of the great and numerous disparities between the Homeric and the contemporary world. This tendency was most notably expressed by Thomas Blackwell, whose *Enquiry into the Life and Writings of Homer* (1735) gave a more detailed answer than ever before to the much-debated question of why no later poet had been able to achieve the greatness of an *Iliad* or an *Odyssey*. Blackwell's main thesis was that Homer had received unique poetic advantages from his social environment, advantages which could not be duplicated in eighteenth-century England; living in a period of transition between complete barbarism and the sloth of settled commercial civilisation, Homer had rejoiced in a naturally heroic culture when 'living by Plunder gave a Reputation for Spirit and Bravery'. Nor was Homer's audience composed of 'the Inhabitants of a *great luxurious City*', but of simpler and more martial folk who wanted to listen to tales of 'the Prowess of their Ancestors'.[2]

Three of the applications which Blackwell makes of this contrast are very relevant to the differences between the epic and the novel in general, and to the conditions underlying Richardson's literary innovations in particular. Homer's poems, Blackwell writes, were 'made to be *recited*, or sung to a *Company*; and not read in private, or perused in a Book'. Secondly, 'the *natural Greek* . . . covered none of his Sentiments' and for this reason Blackwell prefers them to his contemporaries 'with more refined but *double* characters'. Lastly, since epic portrays '*more natural* Manners', it follows not only that the contemporary writer must '*unlearn* [his] daily way of life' if he is to 'poetize in the higher strains', but that the reader of epic must project himself into persons and situations that he is likely to find both unusual and unpleasant. So Blackwell, with all his enthusiasm for Homer, cannot but conclude that although his patron 'may

---

[1] *Correspondence*, II, 252 (July 20, 1750).   [2] 2nd ed., 1736, pp. 16, 123.

regret the Silence of the Muses, yet I am persuaded your Lordship will join in the Wish, *That we may never be the proper Subject of an* Heroic Poem'.[1]

Blackwell's views go far to explain the unpopularity of the epic with the reading public of his day, and the popularity of the novel. That the epic was unpopular can be surmised, for example, from Richardson's suggestion to Aaron Hill in 1744 that when he published his *Gideon, An Epic Poem*, he should not 'call it epic in the title page, since hundreds who see the title, will not, at the same time, have seen your admirable definition of the word'.[2] This unpopularity must have been connected with the fact that reading epic meant a continuous effort to exclude the normal expectations of everyday contemporary life —the very expectations which the novel exploited. Addison had already said in the *Spectator* that when reading Homer it was difficult not to feel that 'you were reading the History of another Species':[3] while Voltaire, in his early *Essay on Epic Poetry* (1727), had specifically contrasted the very different ways that the *Iliad* and Madame de La Fayette's *Zaïde* were read by his contemporaries: 'it is very strange, yet true, that among the most learned, and the greatest Admirers of Antiquity, there is scarce one to be found, who ever read the *Iliad*, with that Eagerness and Rapture, which a Woman feels when she reads the Novel of Zaïda'.[4]

Not only must the feminine devotees of *Zaïde*—and *Pamela*—have found it difficult to identify themselves with Homer's characters; they must also have been shocked by his treatment of their sex. Greek men, Blackwell tells us, were not ashamed of 'their natural appetites';[5] and, as James Macpherson was later to say, 'Homer, of all ancient poets, uses the sex with least ceremony'.[6] This scandalous indelicacy supplies a further reason for Richardson's antipathy—it is noticeable that his attacks on the epic were stimulated by a feminine correspondent, and expressed mainly through his female characters. In *Sir Charles Grandison*, for instance, Harriet Byron is a strong supporter of the claims of Christian epic and of Milton, as against Homer, and she cites Addison's papers in the *Spectator*, as well

[1] Pp. 122, 340, 24, 25, 28.   [2] *Correspondence*, I, 122.   [3] No. 209.
[4] Florence D. White, *Voltaire's Essay on Epic Poetry: A Study and an Edition* (Albany, 1915), p. 90.   [5] Enquiry, p. 340.
[6] *Temora, an Ancient Epic Poem* (1763), p. 206, n.; cited by Foerster, *Homer*, p. 57.

as 'the admirable Mr. Deane', to support her position; on the other hand, Homer gets the most damaging kind of support—the praise of pedantic males like Mr. Walden, or of forward and masculine disgraces to the female sex such as Miss Barnevelt, of whom Miss Byron reports to Miss Selby, in tones that echo Richardson's own ejaculatory horror to Lady Bradshaigh, that 'Achilles, the savage Achilles, charmed her'.[1] Even more damning, perhaps, is the fact that in *Clarissa* the infamous Lovelace is tarred with the epic feather. He justifies his treatment of Clarissa by Virgilian precedent, asking Belford whether he is not 'as much entitled to forgiveness on Miss Harlowe's account, as Virgil was on Queen Dido's?'; and is even impudent enough to argue that since he does not have 'half the obligation to her that Aeneas had to the Queen of Carthage', there is no reason why it should not be 'the *pious* Lovelace, as well as the *pious* Aeneas'.[2]

A late eighteenth-century essayist, Martin Sherlock, expressed a fairly widely held view when he wrote that Richardson's 'misfortune was that he did not know the Ancients'.[3] The opposite is much more likely to be the case, at least as far as his literary originality is concerned, and it is significant that in his later years Richardson became an ardent supporter of the Moderns against the Ancients. This is made clear by the part he played in the composition of Edward Young's *Conjectures on Original Composition in a Letter to the Author of Sir Charles Grandison* (1759), where, as A. D. McKillop has shown,[4] he was responsible for a general sharpening of Young's polemic in the direction of a new anti-classical hierarchy of literary values. One celebrated passage of the *Conjectures* which was actually written by Richardson suggests that he was also aware of having a personal stake in the controversy:

> After all, the first ancients had no merit in being originals: they could not be imitators. Modern writers have a choice to make; and therefore have a merit in their power. They may soar in the regions of liberty, or move in the soft fetters of easy imitation; and imitation has as many plausible reasons to urge, as pleasure had

---

[1] *Grandison*, I, 67-86. [2] *Clarissa*, IV, 30-31; see also II, 424; IV, 451.
[3] In *Lettres d'un voyageur anglais* (1779), trans. Duncombe, *cit.* John Nichols, *Literary Anecdotes of the Eighteenth Century* (1812), IV, 585.
[4] 'Richardson, Young, and the *Conjectures*', *MP*, XXII (1925), 393-399.

to offer Hercules. Hercules made the choice of an hero, and so became immortal.[1]

Richardson's ulterior purpose is transparent. He had been an original, not willy-nilly, like Homer, but by a deliberate rejection of previous models. The new literary Hercules was, of course, being brave after the event, since we have no evidence of his serious concern with classical models until after the completion of *Clarissa*. But we must accede to part of Richardson's plea: the originality which secured his immortality was connected, whether by accident or design, with his neglect of established literary models in favour of his own vivid awareness of life, and the unconventional but peculiarly appropriate methods which enabled him to express it directly and naturally.

III

Unlike Defoe and Richardson, Fielding was steeped in the classical tradition, and though he was by no means a slavish supporter of the Rules, he felt strongly that the growing anarchy of literary taste called for drastic measures. In the *Covent Garden Journal*, for example, he proposed that 'No author is to be admitted into the Order of Critics, until he hath read over, and understood, Aristotle, Horace, and Longinus, in their original Language'.[2] Similar qualifications, he felt, were particularly necessary to preserve the new realm of fiction against what George Eliot once eloquently described as 'the intrusions of mere left-handed imbecility'; 'a good share of learning', he suggested in *Tom Jones*, was an essential prerequisite for those who wished to write 'such histories as these',[3] and such learning was undoubtedly intended to include a knowledge of Latin and Greek.

It is therefore wholly in keeping with his general outlook that in *Joseph Andrews* (1742), his first work in the novel genre, Fielding should have been at pains to justify his enterprise both to himself and to his literary peers by bringing it into line with the classical critical tradition. Nor could there be much doubt as to what direction such a justification should take. Many previous writers and critics of fiction, notably of the seventeenth-century French romances, had assumed that any imitation of

[1] Young, *Works* (1773), V, 94.   [2] No. 3 (1752).   [3] Bk. IX, ch. 1.

human life in narrative form ought to be assimilated as far as possible to the rules that had been laid down for the epic by Aristotle and his innumerable interpreters; and Fielding— apparently quite independently—started from the same point of view.[1]

He began his Preface by suggesting, somewhat patronisingly perhaps, that 'As it is possible the mere English reader may have a different idea of romance from the author of these little volumes . . . it may not be improper to premise a few words concerning this kind of writing, which I do not remember to have seen hitherto attempted in our language'. He then continued:

> The Epic, as well as the Drama, is divided into tragedy and comedy. Homer, who was the father of this species of poetry, gave us a pattern of both these, though that of the latter kind is entirely lost; which Aristotle tells us, bore the same relation to comedy which his *Iliad* bears to tragedy. . . .
>
> And farther, as this poetry may be tragic or comic, I will not scruple to say it may be likewise either in verse or prose; for though it wants one particular, which the critic enumerates in the constituent parts of an epic poem, namely metre; yet, when any kind of writing contains all its other parts, such as fable, action, characters, sentiments, and diction, and is deficient in metre only; it seems, I think, reasonable to refer it to the epic; at least as no critic hath thought proper to range it under any other head, or to assign it a particular name to itself.

Fielding's argument here for 'referring' his novel to the epic genre is unimpressive: *Joseph Andrews*, no doubt, has five out of the six parts under which Aristotle considered epic; but then it is surely impossible to conceive of any narrative whatever which does not in some way contain 'fable, action, characters, sentiments, and diction'.

The possession of these five elements certainly does nothing to elucidate the distinction which Fielding goes on to make between the prose epic and French romances:

> Thus the *Telemachus* of the archbishop of Cambray appears to me of the epic kind, as well as the *Odyssey* of Homer; indeed, it is much fairer and more reasonable to give it a name common with that species from which it differs only in a single instance,

---

[1] See René Bray, *La Formation de la doctrine classique en France* (Paris, 1927), pp. 347-349; Arthur L. Cooke, 'Henry Fielding and the Writers of Heroic Romance', *PMLA*, LXII (1947), 984-994.

than to confound it with those which it resembles in no other. Such are those voluminous works, commonly called Romances, namely *Clelia*, *Cleopatra*, *Astrae*, *Cassandra*, the *Grand Cyrus*, and innumerable others, which contain, as I apprehend, very little instruction or entertainment.

Fielding's distinction between Fénelon's *Télémaque* and the French heroic romances, it will be observed, is entirely based on the introduction of a new factor, 'instruction or entertainment', which is obviously a question of personal value judgements, and therefore very difficult to fit into any general analytic scheme. It is not surprising, therefore, that when Fielding goes on to distinguish his own 'comic epic in prose' from serious epic and its prose analogues he makes no use of this criterion either; instead he applies the Aristotelian distinction between the serious and the comic modes in a way that would actually put all the French romances in the same category as the *Odyssey* and *Télémaque*:

> Now a comic romance is a comic epic poem in prose; differing from comedy, as the serious epic from tragedy: its action being more extended and comprehensive; containing a much larger circle of incidents, and introducing a greater variety of characters. It differs from the serious romance in its fable and action, in this; that as in the one these are grave and solemn, so in the other they are light and ridiculous; it differs in its characters, by introducing persons of inferior . . . manners, whereas the grave romance sets the highest before us; lastly, in its sentiments and diction, by preserving the ludicrous instead of the sublime.

This completes Fielding's critical exposition of the epic analogy in the Preface to *Joseph Andrews*. It is obvious that the whole operative force of the argument depends on the term comic, and the remainder of the preface, comprising some five-sixths of the total, is engaged in developing his ideas of 'the ludicrous'. This, of course, is inevitably accompanied by the dropping of the epic analogy; for, since Homer's *Margites* was lost, and the comic epic received but a bare mention in the *Poetics*, Fielding's attempts to bring his novel into line with classical doctrine could not be supported either by existing literary parallel or theoretical precedent.

Before considering the practical effects of the epic analogy on the novels, it should perhaps be pointed out that what has been reproduced above constitutes almost everything that Fielding said about the comic epic in prose. *Joseph Andrews* was a hurriedly composed work of somewhat mixed intentions, begun as a parody of *Pamela* and continued in the spirit of Cervantes; and this perhaps suggests that not too much importance should be attached to its Preface, which does not really adumbrate a whole theory of fiction; it merely, as Fielding himself says, contains 'some few very short hints'. The formula of 'the comic epic poem in prose' is only such a hint; and although Fielding referred to it briefly in his preface to his sister Sarah's *David Simple* (1744), and subsequently called *Tom Jones* (1749) a 'heroic, historical, prosaic poem' and a specimen of 'prosai-comi-epic writing',[1] he did not develop or modify his early formula in his later writings; indeed, he paid very little further attention to it.

IV

Since it was a comic variant of epic that Fielding wished to produce he was debarred from imitating two at least of its component parts—characters and sentiments; heroic persons and sublime thoughts obviously had no place in *Joseph Andrews* or *Tom Jones*. Some aspects of epic plot could, however, be adapted to his purpose, and epic diction could be used in burlesque form.

Even as regards plot, it is true, the differences were bound to be more marked than the similarities: comic characters could hardly be allowed to perform heroic acts, and whereas epic plots were based on history or legend, Fielding had to invent his stories. The most that he could do, therefore, was to retain some other general features of the epic plot while altering the content. The best example of this is probably *Tom Jones*, whose action has epic quality at least in the sense that it presents a sweeping panorama of a whole society, as opposed to Richardson's

---

[1] Bk. IV, ch. 1; Bk. V, ch. 1. It is interesting, incidentally, to observe that these references occur early; after the first six books of *Tom Jones* Fielding changes over to a more completely dramatic method, as W. L. Cross points out (*History of Henry Fielding*, II, 179). Further evidence for believing that Fielding did not take the epic analogy seriously enough to explore the critical issues fully is afforded by the fact that he took no account either of Aristotle's mention of the form of literature which represented men 'as they are in real life' (*Poetics*, ch. 2), which would presumably be the category into which *Amelia* at least would fall, or of the contemporary controversy as to whether an 'epic in prose' was not a contradiction in terms (see H. T. Swedenberg, *The Theory of the Epic in England, 1650–1800* (Berkeley and Los Angeles, 1944), pp. 155, 158–159).

detailed picture of a very small social group.

But although the magnitude and variety of the structure of *Tom Jones* fit in very well with the chief connotation of the term 'epic' today, it is, after all, mainly a question of scale, and it cannot be held as evidence of any specific indebtedness on Fielding's part to an epic prototype. There are, however, at least two other more definite ways in which Fielding transposed characteristic features of the epic plot into a comic context: his use of surprise, and his introduction of mock-heroic battles.

It was generally agreed in neo-classical theory that the action of epic was characterised by two elements—verisimilitude and the marvellous: the ways in which these incongruous bedfellows could be happily mated had taxed all the ingenuity of the Renaissance critics, and their somewhat sophistic arguments had later been retailed by many of the French writers of romance. Fielding attacked the problem in the introductory chapter to the eighth book of *Tom Jones*. He began by excusing the incredible episodes in Homer on the grounds that he 'wrote to heathens, to whom poetical fables were articles of faith'; even so, Fielding could not refrain from wishing that Homer could have known and obeyed Horace's rule prescribing that supernatural agents be introduced 'as little as possible'. In any case, Fielding proceeded, writers of epic and genuine historians were able to introduce unlikely events much more plausibly than novelists, since they recorded 'public transactions' which were already known, whereas 'we who deal in private character . . . have no public notoriety, no concurrent testimony, no records to support and corroborate what we deliver'. He concluded that it 'becomes' the novelist 'to keep within the limits not only of possibility, but of probability too'.

Fielding, then, prescribed a greater emphasis on verisimilitude for the new genre than that current in epic or romance. He qualified this, however, by admitting that since 'the great art of poetry is to mix truth with fiction, in order to join the credible with the surprising', 'complaisance to the scepticism of the reader' should not be taken to a point at which the only characters or incidents permitted are 'trite, common, or vulgar; such as may happen in every street, or in every house, or which may be met with in the home articles of a newspaper'.

What Fielding actually means by 'the surprising' is made clear by the context: he is referring primarily to the series of coincidences whereby Tom Jones successively meets the beggar who has picked up Sophia's pocket-book, the Merry Andrew who has seen her pass along the road, and her actual guide for part of the route; more generally, to the way that hero and heroine continually cross each other's path on their journey to London without ever meeting. Fielding valued such devices because they made it possible to weave the whole narrative into a very neat and entertaining formal structure; but although such apposite juxtapositions of persons and events do not violate verisimilitude so obviously as the supernatural interventions that are common in Homer or Virgil, it is surely evident that they nevertheless tend to compromise the narrative's general air of literal authenticity by suggesting the manipulated sequences of literature rather than the ordinary processes of life. Thus even Fielding's relatively inconspicuous concessions to the doctrine of the marvellous tended to confirm, as far as the novel was concerned, the reality of the dilemma of the would-be writer of epic in modern times which Blackwell had stated in his *Enquiry*: 'The marvellous and wonderful is the nerve of the epic strain: but what marvellous things happen in a well ordered state? We can hardly be surprised.'[1]

Fielding's most obvious imitation of the epic model in the action of his novels—the mock-heroic battles—is also somewhat at variance both with the dictates of formal realism and with the life of his time. Either because the events themselves are inherently improbable—as is the case, for instance, with the fight between Joseph Andrews and the pack of hounds that is pursuing Parson Adams[2]—or because they are narrated in such a way as to deflect our attention from the events themselves to the way that Fielding is handling them and to epic parallels involved. This is actually the case in the episode from *Joseph Andrews*, and it is even more obviously so in Moll Seagrim's celebrated churchyard battle in *Tom Jones*.[3] The spectacle of a village mob assaulting a pregnant girl after church service is in itself anything but amusing, and only Fielding's burlesque manner, his 'Homerican style', enables him to maintain the comic note. It is certain that this and some other episodes would be quite unacceptable if Fielding directed our attention wholly to the actions and feelings of the participants; and, even so, it may be

[1] P. 26.   [2] *Joseph Andrews*, Bk. III, ch. 6.
[3] *Tom Jones*, Bk. V, ch. 8.

doubted whether the Moll Seagrim scene, at least, coming from so humane a man as Fielding, does not give some colour to Richardson's objections to the bellicose influence of epic.

Fielding's Homerican style itself suggests a somewhat ambiguous attitude to the epic model: were it not for the Preface we would surely be justified in taking *Joseph Andrews* as a parody of epic procedures rather than as the work of a writer who planned to use them as a basis for the new genre: and even if we take account of the Preface, Fielding's novel surely reflects the ambiguous attitude of his age, an age whose characteristic literary emphasis on the mock-heroic reveals how far it was from the epic world it so much admired.

The reasons for this ambivalence, indeed, are evident in the Preface to *Joseph Andrews*, where Fielding by implication admits that the direct imitation of the epic was in opposition to the imitation of 'nature' when he states that although he has allowed 'parodies or burlesque imitations' in his diction, chiefly for the 'entertainment' of 'the classical reader', he has 'carefully excluded' them from his sentiments and characters because it is his major intention to confine himself 'strictly to nature, from the just imitation of which will flow all the pleasure we can . . . convey to the sensible reader'. The difficulty with such a dual attitude, of course, is that, as a good Aristotelian like Fielding must have known, no single component of a literary work can in fact be treated as an independent entity. He argues in *Tom Jones*, for example, that without 'sundry similes, descriptions, and other kind of poetical embellishments the best narrative of plain matter of fact must overpower every reader'; but when he goes on to inform us that the introduction of the heroine requires 'the utmost solemnity in our power, with an elevation of style, and all other circumstance proper to raise the veneration of our reader',[1] and follows this with a chapter entitled 'A Short Hint of what we can do in the Sublime, and a Description of Miss Sophia Western', which begins: 'Hushed be every ruder breath. May the heathen ruler of the winds confine in iron chains the boisterous limbs of noisy Boreas'—it is surely evident that Fielding has achieved his 'poetical embellishment' at a very considerable price: Sophia never wholly recovers from so artificial an introduction, or at least never

[1] Bk. IV, ch. 1.

wholly disengages herself from the ironical attitude which it has induced.

A similar diminution of the reader's belief in the authenticity of the character or the action occurs whenever the usual tenor of Fielding's narrative is interrupted by the stylistic devices of epic; this surely underlines the fact that the conventions of formal realism compose an inseparable whole, of which the linguistic one is an integral part; or, as one of his contemporaries, Lord Monboddo, put it, Fielding's abandonment of his 'simple and familiar' style impaired 'the probability of the narrative, which ought to be carefully studied in all . . . imitations of real life and manners'.[1]

V

Fielding's last novel, *Amelia* (1751), is wholly serious in moral purpose and narrative manner; and its allegiance to the epic model is of a very different kind. There is no reference to the formula of the comic epic in prose, and both mock-heroic incidents and epic diction have been abandoned; in their place, as Fielding announced in the *Covent Garden Journal*, Virgil's *Aeneid* 'was the noble model, which I have made use of on this occasion'.[2] Booth also is an unemployed soldier, the episode in Newgate with Miss Matthews refers to the loves of Aeneas and Dido in the cave, and there are some other slight parallels which have been outlined by George Sherburn.[3]

It will be noted that this kind of analogy involves no more than a kind of narrative metaphor which assists the imagination of the writer to find a pattern for his own observation of life without in any way detracting from the novel's appearance of literal veracity: nor does the reader need to know about the analogy to appreciate *Amelia*, as he does with the burlesque passages in Fielding's earlier novels. For these reasons *Amelia* may be regarded as the work in which the influence of the epic on Fielding was most fruitful; and it is certainly here that he had his most illustrious successor. When T. S. Eliot, with that leap into hyperbole which seems mandatory whenever the relation of novel and epic is being mooted, writes that James Joyce's use of the epic parallel in *Ulysses* 'has the importance of

[1] *Of the Origin and Progress of Language* (Edinburgh, 1776), III, 296-298.
[2] No. 8 (1752).
[3] 'Fielding's *Amelia*: An Interpretation', *ELH*, III (1936), 3-4.

a scientific discovery',[1] and claims that 'no one else has built a novel upon such a foundation before', he is surely being distinctly unfair to Fielding's no doubt fragmentary application of a similar idea.

After *Amelia*, Fielding continued to move away from his earlier literary outlook. He came to see the insufficiency of his early views of affectation as the only source of the ridiculous, and therefore of comedy, and his increasingly serious moral outlook even made him find much to regret in two of his early comic favourites, Aristophanes and Rabelais.[2] At the same time his attitude towards epic changed, a change whose climax comes in the Preface to *The Journal of a Voyage to Lisbon*:

> But, in reality, the *Odyssey*, the *Telemachus*, and all of that kind, are to the voyage-writing I here intend, what romance is to true history, the former being the confounder and corrupter of the latter. I am far from supposing that Homer, Hesiod, and the other ancient poets and mythologists, had any settled design to pervert and confuse the records of antiquity; but it is certain that they have effected it; and for my part I must confess that I should have honoured and loved Homer more had he written a true history of his own times in humble prose, than those noble poems that have so justly collected the praise of all ages; for, though I read these with more admiration and astonishment, I still read Herodotus, Thucydides, and Xenophon with more amusement and more satisfaction.

The statement must be taken in its context. The *Odyssey* is obviously an unsatisfactory model for an account of an eighteenth-century voyage to Lisbon. Still, to couple *Télémaque* and the *Odyssey* as romances, represents a total reversal of Fielding's position in *Joseph Andrews*. The contrast between both of them, on the one hand, and 'true history' on the other is also taken far beyond what was needed for a prefatory explanation of the type of writing which he was proposing to follow; and Fielding comes very close to Defoe's position when he speaks of the way that Homer and the other 'original poets' corrupted historical truth. The reason he gives for their doing so is an interesting one: 'they found the limits of nature too straight for the immensity of their genius, which they had not room to exert without

---

[1] '*Ulysses*, Order and Myth', *Dial*, 1923; quoted from *Forms of Modern Fiction*, ed. O'Connor (Minneapolis, 1948), p. 123.

[2] See *Covent Garden Journal*, Nos. 10 and 55 (1752).

extending fact by fiction: and that especially at a time when the manners of men were too simple to afford that variety which they have since offered in vain to the choice of the meanest writers'.

Fielding, then, eventually came to see his own society as offering sufficient interest and variety to make possible a literary genre exclusively devoted to engaging the reader in a closer scrutiny of 'nature' and of modern 'manners' than had ever been attempted before: and his own literary development was certainly in this direction. *Amelia* is, as has often been said, much closer to Richardson's close study of domestic life than his previous works; and although Fielding did not live long enough to embody his reorientation in another novel, there seems to be no doubt that he had become conscious of the fact that his earlier applications of the epic analogy had been responsible for his most obvious divergences from the role pr per to the faithful historian of the life of his time—a realisation, incidentally, which is implicit in his ironical defence of the epic diction in *Tom Jones* which was introduced, he explained, so that it 'might be in no danger of being likened to the labours of [modern] historians'.[1]

At the same time the extent of the influence of the epic analogy on Fielding's earlier novels must not be exaggerated. He called *Tom Jones* 'A History', and habitually described his role as that of historian or biographer whose function was to give a faithful presentation of the life of his time. Fielding's conception of this role, it is true, was different from that of Defoe or Richardson, but the difference is mainly connected, not with his attempt to imitate epic, but with the general influence of the neo-classical tradition on every aspect of his work. The most specific literary debt manifested in *Tom Jones*, indeed, is not to epic but to drama: not so much because his main critical source, Aristotle's *Poetics*, was primarily concerned with drama and gave epic a secondary place, as because Fielding had been a dramatist himself for over a decade before attempting fiction. The remarkable coherence of the plot of *Tom Jones* surely owes little to the actual example of Homer or Virgil, and little more to Aristotle's insistence that 'in the Epic as in Tragedy, the story should be constructed on dramatic principles';[2] it is very

[1] Bk. IV, ch. 1. On this see Robert M. Wallace, 'Fielding's Knowledge of History and Biography', *SP*, XLIV (1947), 89-107.   [2] *Poetics*, ch. 23.

palpably the product of Fielding's experience as a practising dramatist. It is also highly likely, incidentally, that some of the other features of his novels, such as the coincidences and discoveries which provide surprise at the cost of a certain loss of authenticity, are also a legacy from the drama rather than from the epic; and even the burlesque and mock-heroic elements had appeared long ago in many of his plays, such as *Tom Thumb, a Tragedy* (1730).

Why, then, it may be asked, has the formula of the comic epic in prose so 'obsessed critics of novels', to use George Sherburn's phrase?[1] It no doubt makes an immediate appeal to those who, like Peacock's Dr. Folliott, habitually manifest 'a safe and peculiar inaccessibility to ideas except such as are recommended by an almost artless simplicity or a classical origin';[2] and this perhaps gives a clue both to the reason why Fielding was led to invent the formula and to why it later flourished.

In 1742 the novel was a form in grave disrepute, and Fielding probably felt that to enlist the prestige of epic might help win for his first essay in the genre a less prejudiced hearing from the *literati* than might otherwise have been expected. In this Fielding was actually following the example of the French writers of romance a century earlier; they, too, had laid claim to the epic filiation in prefatory asseverations which were not so much accurate analyses of their achievement as attempts to assuage their own anxieties and those of their readers about the uncanonised nature of what was to follow in the text. Nor have such attempts to dissipate the odour of unsanctity in which prose fiction seems destined to have its being ceased even in our day—F. R. Leavis's 'The Novel as Dramatic Poem' would seem to be an analogous attempt to smuggle the novel into the critical Pantheon under the disguise of an ancient and honoured member.

At the same time, however, the fact that the formulae both of Fielding and of Leavis connect the novel with major poetic forms suggests an effort to put the genre into the highest possible literary context. Obviously both the creation and the criticism of the novel cannot but gain from this, and it is indeed likely that the most positive gain which Fielding derived from thinking about his narrative in terms of epic was that it encouraged him

---

[1] 'Fielding's *Amelia*', p. 2.
[2] Carl van Doren, *Life of Thomas Love Peacock* (London, 1911), p. 194.

to as intense and serious a travail as the loftiest literary forms were presumed to demand.

Apart from this it is likely that the epic influence on Fielding was very slight, mainly retrograde, and of little importance in the later tradition of the novel. To call Fielding, as Ethel Thornbury does in her monograph on the subject, 'the founder of the English Prose epic'[1] is surely to award him a somewhat sterile paternity; Fielding's greatest followers, Smollett, Dickens and Thackeray, do not, for example, imitate the very few specifically epic features in his work. But, as we have seen, the idea of 'the comic epic in prose' is by no means Fielding's major claim on our attention: its main function was to suggest one of the high standards of literary achievement which he wished to keep in mind when he began on his new path in fiction; it was certainly not intended as yet another of the innumerable eighteenth-century 'Receits to make an Epick Poem'; and this is fortunate, for, in literature at least, the nostrum killeth but the nostalgia may give life.

---

[1] *Henry Fielding's Theory of the Comic Prose Epic.* Madison, 1931, p. 166.

CHAPTER IX

Fielding as Novelist: 'Tom Jones'

LITERATURE yields few more interesting *causes célèbres* than the debate over the respective merits of the novels of Fielding and Richardson, a debate which continues today[1] even though during the last century or so the supporters of Fielding have been in almost complete command of the field. The main reason for the vitality of the controversy is the exceptional range and variety of the issues—the opposition is not only between two kinds of novel, but between two kinds of physical and psychological constitution and between two social, moral and philosophical outlooks on life. Not only so: the dispute has the advantage of a spokesman whose strong and paradoxical support for Richardson acts as a perennial provocation to the supporters of Fielding, who are dismayed to find Dr. Johnson, the authoritative voice of neo-classicism, pronouncing anathema on the last full embodiment of the Augustan spirit in life and literature.[2]

One way of resolving this last difficulty has been to suggest that Dr. Johnson's attitude should not be taken too seriously because it was dictated by friendship and personal obligation —Richardson had once saved him from being arrested for debt. Johnson's critical judgement, however, was not usually at the mercy of such considerations, and the supposition in any case runs counter to the fact that his enthusiastic endorsement of Richardson's novels was accompanied by a merciless awareness of the shortcomings of the man—witness his lethal jibe that Richardson 'could not be content to sail quietly down the stream of reputation without longing to taste the froth from every stroke of the oar'.[3]

We should, then, consider Johnson's preference seriously, particularly in view of the consistency with which he recurred

---

[1] See, for example, Frank Kermode, 'Richardson and Fielding', *Cambridge Journal*, IV (1950), 106-114: and, for a detailed account of their literary reputations, F. T. Blanchard, *Fielding the Novelist: A Study in Historical Criticism* (New Haven, 1926).

[2] See Robert E. Moore, 'Dr. Johnson on Fielding and Richardson', *PMLA*, LXVI (1951), 162-181.   [3] *Johnsonian Miscellanies*, ed. Hill, I, 273-274.

to his main charge. 'All the difference between the characters of Fielding and those of Richardson', he maintained, according to Boswell, was that between 'characters of manners' and 'characters of nature'. 'Characters of manners', of course, Johnson ranked much lower on the grounds that although 'very entertaining . . . they are to be understood by a more superficial observer than characters of nature, where a man must dive into the recesses of the human heart'. This distinction between Richardson and Fielding was more memorably expressed when Johnson said that 'there was as great a difference between them as between a man who knew how a watch was made, and a man who could tell the hour by looking on the dial plate';[1] and the same idea is present in the even more plainly invidious statement reported by Mrs. Thrale that 'Richardson had picked the kernel of life . . . while Fielding was contented with the husk'.[2]

This basic distinction does not involve any direct divergence from critical orthodoxy, but it perhaps does so implicitly, since the basis of Richardson's 'diving into the recesses of the human heart' was his detailed description of individual states of mind, a description which requires a minute particularity in the presentation of character, and which is therefore contrary to the usual neo-classical bias towards the general and the universal. There is no doubt that Johnson's theoretical presuppositions were strongly in this direction, as he often proclaimed the doctrine that the poet 'must not dwell on the minuter distinctions by which one species differs from another'.[3] Yet his operative premises for fiction were apparently quite different, since he reproached Fielding for his reluctance to dwell on these very distinctions, telling Mrs. Thrale, for example, that 'Fielding could describe a horse or an ass, but he never reached to a mule'.[4]

It would seem, then, that Johnson's vigorously independent literary sensibility tended to confirm at least one of the elements of the opposition described in the first chapter between neo-classical theory and the novel's formal realism. As for the discrepancy between Johnson's literary theory and his practical judgement, it need occasion little surprise: any body of doctrine is ambiguous in some of its applications, and especially when it

[1] *Life of Johnson*, ed. Hill-Powell, II, 48-49.
[2] *Johnsonian Miscellanies*, ed. Hill, I, 282.
[3] *Rambler*, No. 36 (1750); see also *Rasselas*, ch. 10.
[4] *Thraliana*, ed. Balderston, I, 555.

is applied in areas for which it was not originally designed. In any case, Johnson's neo-classicism was not a simple thing (neither, for that matter, was neo-classicism); and his divergence from his usual principles in the present instance must surely be regarded as yet another example of how the radical honesty of his literary insight raised fundamental issues so forcibly that later criticism cannot but use his formulations as points of departure; any comparison between the two first masters of the novel form certainly must begin from the basis which he provided.

I

Tom Jones and *Clarissa* have sufficient similarity of theme to provide several closely parallel scenes which afford a concrete illustration of the differences between the methods of Fielding and Richardson as novelists. Both, for example, show us scenes where the heroine is forced to receive the addresses of the hated suitor their parents have chosen for them, and both also portray the later conflict between father and daughter which their refusal to marry this suitor provokes.

Here, first, is how Fielding describes the interview between Sophia Western and the odious Blifil:

> Mr. Blifil soon arrived; and Mr. Western soon after withdrawing, left the young couple together.
>
> Here a long silence of near a quarter of an hour ensued; for the gentleman, who was to begin the conversation, had all that unbecoming modesty which consists in bashfulness. He often attempted to speak, and as often suppressed his words just at the very point of utterance. At last, out they broke in a torrent of far-fetched and high-strained compliments, which were answered on her side by downcast looks, half bows, and civil monosyllables.— Blifil, from his inexperience in the ways of women, and from his conceit of himself, took this behaviour for a modest assent to his courtship; and when, to shorten a scene which she could no longer support, Sophia rose up and left the room, he imputed that, too, merely to bashfulness, and comforted himself that he should soon have enough of her company.
>
> He was indeed perfectly well satisfied with his prospect of success; for as to that entire and absolute possession of the heart of his mistress, which romantic lovers require, the very idea of it never entered his head. Her fortune and her person were the

sole objects of his wishes, of which he made no doubt soon to obtain the absolute property; as Mr. Western's mind was so earnestly bent on the match; and as he well knew the strict obedience which Sophia was always ready to pay to her father's will, and the greater still which her father would exact, if there was occasion . . .[1]

Structurally, the scene is based on that typical device of comedy, total ignorance by one character of the intentions of the other as a result of a misunderstanding between third parties —Squire Western has been misled by the ineffable Mistress Western into thinking that Sophia loves Blifil, not Tom Jones. It is perhaps because this misunderstanding must be kept up that there is no actual conversation and little feeling of personal contact between the characters concerned. Instead, Fielding, acting as omniscient author, lets us into Blifil's mind, and the meanness of the considerations by which it is governed: at the same time the consistent irony of Fielding's tone suggests to us the probable limits of Blifil's role: we need not fear that he will ever get possession of Sophia's fortune or of her person, for, although he is cast as a villain, it is patently as the villain in comedy.

Blifil's misunderstanding of Sophia's silence leads on to the next comic complication, since it causes him to give Squire Western the impression that his suit has prospered. Western at once goes to rejoice with his daughter, who of course is unaware of how he has been deceived:

Sophia, perceiving her father in this fit of affection, which she did not absolutely know the reason of (for fits of fondness were not unusual in him, though this was rather more violent than ordinary), thought she should never have a better second opportunity of disclosing herself than at present, as far at least as regarded Mr. Blifil; and she too well foresaw the necessity which she should soon be under of coming to a full explanation. After having thanked the squire, therefore, for all his professions of kindness, she added with a look full of inexpressible softness, 'And is it possible that my papa can be so good as to place all his joy in his Sophy's happiness?' which Western having confirmed by a great oath and a kiss, she then laid hold of his hand, and falling on her knees, after many warm and passionate declarations of affection and duty, she begged him 'not to make her the most miserable creature on earth, by forcing her to marry a man she detested. This I entreat of you, dear sir,' said she, 'for your sake, as well as my own, since you are so very kind to tell me your happiness depends on mine.'—'How! What!' says Western, staring wildly. 'O, sir,' continued she, 'not only your poor Sophy's happiness, her very life, her being, depends upon your granting her request. I cannot live with Mr. Blifil. To force me into this marriage would be killing me.'—'You can't live with Mr. Blifil!' says Mr. Western—'No, upon my soul, I can't,' answered Sophia.—'Then die and be d—ned,' cries he, spurning her from him . . . 'I am resolved upon the match, and unless you consent to it, I will not give you a groat, not a single farthing; no, though I saw you expiring in the street, I would not relieve you with a morsel of bread. This is my fixed resolution, and so I leave you to consider on it.' He then broke from her with such violence, that her face dashed against the floor; and he burst directly out of the room, leaving poor Sophia prostrate on the ground.

Fielding's primary aim is certainly not to reveal character through speech and action. We cannot be meant to deduce, for instance, that Sophia knows her father so poorly as to entertain any hopes of being able to hold him down to one position by force of logic; what Fielding tells us about Sophia's decision to break the matter to her father is obviously mainly aimed at heightening the comic reversal that is to follow. Similarly we cannot consider Western's threat—'No, though I saw you expiring in the street, I would not relieve you with a morsel of bread'—as characteristic of the man either in diction or sentiment—it is hackneyed trope that belongs to any such situation in melodrama, not to a particular Squire who habitually speaks the most uncouth Somersetshire jargon, and whose childish intemperateness is not elsewhere shown capable of such an imaginative flight. To say that Sophia's and Western's speeches are grossly out of character would be an exaggeration; but they are undoubtedly directed entirely towards exploiting the comic volte-face and not towards making us witnesses of an actual interview between a father and daughter in real life.

It is probably an essential condition for the realisation of Fielding's comic aim that the scene should not be rendered in all its physical and psychological detail; Fielding must temper our alarm for Sophia's fate by assuring us that we are witnessing, not real anguish, but that conventional kind of comic perplexity which serves to heighten our eventual pleasure at the happy ending, without in the meantime involving any unnecessary expenditure of tears on our part. Fielding's external and somewhat peremptory approach to his characters, in fact, would seem to be a necessary condition of the success of his main comic purpose: attention to the immediate counterpoint of misunderstanding and contradiction must not be dissipated by focussing interest on Sophia's feelings or on any other tangential issue.

A total contrast of purpose and method is offered by the way Richardson presents Clarissa's interview with Solmes, after her maid Hannah has warned her secretly that he is the husband that has been decided on for her. It is thus described in a letter to Anna Howe:

> I went down this morning when breakfast was ready with a very uneasy heart . . . wishing for an opportunity to appeal to my mother, in hopes to engage her interest in my behalf, and purposing to try to find one when she retired to her own apartment after breakfast; but, unluckily, there was the odious Solmes sitting asquat between my mother and sister, with *so much* assurance in his looks! But you know, my dear, that those we love not cannot do anything to please us.
>
> Had the wretch kept his seat, it might have been well enough: but the bent and broad-shouldered creature must needs rise and stalk towards a chair; which was just by that which was set for me.
>
> I removed it to a distance, as if to make way to my own: And down I sat, abruptly I believe; what I had heard all in my head.
>
> But this was not enough to daunt him. The man is a very confident, he is a very bold, staring man! Indeed, my dear, the man is very confident!
>
> He took the removed chair and drew it so near mine, squatting in it with his ugly weight, that he pressed upon my hoop. I was so offended (all I had heard, as I said, in my head) that I removed to another chair. I own I had too little command of myself. It gave my brother and sister too much advantage. I dare say they took it. But I did it involuntarily, I think. I could not help it. I knew not what I did.
>
> I saw that my father was excessively displeased. When angry, no man's countenance ever shows it so much as my father's. Clarissa Harlowe! said he with a big voice—and there he stopped. Sir! said I, trembling and curtsying (for I had not then sat down again): and put my chair nearer the wretch, and sat down—my face, as I could feel, all in a glow.

Make tea, child, said my kind mamma: sit by me, love, and make tea.

I removed with pleasure to the seat the man had quitted; and being thus indulgently put into employment, soon recovered myself; and in the course of the breakfasting officiously asked two or three questions of Mr. Solmes, which I would not have done, but to make up with my father. *Proud spirits may be brought to!* whisperingly spoke my sister to me over her shoulder, with an air of triumph and scorn: but I did not mind her.

My mother was all kindness and condescension. I asked her once if she were pleased with the tea . . .

Small incidents these, my dear, to trouble you with; only as they lead to greater, as you shall hear.

Before the usual breakfast-time was over my father withdrew with my mother, telling her he wanted to speak to her. Then my sister and next my aunt (who was with us) dropped away.

My brother gave himself some airs of insult, which I understood well enough; but which Mr. Solmes could make nothing of: and at last he arose from *his* seat. Sister, says he, I have a curiosity to show you. I will fetch it. And away he went; shutting the door close after him.

I saw what all this was for. I arose; the man hemming up for a speech, rising and beginning to set his splay feet (indeed, my dear, the man in all his ways is hateful to me!) in an approaching posture. I will save my brother the trouble of bringing to me his curiosity, said I. I curtsied—your servant, sir. The man cried, madam, madam, twice, and looked like a fool. But away I went— to find my brother to save my word. But my brother, indifferent as the weather was, was gone to walk in the garden with my sister. A plain case that he had left his *curiosity* with me, and designed to show me no other.[1]

The passage is characteristic of Richardson's very different kind of realism. Clarissa is describing what happened 'this morning', and is 'as minute as' she knows Anna wishes her to be; only so can Richardson convey the physical reality of the scene—the party at breakfast, the jockeying for position over trifles, and all the ordinarily trivial domestic details which bear the main burden of the drama. The letter form gives Richardson access to thoughts and emotions of a kind that cannot issue in speech, and are hardly capable of rational analysis—the flux and reflux of Clarissa's lacerated sensibility as she struggles

[1] I, 68-70.

against parental tyranny on the battlefield of petty circumstance: as a result we have quite a different kind of participation
from that which Fielding produces: not a lively but objective
sense of the total comic pattern, but a complete identification
with the consciousness of Clarissa while her nerves still quiver
from the recollection of the scene, and her imagination recoils
from the thought of her own strained alternation between involuntary revolt and paralysed compliance.

Because Richardson's narrative sequence is based on an
exploration in depth of the protagonist's reaction to experience,
it encompasses many minor shades of emotion and character
that are not found in the passages from *Tom Jones*. Fielding does
not attempt to do more than to make us understand the rational
grounds on which Sophia acts as she does—there is nothing
which would not fit almost any sensible young girl's behaviour
in the circumstances: whereas Richardson's epistolary technique, and the intimacy of Clarissa with Anna, encourages him
to go far beyond this, and communicate a host of things which
deepen and particularise our picture of Clarissa's total moral
being. Her shuddering ejaculation—'Indeed, my dear, the man
is very confident', her scornful comment on her sister's intervention—'I did not mind her', and her admission of involvement in petty family rivalries—she regrets moving away from
Solmes because 'It gave my brother and sister too much advantage'—all these details of characterisation must surely be overlooked by those who describe Richardson as a creator of 'ideal'
characters: there is, of course, great will and tenacity in Clarissa,
but it is very definitely that of an inexperienced young woman,
who has her fair share of sisterly vindictiveness and pert self-
assertion, and who, far from being an idealised figure of virgin
sainthood, is capable of the catty and sardonic emphasis on Mr.
Solmes as a 'curiosity'. Nor is she by any means a disembodied
being; we have no indications of any physical reaction on
Sophia's part towards Blifil, but we are given Clarissa's very
intense one to Solmes—an instinctive sexual revulsion from
'his ugly weight'.

The same setting of personal relationships in a minutely
described physical, psychological and even physiological continuum is shown in the brief scene which is the counterpart of
the second passage quoted from *Tom Jones*. After two private
interviews with her mother, Clarissa has been faced with a

family ultimatum, and her mother is with her to receive an answer:

> Just then, up came my father, with a sternness in his looks that made me tremble. He took two or three turns about my chamber, though pained by his gout. And then said to my mother, who was silent, as soon as she saw him:
> My dear, you are long absent. Dinner is near ready. What you had to say lay in a very little compass. Surely, you have nothing to do but to declare *your* will, and *my* will—but perhaps you may be talking of the preparations. Let us soon have you down—your daughter in your hand, if worthy of the name.
> And down he went, casting his eye upon me with a look so stern that I was unable to say one word to him, or even for a few minutes to my mother.[1]

Richardson and Fielding portray the cruelty of the two fathers very differently; that of Squire Western has an involuntary and exaggerated quality, whereas Mr. Harlowe's is that of ordinary life; the latter's callous resolve seems all the more convincing because it is only manifested in his refusal to speak to Clarissa—our own emotional involvement in the inner world of Clarissa makes it possible for a father's silent look to have a resonance that is quite lacking in the physical and rhetorical hyperbole by which Fielding demonstrates the fury of Squire Western.

II

On further analysis, then, it appears that Johnson's comparison between Richardson and Fielding does not directly raise the question of which was the better psychologist, but depends rather on their quite opposite literary intentions: those of Fielding allotted characterisation a much less important place in his total literary structure, and precluded him even from attempting the effects which were suited to Richardson's very different aim. The full implications of the divergence can perhaps be most clearly and inclusively demonstrated in Fielding's handling of the plot in *Tom Jones*, for it reflects the whole of his social, moral and literary outlook.

Fielding's conduct of the action, despite a few excrescences such as the interpolated story of the Man of the Hill, and some

[1] I, 75-76.

signs of haste and confusion in the concluding books,[1] exhibits a remarkably fine control over a very complicated structure, and abundantly justifies Coleridge's famous eulogy: 'What a master of composition Fielding was! Upon my word, I think the *Oedipus Tyrannus*, the *Alchemist*, and *Tom Jones*, the three most perfect plots ever planned.'[2]

Perfect for what? we must ask. Not, certainly, for the exploration of character and of personal relations, since in all three plots the emphasis falls on the author's skilfully contrived revelation of an external and deterministic scheme: in *Oedipus* the hero's character is of minor importance compared with the consequences of his past actions, which were themselves the result of a prophecy made long before his birth; in the *Alchemist* the portrayal of Face and Subtle does not go far beyond the need for suitable instruments to carry out Jonson's complex series of chicaneries; while the plot of *Tom Jones* offers a combination of these features. As in Sophocles, the crucial secret, that of the hero's actual birth, is very elaborately prepared for and hinted at throughout the action, and its eventual disclosure brings about the final reordering of all the main issues of the story: while, as in Jonson, this final reordering is achieved through the unmasking of a complicated pattern of villainy and deception.

The three plots are alike in another respect: their basic direction is towards a return to the norm, and they therefore have a fundamentally static quality. In this they no doubt reflect the conservatism of their authors, a conservatism which in Fielding's case is probably connected with the fact that he belonged, not to the trading class like Defoe and Richardson, but to the gentry. The plots of the novels of Defoe and Richardson, as we have seen, mirrored certain dynamic tendencies in the outlook of their class: in *Moll Flanders*, for example, money has a certain autonomous force which determines the action at every turn. In *Tom Jones*, on the other hand, as in the *Alchemist*, money is something that the good characters either have or are given or momentarily lose: only bad characters devote any effort either to getting it or keeping it. Money, in fact, is a useful plot device but it has no controlling significance.

Birth, on the other hand, has a very different status in *Tom*

[1] For a full account see F. H. Dudden, *Henry Fielding* (Oxford, 1952), II, 621-627.
[2] *Cit.* Blanchard, *Fielding*, pp. 320-321.

Jones: as a determining factor in the plot it is almost the equivalent of money in Defoe or virtue in Richardson. In this emphasis,
of course, Fielding reflects the general tenor of the social
thought of his day: the basis of society is and should be a system
of classes each with their own capacities and responsibilities.
The vigour of Fielding's satire on the upper classes, for example,
should not be interpreted as the expression of any egalitarian
tendency: it is really a tribute to the firmness of his belief in the
class premise. It is true that in *Amelia* he goes so far as to say that
'of all kinds of pride, there is none so unChristian as that of
station'.[1] But that, of course, is only a matter of *noblesse oblige*;
and in *Tom Jones* Fielding also wrote that 'liberality of spirits'
was a quality which he had 'scarce ever seen in men of low
birth and education'.[2]

This class fixity is an essential part of *Tom Jones*. Tom may
think it unfortunate that, as a foundling of presumed low
ancestry, he cannot marry Sophia; but he does not question the
propriety of the assumption on which their separation is decreed.
The ultimate task of Fielding's plot therefore is to unite the
lovers without subverting the basis of the social order; and this
can only be done by revealing that Mr. Jones, though illegitimate, is genteel. This, however, is not wholly a surprise to the
perceptive reader, for whom Tom's eminent 'liberality of
spirit' has already suggested his superior pedigree; the recent
Soviet critic, therefore, who sees the story as the triumph of a
proletarian hero[3] is neglecting, not only the facts of his birth,
but its continuing implications for his character.

Fielding's conservatism accounts for another and much more
general difference between the plots of *Tom Jones* and *Clarissa*:
for whereas Richardson depicts the crucifixion of the individual
by society, Fielding portrays the successful adaptation of the
individual to society, and this entails a very different relation
between plot and character.

In *Clarissa* the individual must be given priority in the total
structure: Richardson merely brings together certain individuals, and their proximity is all that is necessary to set off
an extended chain reaction which then proceeds under its own

[1] Bk. VII, ch. 10.
[2] Bk. IX, ch. 1. See also A. O. Lovejoy, *The Great Chain of Being* (Harvard,
1936), pp. 224, 245.
[3] A. Elistratov, 'Fielding's Realism', in *Iz Istorii Angliskogo Realizma* [On the
History of English Realism] (Moscow, 1941), p. 63.

impetus and modifies all the characters and their mutual relationships. In *Tom Jones*, on the other hand, society and the larger order which it represents must have priority, and the plot's function, therefore, is to perform a physical rather than a chemical change: it acts as a kind of magnet that pulls every individual particle out of the random order brought about by temporal accident and human imperfection and puts them all back into their proper position. The constitution of the particles themselves—the characters—is not modified in the process, but the plot serves to reveal something much more important— the fact that all human particles are subject to an ultimate invisible force which exists in the universe whether they are there to show it or not.

Such a plot reflects the general literary strategy of neo-classicism; just as the creation of a field of force makes visible the universal laws of magnetism, so the supreme task of the writer was to make visible in the human scene the operations of universal order—to unveil the handiwork of Pope's 'Unerring Nature, still divinely bright,/One clear, unchanged and universal light'.

This much wider perspective on character obviously reduces the importance which will be attached to the nature and actions of any particular individual entity—they are mainly interesting as manifestations of the great pattern of Nature. This informs Fielding's treatment of every aspect of characterisation—not only the extent to which his *dramatis personae* are individualised, but the degree of attention paid to their subjective lives, to their moral development, and to their personal relationships.

Fielding's primary objectives in the portrayal of character are clear but limited: to assign them to their proper category by giving as few diagnostic features as are necessary for the task. Such was his conception of 'invention' or 'creation': 'a quick and sagacious penetration into the true essence of all the objects of our contemplation'.[1] This meant in practice that once the individual had been appropriately labelled the author's only remaining duty was to see that he continued to speak and act consistently. As Aristotle put it in the *Poetics*, 'character' is 'that which reveals the moral purpose', and consequently 'speeches . . . which do not make this manifest . . . are not expressive of character'.[2] Parson Supple must never cease to be supple.

[1] Bk. IX, ch. 1.   [2] Ch. 6, No. 17.

So it is that Fielding does not make any attempt to individualise his characters. Allworthy is sufficiently categorised by his name, while that of Tom Jones, compounded as it is out of two of the commonest names in the language, tells us that we must regard him as the representative of manhood in general, in accordance with his creator's purpose to show 'not men, but manners; not an individual, but a species'.[1]

The scope of the word 'manners' has dwindled so drastically in the last few centuries—no doubt as a result of the way individualism has reduced the areas in which identity of thought and action is generally expected—that the phrase 'characters of manners' no longer means very much. It can perhaps be best explained in terms of the contrast with Richardson's 'characters of nature'. Richardson's literary objective, as B. W. Downs has pointed out,[2] is not so much character—the stable elements in the individual's mental and moral constitution—as personality: he does not analyse Clarissa, but presents a complete and detailed behavioural report on her whole being: she is defined by the fullness of our participation in her life. Fielding's purpose, on the other hand, is analytic: he is not interested in the exact configuration of motives in any particular person's mind at any particular time but only in those features of the individual which are necessary to assign him to his moral and social species. He therefore studies each character in the light of his general knowledge of human behaviour, of 'manners', and anything purely individual is of no taxonomic value. Nor is there any need to look inside: if, as Johnson said, Fielding gives us the husk, it is because the surface alone is usually quite sufficient to identify the specimen—the expert does not need to assay the kernel.

There are many other reasons for Fielding's predominantly external approach to character, reasons of a social and philosophical as well as of a literary order. To begin with, the opposite approach involved a breach of decorum: as Fielding's cousin Lady Mary Wortley Montagu pointed out, it was very bad manners for Richardson's heroines to 'declare all they think', since 'fig leaves are as necessary for our minds as our bodies'.[3] It was also consistent with the classical tradition as a whole, as we have seen, to avoid the intimate and confessional

---

[1] *Joseph Andrews*, Bk. III, ch. 1.   [2] *Richardson*, pp. 125-126.
[3] *Letters and Works*, II, 291.

approach to personality; and in any case the philosophical problems of self-consciousness had only begun to receive attention
some six centuries after Aristotle in the works of Plotinus.[1]
Lastly, as was evident in the treatment of Blifil and Sophia,
Fielding's comic purpose itself required an external approach,
and for a compelling reason. If we identify ourselves with the
characters we shall not be in any mood to appreciate the humour
of the larger comedy in which they are risible participants: life,
we have been told, is a comedy only to the man who thinks, and
the comic author must not make us feel every stroke of the lash
as his characters squirm under his corrective rod.

At all events, Fielding avowedly and even ostentatiously
refused to go too deep into the minds of his characters, on the
general grounds that 'it is our province to relate facts, and we
shall leave causes to persons of much higher genius'. We have
noted how little was said about the feelings, as opposed to the
rational determinations, of Blifil and Sophia. This was quite
conscious on Fielding's part: he had already remarked ironically
of Blifil that 'it would be an ill office in us to pay a visit to the
inmost recesses of his mind, as some scandalous people search
into the most secret affairs of their friends, and often pry into
their closets and cupboards, only to discover their poverty and
meanness to the world'; similarly when Fielding came to present
Sophia's feelings when she first learned of Tom's love, he
excused himself in the words: 'as to the present situation of her
mind I shall adhere to the rule of Horace, by not attempting
to describe it, from despair of success'.[2]

Fielding's avoidance of the subjective dimension, then, is
quite intentional: but that does not, of course, mean that it has
no drawbacks, for it undoubtedly has, and they become very
apparent whenever important emotional climaxes are reached.
Coleridge, for all his love of Fielding, pointed out that in the
soliloquies between Sophia and Tom Jones before their final
reconciliation, nothing could be 'more forced and unnatural:
the language is without vivacity or spirit, the whole matter is
incongruous, and totally devoid of psychological truth'.[3] In fact,
Fielding merely gave us a stock comic scene: elevated sentiments
of penitent ardour on the hero's part were countered by wronged
womanhood's equally elevated scorn of her faithless suitor.

[1] See A. E. Taylor, *Aristotle* (London, 1943), p. 108.
[2] Bk. II, ch. 4; Bk. IV, chs. 3, 14. [3] *Cit.* Blanchard, *Fielding*, p. 317.

273

Soon after, of course, Sophia accepts Tom, and we are surprised by her very sudden and unexplained reversal: the dénouement has been given a certain comic life, but at the expense of the reality of emotions involved.

This emotional artificiality is very general in *Tom Jones*. When the hero, for instance, is expelled from Allworthy's house we are told that '. . . he presently fell into the most violent agonies, tearing his hair from his head, and using most other actions which generally accompany fits of madness, rage and despair'; and later that he read Sophia's parting letter 'a hundred times over, and kissed it a hundred times as often'.[1] Fielding's use of these hackneyed hyperboles to vouch for the intensity of the emotions of his characters underlines the price that he pays for his comic approach: it denies him a convincing and continuous access to the inner life of his characters, so that whenever he has to exhibit their emotional life, he can only do it externally by making them have exaggerated physical reactions.

The fact that Fielding's characters do not have a convincing inner life means that their possibilities of psychological development are very limited. Tom Jones's character, for example, exhibits some development, but it is of a very general kind. Tom's early imprudences, his youthful lack of worldly wisdom, and his healthy animality, for example, lead to his disgrace, his expulsion from the Allworthy household, his subsequent difficulties on the road and in London, and his apparently irrecoverable loss of Sophia's love. At the same time his good qualities, his courage, honour and benevolence, all of which have been glimpsed at the beginning, eventually combine to extricate him from the nadir of his misfortunes, and restore him to the love and respect of those who surround him. But although different qualities come to the fore at different times they have all been present from the beginning, and we have not been taken close enough to Tom's mind to be able to do anything but take on trust Fielding's implication, which is that his hero will be able to control his weaknesses by the wisdom he has learned of experience.

In taking this essentially static view of human nature Fielding was following the time-hallowed Aristotelian view, which was actually held with much greater rigidity by most of the

[1] Bk. VI, ch. 12.

philosophers and literary critics of his time.[1] It is, of course, an a-historical view of character, as Fielding showed in *Joseph Andrews*, when he asserted that his characters were 'taken from the life', but added that the particular lawyer in question was 'not only alive, but hath been so this four thousand years'.[2] It follows logically that if human nature is essentially stable, there is no need to detail the processes whereby any one example of it has reached its full development; such processes are but temporary and superficial modifications of a moral constitution which is unalterably fixed from birth. Such, for example, is the premise of the way that although Tom and Blifil share the same mother and are brought up in the same household by the same tutors, their respective courses are unalterably set in different directions from the very beginning.

Once again the contrast with Richardson is complete. Much of our sense of Clarissa's psychological development arises from the way that her experience brings a continual deepening of her understanding of her own past: as a result character and plot are indivisible. Tom Jones, on the other hand, is not in touch with his own past at all: we feel a certain unreality in his actions because they always seem to be spontaneous reactions to stimuli that the plot has been manipulated to provide; we have no sense that they are manifestations of a developing moral life. We cannot but feel surprise, for instance, when, immediately after accepting 50 pounds from Lady Bellaston, Tom gives his famous lecture to Nightingale on sexual ethics.[3] It is not that the two actions are inherently contradictory—Tom's ethics have throughout been based on the much greater heinousness of harming others than of failing to live up to one's moral code oneself; but if we had been given some indication that Tom was aware of the apparent contradictions between his speech and his own past practice he might have sounded less priggish and more convincing. Actually, of course, separate parts of Tom's nature can hold very little converse with each other, because there is only one agency for such converse—the individual consciousness through which the whole repertoire of past actions operates—and Fielding does not take us into this consciousness because he believes that individual character is a specific

[1] See Leslie Stephen, *English Thought in the Eighteenth Century* (London, 1902), II, 73-74; R. Hubert, *Les Sciences sociales dans l'Encyclopédie* (Paris, 1923), pp. 167 ff.
[2] Bk. II, ch. 1.   [3] Bk. XIV, ch. 7.

combination of stable and separate predispositions to action' rather than the product of its own past.

For the same reasons personal relationships are also relatively unimportant in *Tom Jones*. If there is a controlling force independent of the individual actors and their positions with respect to each other, and if their own characters are innate and unchanging, there is no reason why Fielding should give close attention to their mutual feelings, since they cannot play a decisive role. Here, again, the scene between Sophia and Blifil was typical in that it reflected the extent to which the structure of *Tom Jones* as a whole depends on the lack of any effective communication between the characters: just as Blifil must misunderstand Sophia, so Allworthy must fail to see Blifil in his true light, and Tom must be unable either to understand Blifil's true nature or to explain himself properly either to Allworthy or Sophia until the closing scenes. For, since Fielding's view of human life and his general literary purpose did not permit him to subordinate his plot to the deepening exploration of personal relationships, he needed a structure based on an elaborate counterpoint of deception and surprise, and this would be impossible if the characters could share each other's minds and take their fates into their own hands.

There is, then, an absolute connection in *Tom Jones* between the treatment of plot and of character. Plot has priority, and it is therefore plot which must contain the elements of complication and development. Fielding achieves this by superimposing on a central action that is, in essentials as simple as that in *Clarissa*, a very complex series of relatively autonomous subplots and episodes which are in the nature of dramatic variations on the main theme. These relatively independent narrative units are combined in a concatenation whose elaboration and symmetry is suggested in the most obvious outward aspect of the book's formal order: unlike the novels of Defoe and Richardson, *Tom Jones* is carefully divided into compositional units of different sizes—some two hundred chapters which are themselves grouped into eighteen books disposed into three groups of six, dealing respectively with the early lives, the journeys to London, and the activities on arrival, of the main characters.

This extreme diversification of the narrative texture reinforces, of course, Fielding's tendency not to dwell for long on any one

scene or character. In the passages quoted, for example, there
was none of the intensive treatment which Richardson gave to
Clarissa's interview with Solmes; most of Fielding's time was
spent on making clear the initial misunderstanding, and the
scale of the scene allowed no more in the way of characterisation
than a designing hypocrite, a trapped maiden and a heavy
father. But even if there had been any full absorption in the
feelings of Sophia, for example, it would soon have been termin-
ated by the management of the ensuing scenes: for, just as we
left Sophia immediately after Squire Western had stormed out
of the room, and were thus spared any prolonged awareness of
her sufferings, so in the next chapter our attention was soon
switched away from her parting interview with Tom Jones by
Fielding's announcement that '. . . the scene, which I believe
some of my readers will think had lasted long enough, was interrupted by one of so different a nature, that we shall reserve the
relation of it for a different chapter'.[1]

This is typical of the narrative mode of *Tom Jones*: the
author's commentary makes no secret of the fact that his aim is
not to immerse us wholly in his fictional world, but rather to
show the ingenuity of his own inventive resources by contriv-
ing an amusing counterpoint of scenes and characters; quick
changes are the essence of Fielding's comic manner, and a new
chapter will always bring a new situation for the characters, or
present different characters in a similar scene for ironical contrast. In addition, by a great variety of devices, of which the
chapter headings are usually significant pointers, our attention
is continually drawn to the fact that the ultimate cohesive force
of the book resides not in the characters and their relationships,
but in an intellectual and literary structure which has a considerable degree of autonomy.

The effects of this procedure and its relationship to Fielding's
treatment of character can be summarised in relation to a brief
scene which occurs after Tom has heard that Allworthy is to
recover from his illness. He takes a walk 'in a most delicious
grove', and contemplates the cruelty of fortune which separates
him from his beloved Sophia:

Was I but possessed of thee, one only suit of rags thy whole estate,
is there a man on earth whom I would envy! How contemptible

[1] Bk. VI, ch. 8.

277

would the brightest Circassian beauty, dressed in all the jewels of the Indies, appear to my eyes! But why do I mention another woman? Could I think my eyes capable of looking at any other with tenderness, these hands should tear them from my head. No, my Sophia, if cruel fortune separates us for ever, my soul shall dote on thee alone. The chastest constancy will I ever preserve to thy image . . .

At these words he started up and beheld—not his Sophia—no, nor a Circassian maid richly and elegantly attired for the grand Signior's seraglio . . .

but Molly Seagrim, with whom, 'after a parley' which Fielding omits, Tom retires to 'the thickest part of the grove'.[1]

The least convincing aspect of the episode is the diction: the speech habits manifested here obviously bear little relation to those we expect of Tom Jones. But, of course, they are a stylistic necessity for Fielding's immediate purpose—the comic deflation of the heroic and romantic pretences of the human word by the unheroic and unromantic eloquence of the human deed. Tom Jones is no more than a vehicle for the expression of Fielding's scepticism about lovers' vows; and he must be made to speak in terms that parody the high-flown rhetoric of the pastoral romance to give point to the succeeding wayside encounter which belongs to the very different world of the *pastourelle*. Nor can Fielding pause to detail the psychological processes whereby Tom is metamorphosed from Sophia's romantic lover to Moll's prompt gallant: to illustrate the commonplace that 'actions speak louder than words', the actions must be very silent and they must follow very hard upon very loud words.

The relation of this episode to the larger structure of the novel is typical. One of Fielding's general organising themes is the proper place of sex in human life; this encounter neatly illustrates the conflicting tendencies of headstrong youth, and shows that Tom has not yet reached the continence of moral adulthood. The scene, therefore, plays its part in the general moral and intellectual scheme; and it is also significantly connected with the workings of the plot, since Tom's lapse eventually becomes a factor in his dismissal by Allworthy, and therefore leads to the ordeals which eventually make him a worthier mate for Sophia.

At the same time Fielding's treatment of the scene is also

[1] Bk. V, ch. 10.

typical in avoiding any detailed presentation of Tom's feelings either at the time or later—to take his hero's faithlessness too seriously would jeopardise Fielding's primarily comic intention in the episode, and he therefore manipulates it in such a way as to discourage us from giving it a significance which it might have in ordinary life. Comedy, and especially comedy on an elaborate scale, often involves this kind of limited liability to psychological interpretation: it applies to Blifil's malice and to Sophia's sufferings in the scenes quoted earlier, and Allworthy's sudden illness and recovery, which have led to Tom's lapse, must be placed in the same perspective. We must not dwell on the apparent fact that Allworthy is incapable of distinguishing between a cold and a mortal illness, since we are not intended to draw the implications for his character that he is either an outrageous hypochondriac or lamentably unskilled in choosing physicians: Allworthy's illness is only a diplomatic chill, and we must not infer anything from it except a shift in Fielding's narrative policy.

Tom Jones, then, would seem to exemplify a principle of considerable significance for the novel form in general: namely, that the importance of the plot is in inverse proportion to that of character. This principle has an interesting corollary: the organisation of the narrative into an extended and complex formal structure will tend to turn the protagonists into its passive agents, but it will offer compensatingly greater opportunities for the introduction of a variety of minor characters, whose treatment will not be hampered in the same way by the roles which they are allotted by the complications of the narrative design.

The principle and its corollary would seem to lie behind Coleridge's contrast of the 'forced and unnatural quality' of the scenes between the protagonists in *Tom Jones* and Fielding's treatment of the 'characters of postilions, landlords, landladies, waiters' where 'nothing can be more true, more happy or more humorous'.[1] These minor characters figure only in scenes which require exactly the amount of psychological individuality which they are possessed of; relieved of any responsibility for carrying out the major narrative design Mrs. Honour can get herself dismissed from the Western household by methods which are at

[1] *Cit.* Blanchard, *Fielding*, p. 317.

once triumphantly comic, sociologically perceptive and eminently characteristic;[1] nor is there any question of the violence to character and probability which colours the ways whereby Tom Jones, for example, or Sophia leave home.

Such is the pattern of most comic novels with elaborate plots, from Fielding and Smollett to Dickens: the creative emphasis is on characters who are minor at least in the sense that they are not deeply involved in the working out of the plot; whereas the Tom Jones's, the Roderick Randoms and the David Copperfields are less convincing as characters because their personalities bear little direct relation to the part they must play, and some of the actions in which the plot involves them suggests a weakness or folly which is probably at variance with the actual intentions of their author towards them.

On the other hand, the type of novel which is perhaps most typical of the genre, and which achieves effects which have not been duplicated in any other literary form, has used a very different kind of plot. From Sterne and Jane Austen to Proust and Joyce the Aristotelian priority of plot over character has been wholly reversed, and a new type of formal structure has been evolved in which the plot attempts only to embody the ordinary processes of life and in so doing becomes wholly dependent on the characters and the development of their relationships. It is Defoe and above all Richardson who provide this tradition with its archetypes, just as it is Fielding who provides that for the opposite tradition.

III

Johnson's most famous criticism of Fielding's novels is concerned with their basic technique, but from his own point of view it was probably their moral shortcomings which were the decisive factor. It is certainly this with which he was concerned in his only published reference to Fielding, although even here it is only by implication. In the *Rambler* (1750) Johnson attacked the effects of 'familiar' histories' whose wicked heroes were made so attractive that 'we lose abhorrence of their faults', apparently with *Roderick Random* (1748) and *Tom Jones* (1749) chiefly in mind.[2] He certainly later told Hannah More that he 'scarcely knew a more corrupt work' than *Tom Jones*,[3] and, on

[1] Bk. VII, ch. 7.   [2] No. 4.
[3] *Johnsonian Miscellanies*, II, 190.

the other hand, praised *Clarissa* on the significant grounds that 'It was in the power of Richardson alone to teach us at once esteem and detestation; to make virtuous resentment overpower all the benevolence which wit, elegance, and courage naturally excite, and to lose at last the hero in the villain'.[1]

We find it difficult today to share much of Johnson's abhorrence of the morality of *Tom Jones* and are, indeed, more likely to be unjust to Richardson, and to assume without question that his concern, and that of his heroines, for feminine chastity, can only be explained by prurience on his part or hypocrisy on theirs. But this may not be so, and, conversely, we must in fairness recognise that there are many moral offences in *Tom Jones* which receive a much more tolerant treatment than any Puritan moralist would have accorded them. Defoe and Richardson, for example, are unsparing in their denunciation of drunkenness; but when Tom Jones gets drunk in his joy at Allworthy's recovery, Fielding shows no reprobation: it is admittedly an imprudence which later contributes to the hero's expulsion, but Fielding's only direct comment is a humorous editorial development of the *in vino veritas* commonplace.[2]

It is the sexual issue, however, which is crucial, both in the moral scheme of *Tom Jones*, and in the objections of its critics. Fielding certainly does not endorse his hero's incontinence, and Tom himself admits that he has been 'faulty' in this respect; but the general tendency throughout the novel is surely to qualify the condemnation and make unchastity appear a venial sin—even the good Mrs. Miller, for example, seems to think she has put a fairly good face on matters by pleading to Sophia that Tom has 'never been guilty of a single instance of infidelity to her since . . . seeing her in town'.[3]

Fielding's plot obviously does not punish the sexual transgressions either of Tom Jones or of the many other characters who are guilty in this respect so severely as Richardson, for example, would have wished. Even in *Amelia*, where Booth's adultery is both more serious in itself than anything that can be charged against Tom Jones, and is treated much more severely by Fielding, the plot eventually rescues Booth from the consequences of his acts. There is therefore considerable justification for Ford Madox Ford's denunciation of 'fellows like Fielding,

[1] 'Rowe', *Lives of the Poets*, ed. Hill, II, 67.
[2] Bk. V, ch. 9.   [3] Bk. XVIII, ch. 10.

and to some extent Thackeray, who pretend that if you are a gay drunkard, lecher, squanderer of your goods and fumbler in placket holes you will eventually find a benevolent uncle, concealed father or benefactor who will shower on you bags of ten thousands of guineas, estates, and the hands of adorable mistresses—these fellows are dangers to the body politic and horribly bad constructors of plots'.[1]

Ford, of course, chooses to disregard both Fielding's positive moral intentions and the tendency of comic plots in general to achieve a happy ending at the cost of certain lenity in the administration of justice. For—although Fielding was long regarded as something of a debauchee himself and did not indeed have full justice done to his literary greatness until scholarship had cleared him of the charges made by contemporary gossip and repeated by his first biographer, Murphy—Fielding was in fact as much of a moralist as Richardson, although of a different kind. He believed that virtue, far from being the result of the suppression of instinct at the behest of public opinion, was itself a natural tendency to goodness or benevolence. In Tom Jones he tried to show a hero possessed of a virtuous heart, but also of the lustiness and lack of deliberation to which natural goodness was particularly prone, and which easily led to error and even to vice. To realise his moral aim, therefore, Fielding had to show how the good heart was threatened by many dangers in its hazardous course to maturity and knowledge of the world; yet, at the same time and without exculpating his hero, he had also to show that although Tom's moral transgressions were a likely and perhaps even a necessary stage in the process of moral growth, they did not betoken a vicious disposition; even Tom Jones's carefree animality has a generous quality that is lacking in Clarissa's self-centred and frigid virtue. The happy conclusion of the story, therefore, is very far from representing the kind of moral and literary confusion which Ford alleges, and is actually the culmination of Fielding's moral and literary logic.

The contrast between Fielding and Richardson as moralists is heightened by the effects of their very different narrative points of view. Richardson focusses attention on the individual, and whatever virtue or vice he is dealing with will loom very

[1] *The English Novel from the Earliest Days to the Death of Conrad* (London, 1930), p. 93.

large, and have all its implications reflected in the action: Fielding, on the other hand, deals with too many characters and too complicated a plot to give the single individual virtue or vice quite this importance.

Besides this tendency of the plot, it is also part of Fielding's intention as a moralist to put every phenomenon into its larger perspective. Sexual virtue and sexual vice, for example, are placed in a broad moral perspective, and the results do not always produce the kind of emphasis that the sexual reformer would wish. Fielding knows, for example, and wishes to show, that some marriage designs may be more vicious than the most abandoned profligacy: witness Blifil whose 'designs were strictly honourable as the phrase is, that is to rob a lady of her fortune by marriage'. He knows, too, that moral indignation against promiscuity is not necessarily the result of a real love of virtue: witness the passage in which we are told that 'to exclude all vulgar concubinage, and to drive all whores in rags from within the walls is within the power of everyone. This my landlady very strictly adhered to, and this her virtuous guests, who did not travel in rags, would very reasonably have expected from her.'[1] Here Fielding's Swiftian suavity reminds us of the cruelty and injustice with which complacent virtue is too often associated; but a narrow-minded moralist might see behind the irony a shocking failure to condemn 'whores in rags', and even, perhaps, an implicit sympathy for them.

Fielding, then, attempts to broaden our moral sense rather than to intensify its punitive operations against licentiousness. But, at the same time, his function as the voice of traditional social morality means that his attitude to sexual ethics is inevitably normative; it certainly does not, as Boswell said, 'encourage a strained and rarely possible virtue',[2] but rather reflects, as Leslie Stephen put it, 'the code by which men of sense generally govern their conduct, as distinguished from that by which they affect to be governed in language'.[3] Aristotle's Golden Mean is often, perhaps, capable of a certain subversion of rigid ethical principles: and it is perhaps as a good Aristotelian that Fielding comes very close to suggesting that too much chastity in Blifil is as bad as Tom's too little.

[1] Bk. XI, ch. 4; Bk. IX, ch. 3.
[2] *Life of Johnson*, ed. Hill-Powell, II, 49.
[3] *English Thought in the Eighteenth Century*, II, 377.

There is a further reason why Johnson, who was, after all, an ethical rigorist in his own way, should have found *Tom Jones* a corrupt work. Comedy—if only to maintain an atmosphere of good-humour between audience and participants—often involves a certain complicity in acts and sentiments which we might not treat so tolerantly in ordinary life. Perhaps the most insistent note in *Tom Jones* is Fielding's worldly-wise good-humour, and it often persuades us to regard sexual irregularities as ludicrous rather than wicked.

Mrs. Fitzpatrick, for instance, is dismissed with the words: 'she lives in reputation at the polite end of town, and is so good an economist that she spends three times the income of her fortune without running into debt'.[1] Mrs. Fitzpatrick must remain true to character, and yet be included in the happy ending; nor can Fielding upset the conviviality of his final meeting with his readers to express his abhorrence at the lamentable source of income which we must surmise for his character.

On other occasions, of course, Fielding's humour on that perennial comic resource, sex, is much more overt: in *Jonathan Wilde*, for example, when the captain of the ship asks the hero 'if he had no more Christianity in him than to ravish a woman in a storm?'[2] or in *Tom Jones* when Mrs. Honour gives her celebrated retort to Sophia's 'Would you not, Honour, fire a pistol at any one who should attack your virtue?'—'To be sure, ma'am, . . . one's virtue is a dear thing, especially to us poor servants; for it is our livelihood, as a body may say: yet I mortally hate firearms.'[3] There is, of course, the same broadening tendency in Fielding's humour here as in his treatment of moral issues in general: we must not forget that even the most virtuous indignation is capable of elementary logical fallacies, or that humankind's allegiance to virtue is capable of cautious afterthoughts. But the tacit assumption of much of Fielding's humour is surely one which suggests that 'broad-mindedness' in its modern sense, which typically tends to have a sexual reference, is part of the expansion of sympathy to which his novels as a whole invite us: a relish for wholesome bawdy, in fact, is a necessary part of the moral education of a sex-bedevilled humanity: such, at least, was the classical role of comedy, and Fielding was perhaps the last great writer who continued that tradition.

[1] Bk. XVIII, ch. 13.   [2] Bk. II, ch. 10.   [3] Bk. VII, ch. 7.

IV

As far as most modern readers are concerned it is not Fielding's moral but his literary point of view which is open to objection. For his conception of his role is that of a guide who, not content with taking us 'behind the scenes of this great theatre of nature',[1] feels that he must explain everything which is to be found there; and such authorial intrusion, of course, tends to diminish the authenticity of his narrative.

Fielding's personal intrusion into *Tom Jones* begins with his dedication to the Honourable George Lyttleton, a dedication, it must be admitted, which goes far to justify Johnson's definition of this form of writing—'a servile address to a patron'. There are numerous further references in the body of his work to others among Fielding's patrons, notably Ralph Allen and Lord Chancellor Hardwicke, not to mention other acquaintances whom Fielding wished to compliment, including one of his surgeons, Mr. John Ranby, and various innkeepers.

The effect of these references is certainly to break the spell of the imaginary world represented in the novel: but the main interference with the autonomy of this world comes from Fielding's introductory chapters, containing literary and moral essays, and even more from his frequent discussions and asides to the reader within the narrative itself. There is no doubt that Fielding's practice here leads him in completely the opposite direction from Richardson, and converts the novel into a social and indeed into a sociable literary form. Fielding brings us into a charmed circle composed, not only of the fictional characters, but also of Fielding's friends and of his favourites among the poets and moralists of the past. He is, indeed, almost as attentive to his audience as to his characters, and his narrative, far from being an intimate drama which we peep at through a keyhole, is a series of reminiscences told by a genial raconteur in some wayside inn—the favoured and public locus of his tale.

This approach to the novel is quite consistent with Fielding's major intention—it promotes a distancing effect which prevents us from being so fully immersed in the lives of the characters that we lose our alertness to the larger implications of their actions—implications which Fielding brings out in his capacity of omniscient chorus. On the other hand, Fielding's interventions

[1] Bk. VII, ch. 1.

obviously interfere with any sense of narrative illusion, and break with almost every narrative precedent, beginning with that set by Homer, whom Aristotle praised for saying 'very little *in propria persona*', and for maintaining elsewhere the attitude either of a dispassionate narrator, or of an impersonator of one of the characters.[1]

Few readers would like to be without the prefatory chapters, or Fielding's diverting asides, but they undoubtedly derogate from the reality of the narrative: as Richardson's friend, Thomas Edwards, wrote, 'we see every moment' that it is Fielding who 'does *personam gerere*', whereas Richardson is 'the thing itself'.[2] So, although Fielding's garrulity about his characters and his conduct of the action initiated a popular practice in the English novel, it is not surprising that it has been condemned by most modern critics, and on these grounds. Ford Madox Ford, for instance, complained that the 'trouble with the English nuvvelist from Fielding to Meredith, is that not one of them cares whether you believe in their characters or not';[3] and Henry James was shocked by the way Trollope, and other 'accomplished novelists', concede 'in a digression, a parenthesis or an aside' that their fiction is 'only make-believe'. James went on to lay down the central principle of the novelist's attitude to his creation, which is very similar to that described above as inherent in formal realism: Trollope, and any novelist who shares his attitude, James says,

> admits that the events he narrates have not really happened, and that he can give the narrative any turn the reader may like best. Such a betrayal of a sacred office seems to me, I confess, a terrible crime; it is what I mean by the attitude of apology, and it shocks me every whit as much in Trollope as it would have shocked me in Gibbon or Macaulay. It implies that the novelist is less occupied in looking for the truth (the truth of course I mean, that he assumes, the premises that we must grant him, whatever they may be) than the historian, and in so doing it deprives him at a stroke of all his standing room.[4]

There is not, of course, any doubt as to Fielding's intention of 'looking for the truth'—he tells us indeed in *Tom Jones* that 'we determined to guide our pen throughout by the directions of

[1] *Poetics*, chs. 24, 3.   [2] McKillop, *Richardson*, p. 175.
[3] *English Novel*, p. 89.
[4] 'The Art of Fiction' (1884); cited from *The Art of Fiction*, ed. Bishop, p. 5.

truth'. But he perhaps underestimated the connection between truth and the maintenance of the reader's 'historical faith'. This, at least, is the suggestion of a passage towards the end of *Tom Jones* when he proclaims that he will let his hero be hanged rather than extricate him from his troubles by unnatural means 'for we had rather relate that he was hanged at Tyburn (which may very probably be the case) than forfeit our integrity, or shock the faith of our reader'.[1]

This ironical attitude towards the reality of his creation was probably responsible in part for the main critical doubt which *Tom Jones* suggests. It is, in the main, a very true book, but it is by no means so clear that its truth has, to quote R. S. Crane, been 'rendered' in terms of the novel.[2] We do not get the impressive sense of Fielding's own moral qualities from his characters or their actions that we do from the heroic struggles for human betterment which he conducted as a magistrate under the most adverse personal circumstances, or even from the *Journal of a Voyage to Lisbon*; and if we analyse our impression from the novels alone it surely is evident that our residual impression of dignity and generosity comes mainly from the passages where Fielding is speaking in his own person. And this, surely, is the result of a technique which was deficient at least in the sense that it was unable to convey this larger moral significance through character and action alone, and could only supply it by means of a somewhat intrusive patterning of the plot and by direct editorial commentary. As Henry James put it: Tom Jones 'has so much "life" that it amounts, for the effect of comedy and application of satire, almost to his having a mind'; almost, but not quite, and so it was necessary that 'his author—*he* handsomely possessed of a mind—[should have] such an amplitude of reflection for him and round him that we see him through the mellow air of Fielding's fine old moralism . . .'.[3]

All this, of course, is not to say Fielding does not succeed: *Tom Jones* is surely entitled to the praise of an anonymous early admirer who called it 'on the whole . . . the most lively book ever published'.[4] But it is a very personal and unrepeatable kind

[1] Bk. III, ch. 1; Bk. XVII, ch. 1.
[2] 'The Concept of Plot and the Plot of *Tom Jones*', *Critics and Criticism Ancient and Modern* (Chicago, 1952), p. 639.   [3] Preface, *The Princess Casamassima*.
[4] *Essay on the New Species of Writing Founded by Mr. Fielding*, 1751, p. 43.

of success: Fielding's technique was too eclectic to become a permanent element in the tradition of the novel—*Tom Jones* is only part novel, and there is much else—picaresque tale, comic drama, occasional essay.

On the other hand, Fielding's departure from the canons of formal realism indicated very clearly the nature of the supreme problem which the new genre had to face. The tedious asseveration of literal authenticity in Defoe and to some extent in Richardson, tended to obscure the fact that, if the novel was to achieve equality of status with other genres it had to be brought into contact with the whole tradition of civilised values, and supplement its realism of presentation with a realism of assessment. To the excellent Mrs. Barbauld's query as to the grounds on which he considered Richardson to be a lesser writer than Shakespeare, Coleridge answered that 'Richardson is *only* interesting'.[1] This is no doubt unfair as a total judgement on the author of *Clarissa*, but it indicates the likely limits of a realism of presentation: we shall be wholly immersed in the reality of the characters and their actions, but whether we shall be any wiser as a result is open to question.

Fielding brought to the genre something that is ultimately even more important than narrative technique—a responsible wisdom about human affairs which plays upon the deeds and the characters of his novels. His wisdom is not, perhaps, of the highest order; it is, like that of his beloved Lucian, a little inclined to be easy-going and on occasion opportunist. Nevertheless, at the end of *Tom Jones* we feel we have been exposed, not merely to an interesting narrative about imaginary persons, but to a stimulating wealth of suggestion and challenge on almost every topic of human interest. Not only so: the stimulation has come from a mind with a true grasp of human reality, never deceived or deceiving about himself, his characters or the human lot in general. In his effort to infuse the new genre with something of the Shakespearean virtues Fielding departed too far from formal realism to initiate a viable tradition, but his work serves as a perpetual reminder that if the new genre was to challenge older literary forms it had to find a way of conveying not only a convincing impression but a wise assessment of life, an assessment that could only come from taking a much wider view than Defoe or Richardson of the affairs of mankind.

[1] *Cit.* Blanchard, *Fielding*, p. 316.

So, although we must agree with the tenor of Johnson's watch simile, we must also add that it is unfair and misleading. Richardson, no doubt, takes us deeper into the inner workings of the human machine; but Fielding is surely entitled to retort that there are many other machines in nature besides the individual consciousness, and perhaps to express his surprised chagrin that Johnson should apparently have overlooked the fact that he was engaged in the exploration of a vaster and equally intricate mechanism, that of human society as a whole, a literary subject which was, incidentally, much more consonant than Richardson's with the classical outlook which he and Johnson shared.

CHAPTER X

Realism and the Later Tradition: a Note

AFTER Richardson and Fielding the novel played a part of increasing importance in the literary scene. The annual production of works of fiction, which had averaged only about seven in the years between 1700 and 1740, rose to an average of about twenty in the three decades following 1740, and this output was doubled in the period from 1770 to 1800.[1] The quantitative increase, however, was not in any way matched by an increase in quality. With only a few exceptions the fiction of the last half of the eighteenth century, though occasionally of some interest as evidence of the life of the time or of various fugitive literary tendencies such as sentimentalism or Gothic terror, had little intrinsic merit; and much of it reveals only too plainly the pressures towards literary degradation which were exerted by the booksellers and circulating library operators in their efforts to meet the reading public's uncritical demand for easy vicarious indulgence in sentiment and romance.

There were, however, several novelists who rose above the level of mediocrity and worse, novelists such as Smollett, Sterne and Fanny Burney. Smollett has many merits as a social reporter and as a humorist, but the manifest flaws in the central situations and the general structure of all his novels except *Humphrey Clinker* (1771) prevent him from playing a very important role in the main tradition of the novel. Sterne is a very different matter, and although his remarkable literary originality gives his work a wholly personal, not to say eccentric, quality, his only novel, *Tristram Shandy* (1760–1767), offers very provocative solutions of the major formal problems which had been raised by his predecessors; for, on the one hand, Sterne found a way of reconciling Richardson's realism of presentation with Fielding's

---

[1] These figures, presented with the greatest possible reserve, were compiled from A. W. Smith, 'Collections and Notes of Prose Fiction in England, 1660–1714', *Harvard Summaries of Dissertations*, pp. 281-284, 1932; Charlotte E. Morgan, *The Rise of the Novel of Manners, 1600-1740* (New York, 1911), p. 54; Godfrey Frank Singer, *The Epistolary Novel* (Philadelphia, 1933), pp. 99-100; Andrew Block, *The English Novel, 1740-1850, a Catalogue . . .* (London, 1939).

realism of assessment, while, on the other, he showed that there was no necessary antagonism between their respective internal and external approaches to character.

Sterne's narrative mode gives very careful attention to all the aspects of formal realism: to the particularisation of time, place and person; to a natural and lifelike sequence of action; and to the creation of a literary style which gives the most exact verbal and rhythmical equivalent possible of the object described. As a result, many of the scenes in *Tristram Shandy* achieve a living authenticity that combines Defoe's brilliant economy of suggestion with Richardson's more minutely discriminated presentation of the momentary thoughts, feelings and gestures of his characters. So assured, indeed, is this mastery of realistic presentation that, had it been applied to the usual purposes of the novel, Sterne would probably have been the supreme figure among eighteenth-century novelists. But, of course, *Tristram Shandy* is not so much a novel as a parody of a novel, and, with a precocious technical maturity, Sterne turns his irony against many of the narrative methods which the new genre had so lately developed.

This ironical tendency is particularly focussed on the hero himself. Pursuing the naming-convention of formal realism, Sterne tells us exactly how his character was named, and how this alone is a symbol of its bearer's unhappy destiny; and yet, of course, poor Tristram remains an elusive figure, perhaps because philosophy has taught him that personal identity is not so simple a question as is commonly assumed: when the commissary asks him '—And who are you?', he can only reply,'Don't puzzle me',[1] thereby resuming the tenor of Hume's sceptical thoughts on the subject in the *Treatise of Human Nature*.[2] But the main reason why Sterne's hero continues to escape us is that his author plays fast and loose with what is probably the most basic of the problems of formal realism, the treatment of the time dimension in narrative.

The primary temporal sequence of *Tristram Shandy* is based —again in accord with the recent tendencies in the philosophy of the time—on the flow of associations in the consciousness of the narrator. Since everything that occurs in the mind occurs in the present, this enables Sterne to portray some of his scenes with all the vividness which Richardson's 'lively present-tense

[1] Bk. I, ch. 9; Bk. VII, ch. 33.   [2] See Bk. I, pt. 4, sect. vi.

manner' had made possible; at the same time, since Tristram Shandy is recounting the story of his own 'life and opinions', Sterne can also command the longer temporal perspectives of Defoe's autobiographical memoir; while, in addition, he adopts Fielding's innovation in the treatment of time by correlating his fictional actions with an external time-scheme—the chronology of the history of the Shandy household is consistent with the dates of such historical events as Uncle Toby's battles in Flanders.[1]

Sterne, however, is not satisfied with this skilful handling of the time problem, and proceeds to take to its logical extreme the ultimate realist premise of a one-to-one correspondence between literature and reality. He proposes to make an absolute temporal equivalent between his novel and his reader's experience of it by providing an hour's reading matter for every hour in his hero's waking life. But this, of course, is a forlorn enterprise, since it will always take Tristram much more than an hour to write down an account of an hour of his own experience, and so the more he writes and the more we read, the more our common objective recedes.

Thus Sterne, largely by taking the temporal requirements of formal realism more literally than had ever been attempted before—or since—achieves a *reductio ad absurdum* of the novel form itself. At the same time, however, this sly subversion of the proper purposes of the novel has recently bestowed upon *Tristram Shandy* a certain posthumous topicality. Sterne's very flexible handling of the time-scheme of his novel prefigures the break with the tyranny of chronological order in the conduct of narrative which was made by Proust, Joyce and Virginia Woolf, and Sterne therefore found renewed critical favour in the 'twenties as a precursor of the moderns. Nor is this all: the greatest contemporary exponent of philosophical realism, Bertrand Russell, modelled his own statement of the problematic nature of time on *Tristram Shandy* and named his paradox after Sterne's infinitely regressive hero.[2]

Sterne's handling of the temporal dimension in *Tristram Shandy* is of crucial importance in yet another context, since it provides the technical basis for his combination of realism of

[1] See Theodore Baird, 'The Time Scheme of *Tristram Shandy* and a Source', *PMLA*, LI (1936), 803-820.
[2] *Principles of Mathematics* (London, 1937), pp. 358-360.

presentation with realism of assessment. Sterne, like Fielding, was a scholar and a wit, and he was equally anxious to have full freedom to comment on the action of his novel or indeed on anything else. But whereas Fielding had gained this freedom only by impairing the verisimilitude of his narrative, Sterne was able to achieve exactly the same ends without any such sacrifice by the simple but ingenious expedient of locating his reflections in the mind of his hero—the most recondite allusion could thus be laid at the door of the notorious inconsequences of the processes of the association of ideas.

Fielding's realism of assessment did not operate only through direct commentary; his evaluations were also made explicit by organising the narrative sequence into a significant counterpoint of scenes which usually reflected ironically upon each other, although often at the cost of giving the reader a sense of somewhat obtrusive manipulation. Sterne, however, can manipulate until we are giddy without any breach of narrative authenticity, since every transition is part of the hero's mental life which, of course, is very little concerned with chronological order. As a result Sterne is able to arrange the elements of his novel into whatever sequence he pleases, without the arbitrary changes of setting and characters which such a counterpoint would involve in Fielding.

This freedom, however, Sterne treats in exactly the same way as he treats his freedom in the use of the time dimension, and as a result his novel's principle of organisation eventually ceases to be narrative in the ordinary sense. The ultimate implications of Sterne's mastery of the technique for achieving realism of assessment without compromising authenticity are therefore largely negative; but even here, of course, objection is impossible within Sterne's fictional terms, since, although we may be entitled to expect some degree of order in an author, it would hardly be reasonable to expect it from the workings of the mind of Tristram Shandy.

Sterne's narrative methods in general, then, bear a more central relationship to the main traditions of the novel than at first appears; we may feel that he has undermined the methods of Richardson and Fielding rather than reconciled them, but there can at least be no doubt that he is working within the narrative directions which they originated. This continuity in *Tristram Shandy* also extends to subject-matter and to methods of characterisation, although in equally paradoxical ways. One of Sterne's major themes, for example, is very similar to Richardson's central preoccupation: Uncle Toby is as much an embodiment of the eighteenth-century conception of ideal goodness as Clarissa, but at the same time Fielding's criticism of Richardson is implicit in the way that Sterne's masculine embodiment of sexual virtue is pitted against the Widow Wadman's villainous Lovelace. In characterisation, also, *Tristram Shandy* shows a very personal combination of the distinctive emphases of Richardson and Fielding. On the surface it would seem that since the hero's consciousness is the locus of the action, Sterne must be classed as an extreme exponent of the internal and subjective approach to character, an approach, of course, which normally accompanies minute particularity in narrative method. Actually, however, although the behaviour of the main persons of the story is often rendered with a studied attention to every inflection of thought and act, they themselves are fundamentally conceived as general social and psychological types, much in Fielding's manner.

Tristram Shandy, then, suggests that just as the author's freedom to suggest an evaluation of the picture of life which his novel presents need not detract from its appearance of authenticity, so there is no absolute dichotomy between the internal and the external approach to character. This issue is of considerable general importance, since the tendency to make an absolute separation between 'characters of nature' and 'characters of manners' is the eighteenth-century form of a later tendency to equate 'realism' in the novel with an emphasis on society rather than the individual, and to regard those novelists who explore the inner lives of their characters as outside the main realist tradition. That this distinction in the approach to character is an important one cannot be denied, and it is understandable that the literary perspective of the French Realists should so have coloured our sense of the term that we feel that if Balzac is a 'realist' Proust needs some other word to describe him. Nevertheless the basic continuity of the tradition of the novel is made clearer if we remember that these differences in narrative method are differences of emphasis rather than of kind, and that they exist within a common allegiance to the formal or presentational realism which, it has been argued above, is typical of the novel genre as a whole.

This particular critical problem has a close epistemological analogue—dualism. It is significant that it was Descartes, the founder of modern philosophical realism, who raised the dualist issue and made it one of the characteristic preoccupations of the thought of the last three centuries. The two philosophical problems, of course, are closely related, since the epistemological bent of seventeenth-century philosophy naturally tended to focus attention on the problem of how the individual mind can know anything that is external to itself. But although dualism dramatises the opposition between different ways of looking at reality it does not, in fact, lead to any complete rejection of the reality either of the ego or of the external world. Similarly, although different novelists have given different degrees of importance to the internal and the external objects of consciousness, they have never completely rejected either; on the contrary, the basic terms of their inquiry have been dictated by the narrative equivalent of dualism—the problematic nature of the relation between the individual and his environment.

Defoe would seem to occupy a very central position between the subjective and the external orientations of the novelist: the individual ego and the material world, as the result of Defoe's use of formal realism, are both given a greater reality in his novels than in previous fiction. Indeed the fact that his narrative point of view, that of the autobiographical memoir, shows itself to be so well suited to reflect the tension between the inner and the outer world, suggests that the Cartesian shift to the point of view of the perceiving individual ego was itself calculated to make possible a more sharply defined picture of the outer as well as of the inner world.

Later novelists, of course, have exhibited very divergent approaches to this duality, but it is significant that even those who, from Richardson onwards, have laid the greatest stress on the subjective and psychological direction, have also made some of the greatest contributions both to the development of the possibilities of formal realism and to the portrayal of society. Proust, for example, gives us, among other things, a document of Cartesian introspection; but it is an introspection which reveals the external world of the Third Republic as tellingly as the internal world of the memories of the narrator. Henry James's technical triumphs can be seen as the result of an ingenious manipulation of the two dualist extremes: in the later novels the reader is absorbed into the subjective consciousness of one or more of the characters, and from that artfully selected point of disadvantage beholds obliquely and ironically unfolded the vision of the external social facts, the furies of money, class and culture which are the ultimate determinants of subjective experience although hardly glimpsed by their human agents and only fully recognised by the reader when the story is done. Joyce's *Ulysses*, which is in so many ways the climax of the novel's development, is certainly its climax in the treatment of the dualist extremes: in its last two books the graphic presentation of Molly Bloom's daydream and the cataloguing of the contents of her husband's drawers are defiantly unadulterated examples of the adjustment of narrative manner to the subjective and the objective poles of dualism.

The example of Sterne, then, and the analogy of philosophical dualism, tend to support the view that the two major differences of narrative method between the novels of Richardson and Fielding are by no means manifestations of two opposite and irreconcilable kinds of novel, but merely rather clearly contrasted solutions of problems which pervade the whole tradition of the novel and whose apparent divergencies can in fact be harmoniously reconciled. Indeed, the full maturity of the genre itself, it can be argued, could only come when this reconciliation had been achieved, and it is probable that it is largely to her successful resolution of these problems that Jane Austen owes her eminence in the tradition of the English novel.

In this as in much else Jane Austen was the heir of Fanny Burney, herself no inconsiderable figure in bringing together the divergent directions which the geniuses of Richardson and Fielding had imposed upon the novel. Both women novelists followed Richardson—the Richardson of the less intense domestic conflicts of *Sir Charles Grandison*—in their minute presentation of daily life. At the same time Fanny Burney and Jane Austen followed Fielding in adopting a more detached attitude to their narrative material, and in evaluating it from a comic and objective point of view. It is here that Jane Austen's technical genius manifests itself. She dispensed with the participating narrator, whether as the author of a memoir as in Defoe, or as letter-writer as in Richardson, probably because both of these roles make freedom to comment and evaluate more difficult to arrange; instead she told her stories after Fielding's manner, as a confessed author. Jane Austen's variant of the commenting narrator, however, was so much more discreet that it did not substantially affect the authenticity of her narrative. Her analyses of her characters and their states of mind, and her ironical juxtapositions of motive and situation are as pointed as anything in Fielding, but they do not seem to come from an intrusive author but rather from some august and impersonal spirit of social and psychological understanding.

At the same time, Jane Austen varied her narrative point of view sufficiently to give us, not only editorial comment, but much of Defoe's and Richardson's psychological closeness to the subjective world of the characters. In her novels there is usually one character whose consciousness is tacitly accorded a privileged status, and whose mental life is rendered more completely than that of the other characters. In *Pride and Prejudice* (published 1813), for example, the story is told substantially from the point of view of Elizabeth Bennet, the heroine; but the identification is always qualified by the other role of the narrator acting as dispassionate analyst, and as a result the reader does not lose his critical awareness of the novel as a whole. The same strategy as regards point of view is employed with supreme brilliance in *Emma* (1816), a novel which combines Fielding's characteristic strength in conveying the sense of society as a whole, with something of Henry James's capacity for locating the essential structural continuity of his novel in the reader's growing awareness of the full complexity of the personality and situation of the character through whom the story is mainly told: the unfolding of Emma Woodhouse's inner being has much of the drama of progressive revelation with which James presents Maisie Farange or Lambert Strether.

Jane Austen's novels, in short, must be seen as the most successful solutions of the two general narrative problems for which Richardson and Fielding had provided only partial answers. She was able to combine into a harmonious unity the advantages both of realism of presentation and realism of assessment, of the internal and of the external approaches to character; her novels have authenticity without diffuseness or trickery, wisdom of social comment without a garrulous essayist, and a sense of the social order which is not achieved at the expense of the individuality and autonomy of the characters.

Jane Austen's novels are also the climax of many other aspects of the eighteenth-century novel. In their subjects, despite some obvious differences, they continue many of the characteristic interests of Defoe, Richardson and Fielding. Jane Austen faces more squarely than Defoe, for example, the social and moral problems raised by economic individualism and the middle-class quest for improved status; she follows Richardson in basing her novels on marriage and especially on the proper feminine role in the matter; and her ultimate picture of the proper norms of the social system is similar to that of Fielding although its application to the characters and their situation is in general more serious and discriminating.

Jane Austen's novels are also representative in another sense; they reflect the process whereby, as we have seen, women were playing an increasingly important part in the literary scene. The majority of eighteenth-century novels were actually written by women, but this had long remained a purely quantitative assertion of dominance; it was Jane Austen who completed the work that Fanny Burney had begun, and challenged masculine prerogative in a much more important matter. Her example suggests that the feminine sensibility was in some ways better equipped to reveal the intricacies of personal relationships and was therefore at a real advantage in the realm of the novel. The reasons for the greater feminine command of the area of personal relationships would be difficult and lengthy to detail; one of the main ones is probably that suggested by John Stuart Mill's statement that 'all the education that women receive from society inculcates in them the feeling that the individuals connected with them are the only ones to whom they owe any duty'.[1] As to the connection of this with the novel, there can surely be little doubt. Henry James, for example, alluded to it in a tribute which is characteristic in its scrupulous moderation: 'Women are delicate and patient observers; they hold their noses close, as it were, to the texture of life. They feel and perceive the real with a kind of personal tact, and their observations are recorded in a thousand delightful volumes.'[2] More generally, James elsewhere linked the 'immensely great con-

[1] *The Subjection of Women* (London, 1924), p. 105.
[2] 'Anthony Trollope', *Partial Portraits* (London, 1888), p. 50. One comparative study of conversations showed that 37 per cent of women's conversations were about persons as against 16 per cent of men's (M. H. Landis and H. E. Burtt, 'A Study of Conversations', *J. Comp. Psychology*, IV (1924), 81-89).

spicuity of the novel' in modern civilisation to the 'immensely great conspicuity of the attitude of women'.[1]

In Jane Austen, Fanny Burney and George Eliot the advantages of the feminine point of view outweigh the restrictions of social horizon which have until recently been associated with it. At the same time it is surely true that the dominance of women readers in the public for the novel is connected with the characteristic kind of weakness and unreality to which the form is liable—its tendency to restrict the field on which its psychological and intellectual discriminations operate to a small and arbitrary selection of human situations, a restriction which, since Fielding, has affected all but a very few English novels with a certain narrowing of the framework of experience and permitted attitude.

There is, then, a real continuity both in narrative method and in social background between the early eighteenth-century novelists and their major successors. As a result, although one cannot properly speak of a school of eighteenth-century novelists, one can, by adopting a larger perspective and comparing them either with any previous writers of fiction or with their contemporaries abroad, see that they constitute a literary movement whose members had a good deal in common. This kinship was very evident to the early nineteenth-century critics of the novel: Hazlitt, for example, tended to see Richardson, Fielding and Sterne as alike in their unprecedented fidelity to 'human nature as it is'.[2] The family resemblance was seen even more clearly abroad. In France, as George Saintsbury pointed out, the relation between literature and life in fiction remained much more distant and formal throughout the eighteenth century.[3] Consequently English pre-eminence in the genre was freely granted from the middle of the century onwards, with Fielding, Sterne and, above all, Richardson as the major figures: Diderot even expressed a wish that some new name could be found to distinguish the novels of Richardson from the 'romans' of his native tradition;[4] and for many French and German readers the great differences between Richardson and

---

[1] 'Mrs. Humphry Ward', *Essays in London* (London, 1893), p. 265.
[2] See Charles I. Patterson, 'William Hazlitt as a Critic of Prose Fiction', *PMLA*, LXVIII (1953), 1010.
[3] *History of the French Novel* (London, 1917), I, 469.
[4] *Œuvres*, ed. Billy, p. 1089.

Fielding, for example, were of minor importance compared with the fact that both were much more realistic than their foreign counterparts.[1]

French testimony to the supremacy of the English novel in the eighteenth century was accompanied by explanations of the phenomenon which were in substantial agreement with the connections suggested above between social change and the rise of the new form. Thus the first important study of the novel in its larger social background, Madame de Staël's *De la littérature, considérée dans ses rapports avec les institutions sociales* (1800), anticipated many of the elements of the present analysis;[2] while de Bonald, who seems to have been the first critic to use the formula 'La littérature est l'expression de la société', presented a substantially similar picture of the historical causes of the accepted English eminence in the novel in his *Du style et de la littérature* (1806). He took it for granted that the novel was essentially concerned with private and domestic life: what could be more natural, therefore, than that a distinctively commercial, bourgeois and urban society which laid so much stress on family life, and which was, moreover, so notoriously poor in the nobler forms of literary expression, should have triumphed in a familiar and domestic genre.[3]

The course of French literature provides confirmation of another kind as to the importance both of the social and the literary factors whose connection with the early development of the novel in England has been presented here. The first great efflorescence of the genre in France which began with Balzac and Stendhal occurred only after the French Revolution had placed the French middle class in a position of social and literary power which their English counterparts had achieved exactly a century before in the Glorious Revolution of 1689. And if Balzac and Stendhal are greater figures in the tradition of the European novel than any English novelist of the eighteenth century, it is surely in part due to the historical advantages which they enjoyed: not only because the social changes with which they were concerned had found much more dramatic expression than in England, but because, on the literary side, they

---

[1] See, for example, L. M. Price, *English Literature in Germany* (Berkeley and Los Angeles, 1953), p. 180.

[2] See especially Part I, ch. 15: 'De l'imagination des Anglais dans leurs poésies et leurs romans'.   [3] *Œuvres complètes* (Paris, 1864), III, col. 1000.

were the beneficiaries, not only of their English predecessors, but of a critical climate which was much more favourable to the development of formal realism than was that of neo-classicism.

It has been part of the present argument that the novel is more intimately related to the general literary and intellectual situation than is always remembered, and the close connection of the first great French Realists with Romanticism is an example of this. Romanticism, of course, was characterised by the emphasis on individualism and on originality which had found its first literary expression in the novel: and many romantic writers expressed themselves with particular vigour against those elements in classical critical theory which were inimical to formal realism. In the Preface to the *Lyrical Ballads* (1800), for example, Wordsworth proclaimed that the writer must 'keep his eye on the object' and present the experiences of common life in 'the real language of men'; while the French break with the literary past found its most dramatic expression with the presentation of *Hernani* (1830) where Victor Hugo defied the hallowed decorums which restricted the manner in which the literary object was supposed to be portrayed.

Such are some of the larger literary perspectives which the early eighteenth-century novelists suggest. Compared with Jane Austen, or with Balzac and Stendhal, Defoe, Richardson and Fielding all have fairly obvious technical weaknesses. Historically, however, they have two kinds of importance: the obvious importance that attaches to writers who made the major contribution to the creation of the dominant literary form of the last two centuries; and the equally great importance which arises from the fact that, assisted, no doubt, by the fact that they were essentially independent innovators, their novels provide three rather sharply defined images of the form in general, and constitute a remarkably complete recapitulation of the essential diversities in its later tradition. They also, of course, make a more absolute claim upon us. In the novel, more perhaps than in any other literary genre, the qualities of life can atone for the defects of art: and there can be little doubt that Defoe, Richardson and Fielding all earned themselves a more secure literary immortality than many later novelists who were possessed of much greater technical sophistication, by expressing their own sense of life with a completeness and conviction which is very rare, and for which one is grateful.

INDEX

Titles are not normally indexed separately, but under author;
fictional characters, editors, compilers, editions, and modern
periodicals are not indexed as such.

Reynolds, Myra, *The Learned Lady in England, 1650–1760*, 152 n., quoted, 144

Richardson, Samuel, 9, 11, 20, 28, 47, 49, 93, 131, 133, 135-238 *passim*, 254, 257, 290, 291, 293, 294, 296, 297, 298, 299, 300, 301; and social class, 59, 165-7, 213, 220-4, 238, 244-5, 269; on the classics, 194, 243-8; and the critical tradition, 33, 56, 58-9, 192-195, 247-8; and devotional literature, 50; his didactic purpose, 215-219, 235-6, 238; compared to Fielding, 260-8, 275, 280-3, 287-9; on Homer, 243-8; his humour, 210-11; irony in, 211; use of letter form, 192-6, 208-11, 228-30; as Londoner, 180, 181-5, 190; and love, 135-73, 208-38; and marriage, 137-8, 141, 143-4, 145-51, 156-7, 163-4, 166-7, 171, 204, 220-6; use of milieu, 26-7; his names, 19, 236; narrative method, 175-6, 203-4, 208-11; and the novel form, 202, 208, 219, 301; and originality, 14-15, 58, 194, 247-248; particularity of description, 17, 34; and personal relationships, 177, 200-1, 220, 238, 266; his plots, 14, 135, 153-4, 220, 238; as printer, 52, 57, 196-200; prose style, 29-30, 192-7, 219; and Puritanism, 85, 172, 222; and reading public, 45-50, 57-9, 151-4; his formal realism, 32-4, 57, 153-4, 290-2; his religious views, 216-18; and sex, 154-73, 199, 202-4, 209, 220-238; as suburban, 186-8, 190; and time, 24-5, 191-4; and women readers, 151-4; and Young's *Conjectures on Original Composition*, 218, 247-8

Criticism of:
by Mrs. Barbauld, 17, 175-6; by Mrs. Chapone, 58; by Coleridge, 288; by Mrs. Donnellan, 184; in *Eclectic Review*, 216; by Thomas Edwards, 286; by Fielding, 25, 168-70, 211, 235; in *Gentleman's Magazine*, 199; by Hazlitt, 34 n.; by Francis Jeffrey, 175; by Johnson, 219, 228, 260-1, 281; by D. H. Lawrence, 203; by Lady Mary

Richardson, Samuel—*contd.*
Criticism of—*contd.*
Wortley Montagu, 138, 146, 148, 151, 272; by Rousseau, 219; by George Saintsbury, 176; by Martin Sherlock, 247; in *The Tablet*, 168; by Thomas Turner, 217-18

Works:
Clarissa, 19, 24-5, 27, 57, 146, 174, 181-2, 183, 188, 191, 192, 195, 197, 198-9, 201, 208-38 *passim*, 244, 248, 294; characterisation in, 211-15, 218-219, 225-9, 231-8; compared to *Tom Jones*, 260-8, 275, 277, 288; composition of, 208; death of Clarissa, 215-19, 232-4; publication of, 42; quoted, 159, 247

Familiar Letters, aim of, 190; quoted, 159, 169, 195

Sir Charles Grandison, 19, 26, 138, 160, 182, 195, 296; quoted, 146, 147, 151, 157, 243-4, 246

Pamela, 11, 17, 19, 26, 29, 47, 55, 135-73 *passim*, 174, 181, 188, 189, 193, 194, 195, 196, 201-5, 232, 244, 246; characterisation, 168-71; compared to *Clarissa*, 208-9, 216, 220, 228; and *Joseph Andrews*, 239; surprising success of, 55; and waiting maids, 47, 143-4, 148

The Rambler, paper in, 167

Riedel, F. Carl, *Crime and Punishment in the Old French Romances*, 136 n.

Rivington, Charles, bookseller, 55

Robinson, Howard, *The British Post Office: A History*, 189 n.

Robinson, Sir Thomas, quoted, 150

Romances, 11, 28, 41, 136, 165-6; Defoe on, 241; Fielding and French heroic romances, 248-9, 250, 252, 258; Richardson and, 137, 192; *Pamela* and, 153-4, 165, 204-6

Romanticism, and the novel, 301

Rougemont, de, *L'Amour et l'Occident*, quoted, 137

Rousseau, 75, 87; *Émile*, quoted, on *Robinson Crusoe*, 86; *Lettre à d'Alembert*, quoted, on *Clarissa*, 219

Rowe, Nicholas, *Fair Penitent*, and *Clarissa*, 214, 224

Society for the Propagation of
Christian Knowledge, 143
Sophocles, *Oedipus Tyrannus*, 269
Space, particularisation of, 26-7
Spate, O. H. K., 'The Growth of
London, A.D. 1600–1800', in
Historical Geography of England,
178 n., 179 n.
Spectator, The, 18, 36, 50-2, 163, 216,
quoted, 178, 246
Spengler, Oswald, *Decline of the
West*, quoted, 22
Spenser, Edmund, 14, 61; *Faerie
Queene*, 23, 137
Spinster, The (periodical), quoted,
145
Sprat, Bishop Thomas, *History of the
Royal Society*, quoted, 101
Staël, Madame de, *De l'Allemagne*,
quoted, 176, 177, 205-6; *De la lit-
térature . . .*, 135, 300
Stamm, Rudolph, 'Daniel Defoe:
An Artist in the Puritan Tradi-
tion', 85; *Der aufgeklärte Puritan-
ismus Daniel Defoes*, 85 n.
Steele, Richard, 52, 61; *The Chris-
tian Hero*, quoted, 51, 244; *The
Guardian*, quoted, 48-9; *The Ladies'
Library*, 151; *The Lover*, quoted,
159; *The Spinster*, quoted, 145; *The
Tender Husband*, 144, 152, 180
Stendhal, 94, 132, 220, 300, 301; *Le
Rouge et le noir*, 27, 94
Stephen, Leslie, 'Defoe's Novels',
103, quoted, 93, 108; *History of
English Thought in the Eighteenth Century*, 35, 275 n.; on Fielding, 283
Sterne, Laurence, 20, 21, 143, 219,
280, 290-4; his characterisation,
294-5; *Tristram Shandy*, 290-4,
Richardson on, 203
Stiltrennung, 79, 83, 166-7
Strahan, William, printer, 53;
quoted, 37
Subjective, the, in classical literature,
176-7, 205-6, 272-3; development
of in modern civilisation, 176-7;
and the epistolary form, 190-5;
and the novel, 177, 198-200, 202-3,
205-7; in philosophy, 22, 177, 295;
and Puritanism, 74-7, 177; and
the suburb, 186-7; in Defoe, 74-6,
175, 295; in Fielding, 272-6, 278;
in Henry James, 295-6; in James
Joyce, 207, 296; in Proust, 295; in

Richardson, 167-8, 175-7, 191-3,
204-5, 238; in Sterne, 294
Suburban life, development of, 186-
187; Defoe and, 186; Richardson
and, 183, 186-9, 206
Sutherland, Edwin H., *Principles of
Criminology*, 94 n.
Sutherland, James R., 'The Circulation of Newspapers and Literary
Periodicals, 1700–1730', 36 n.;
Defoe, 70 n.
Swedenberg, H. T., *The Theory of
the Epic in England, 1650–1800*,
251 n.
Sweets of Sin, 206
Swift, Jonathan, 29, 146, 147, 283;
Conduct of the Allies, 36; 'Description of the Morning', 28; *Journal
to Stella*, 36 n.; *Letter to a Very
Young Lady on Her Marriage*, quoted,
160; 'A Project for the Advance-
ment of Religion and the Reformation of Manners', quoted,
179

Tablet, or Picture of Real Life, The,
quoted, 168
Talbot, Miss Catherine, quoted, 187
Tate, Allen, 'Techniques of Fiction',
quoted, 27
Tatler, The, 50, 143 n., 163; quoted,
28, 51
Tawney, R. H., *Religion and the Rise
of Capitalism*, 73
Taylor, A. E., *Aristotle*, 273 n.
Taylor, Jeremy, *Rule and Exercises of
Holy Living and Holy Dying*, 217
Taylor, John Tinnon, *Early Opposi-
tion to the English Novel*, quoted, 43
Temple, Sir William, quoted, 143
Texte, Joseph, *Jean-Jacques Rousseau
and the Cosmopolitan Spirit in Litera-
ture*, 17 n.
Thackeray, W. M., 259, 282
Thomson, Clara L., *Richardson*,
quoted, 153, 190
Thomson, James, 147
Thornbury, Ethel M., *Henry Field-
ing's Theory of the Comic Prose Epic*,
quoted, 259
Thrale, Mrs., 191, 261; quoted, 44;
Thraliana, Johnson quoted in, 88,
162, 261
Thucydides, 256
Tibullus, 240